Progress in

EXPERIMENTAL PERSONALITY RESEARCH

VOLUME 6

CONTRIBUTORS TO THIS VOLUME

ARLINE CAPLAN

EDWARD M. ELLS

ERWIN FARKAS

PHILIP H. FRIEDMAN

DUNCAN N. HANSEN

HERBERT M. LEFCOURT

HAROLD F. O'NEIL, JR.

DAVID L. RENNIE

CHARLES D. SPIELBERGER

DONALD R. STIEPER

MARK H. THELEN

PROGRESS IN
Experimental
Personality Research

Edited by Brendan A. Maher

DEPARTMENT OF PSYCHOLOGY
AND SOCIAL RELATIONS
HARVARD UNIVERSITY
CAMBRIDGE, MASSACHUSETTS

VOLUME 6

1972
ACADEMIC PRESS   New York and London

ACADEMIC PRESS, INC.
111 Fifth Avenue, New York, New York 10003

United Kingdom Edition published by
ACADEMIC PRESS, INC. (LONDON) LTD.
24/28 Oval Road, London NW1

LIBRARY OF CONGRESS CATALOG CARD NUMBER: 64-8034

PRINTED IN THE UNITED STATES OF AMERICA

CONTENTS

Recent Developments in the Study of Locus of Control

HERBERT M. LEFCOURT

The Effects of Modeling, Roleplaying, and Participation on Behavior Change

PHILIP H. FRIEDMAN

The Effect of Vicarious Reinforcement on Imitation: A Review of the Literature

MARK H. THELEN AND DAVID L. RENNIE

Anxiety, Drive Theory, and Computer-Assisted Learning

CHARLES D. SPIELBERGER, HAROLD F. O'NEIL, JR., AND DUNCAN N. HANSEN

The Effects of Reinforcement Procedures upon Schizophrenic Patients: A Survey of the Data

DONALD R. STIEPER, EDWARD M. ELLS, ERWIN FARKAS, AND ARLINE CAPLAN

CONTRIBUTORS

Numbers in parentheses indicate the pages on which the authors' contributions begin.

ARLINE CAPLAN, *Veterans Administration, St. Paul, Minnesota* (149)

EDWARD M. ELLS, *Veterans Administration, St. Paul, Minnesota* (149)

ERWIN FARKAS,[1] *Veterans Administration, St. Paul, Minnesota* (149)

PHILIP H. FRIEDMAN, *Family Psychiatric Division, Eastern Pennsylvania Psychiatric Institute, Philadelphia, Pennsylvania* (41)

DUNCAN N. HANSEN, *Psychology Department and Computer Assisted Instruction Center, Florida State University, Tallahassee, Florida* (109)

HERBERT M. LEFCOURT, *Department of Psychology, University of Waterloo, Waterloo, Ontario, Canada* (1)

HAROLD F. O'NEIL, JR., *Psychology Department and Computer Assisted Instruction Center, Florida State University, Tallahassee, Florida* (109)

DAVID L. RENNIE, *Department of Psychology, York University, Toronto, Ontario, Canada* (83)

CHARLES D. SPIELBERGER, *Psychology Department and Computer Assisted Instruction Center, Florida State University, Tallahassee, Florida* (109)

DONALD R. STIEPER, *Veterans Administration, St. Paul, Minnesota* (149)

MARK H. THELEN, *Department of Psychology, University of Missouri at Columbia, Columbia, Missouri* (83)

---

[1] Present address: Rochester State Hospital, Rochester, Minnesota.

PREFACE

One of the major questions that arises in the application of the principles of learning to the study of personality is the role and nature of social reinforcements in the individual case. Among the important contemporary approaches to this problem is one that emphasizes the locus of control of reinforcements—the perception that these are contingent upon the individual's own behavior or that they are dependent upon arbitrary activities of somebody else. Lefcourt's paper provides a review of the empirical findings that have been reported from this line of inquiry.

Another major development in the study of social reinforcement has been the investigation of what is variously termed "modeling," "imitation," or "vicarious reinforcement." Separate papers by Friedman and by Thelen and Rennie are included in this present volume, covering several aspects of a complex set of problems.

In the realm of psychopathology there has been a long-standing interest in the motivational aspects of schizophrenic deficit. This, inevitably, has led to a concern with the effects of different kinds of reinforcement upon schizophrenic performance. A bewildering array of findings has been reported in the literature vastly complicated by many variations in experimental method, subject populations, and the like. Stieper and his colleagues have completed a thorough review of this material and have succeeded in creating order in what was heretofore a chaotic potpourri of data.

Finally, Spielberger and his collaborators provide a coherent account of the relationships between anxiety, general drive theory, and programmed learning.

It is not possible to observe the themes of modern work in personality research without being impressed with the centrality of motivational questions for most investigators. While this is understandable, we must reflect upon the relative lack of attention given to the structural aspects of personality and particularly those traits or tendencies that appear to have serious biological components. We must express the hope that the future will be characterized by a more even distribution of interest across the many fascinating problems that the study of personality presents.

BRENDAN A. MAHER

ix

CONTENTS OF PREVIOUS VOLUMES

RECENT DEVELOPMENTS IN THE STUDY OF LOCUS OF CONTROL

Herbert M. Lefcourt[1]

DEPARTMENT OF PSYCHOLOGY, UNIVERSITY OF WATERLOO,
WATERLOO, ONTARIO, CANADA

I. Introduction

Since the publication of two major review articles (Lefcourt, 1966b; Rotter, 1966) an increasing number of research investigations have been reported which directly pertain to the locus of control construct. Throop and MacDonald (1971) have amassed a bibliography containing 339 separate entries of immediate relevance to the locus of control contruct appearing through 1969. MacDonald has since complied four additional supplements attesting to the continuous growth of research in this area. Several books have been published which focus on related conceptions about self-direction such as hope (Stotland, 1969), personal causation (deCharms, 1968), internalized control of behavior (Aronfreed, 1968), and alienation and value-expectancy disjunction (Jessor, Graves, Hanson,

[1] The author wishes to express appreciation to A. P. MacDonald, without whose bibliographic research this review would have been impossible, to Peter McDonald his helping in gathering the research reports, to Barbara Lefcourt for her careful reading and criticism of the manuscript.

1

& Jessor, 1968). In addition, there have been three separate review articles studying various aspects of locus of control since the publication of the first two reviews (Joe, 1971; Lefcourt, 1966a; Minton, 1967), and there are at least nine different tests of locus of control, as well as revisions of some, in use (Battle & Rotter, 1963; Bialer, 1961; Crandall, Katkovsky, & Crandall, 1965; Dean, 1961; Dies, 1968; Gozali & Bialer, 1968; Harrison, 1968; Nowicki & Strickland, in press; Rotter, 1966).

To construct a review of the totality of recent research, therefore, has become a forbidding task. Nevertheless, there are some themes of importance which have recurred with enough frequency and consistency to allow for at least some partial summarization. The present review is directed toward an evaluation of locus of control investigations which have ramifications for five interrelated areas: (1) the resistance to influence; (2) cognitive activity; (3) deferred gratification, achievement behavior, and the response to success and failure; (4) familial and social antecedents of locus of control; and (5) changes in locus of control.

In view of the volume of research with possible pertinence to these areas, this writer has chosen to restrict himself primarily to those research studies that have used or discussed their results in terms of internal and external control of reinforcement expectancies (I-E). The locus of control construct is an integral part of social learning theory (Rotter, 1954). It refers to the degree to which individuals perceive the events in their lives as being a consequence of their own actions, and thereby controllable (internal control), or as being unrelated to their own behaviors and, therefore beyond personal control (external control). It is a generalized expectancy, as opposed to a specific expectancy, being an abstraction developed from a host of experiences in which expectancies have met with varying degrees of validation. It is but one element of a behavioral prediction formula which also includes reinforcement value and situational determinants. Therefore, when research is presented focusing on locus of control as a sole predictor of a given set of criteria, it necessarily represents a limited approach to the prediction of those criteria, such that high magnitude relationships should not be anticipated.

II. Resistance to Influence

Direct concern with the causes of resistance to influence has been a continuous interest for the social sciences. Psychological investigators examining persuasibility (Hovland & Janis, 1959), authoritarianism (Adorno, Frenkel-Brunswik, Levinson, & Sanford, 1950), conformity (Berg & Bass, 1961), and obedience (Milgram, 1963) have each attempted to shed some light on the problem of how and why people come to lose their freedoms, and fail to resist coercive forces. Fromm (1941) and Arendt (1963) have likewise directed their efforts toward this issue through more social-theoretical approaches. Arendt has convincingly argued that the complicity of a man such as Adolph Eichmann, with such horrendous undertakings as the transportation of victims to concentration camps, derives less from sadism than from banal adherence to social customs; and research by Milgram (1963) indicates that such complicity is not at all a rare phenomenon. Indeed, recent events have suggested that such complicity is endemic to any overly large organization. Therefore, knowledge about how man becomes critical and resistant to undesirable pressures seems to be as vital an issue now as when Fromm wrote his classic on man's escape from freedom.

From a common sense point of view, locus of control would seem to be strongly related to the ability to resist coercion. Persons who view themselves as responsible for their own fates should be more cautious about what they accept from others than should those who do not perceive themselves to be in active control of their fate. The first two investigations to empirically link locus of control to influence resistance were described in the earlier reviews. Odell (1959) had found a significant relationship between Rotter's Internal-External Control Scale and Barron's Independence of Judgment Scale, with subjects high in externality showing a greater likelihood of conformity. Crowne and Liverant (1963) also reported that externals had less confidence in their own judgment abilities in an Asch-type task, wagering less money than internals on the correctness of their judgments when making independent rather than conforming judgments.

Since the publication of these early studies, a fair number of experiments have been reported which bear upon this assumed relationship between locus of control and the resistance to influence. Gore (1963) found that internals and externals differed in their response to an examiner who was administering the TAT when the examiner, through smiles and intonation, attempted to manipulate the subjects. Internals produced shorter TAT stories than externals when the examiner's gestures indicated that subjects were expected to produce longer stories in response to the specific TAT cards being presented. When the examiner made no suggestions, this difference between internals and externals was not obtained.

Two other early investigations, which have only recently been published, employed a verbal conditioning paradigm in which the locus of control was used to predict the response to verbal reinforcements. Strickland (1970) found that I-E was related to the denial of having been influenced by the verbal reinforcements, internals denying influence more often than externals. Strickland also found that internals who were aware of the reinforcement contingency in her study tended to exhibit less conditioning than internals who were unaware of the contingencies, and less than all external subjects regardless of whether or not they were aware of the contingencies. Getter (1966), also using a verbal reinforcement procedure, found that the most responsive "conditioners" were his most external subjects. Getter's more internal subjects produced the conditioned response largely during extinction trials, after the experimenter had ceased his own reinforcing responses.

In each of these studies, then, there is some indication that internals behave in a somewhat oppositional manner, doing the reverse of what others would trick them into doing. Biondo and MacDonald (1971) have more recently examined the effect of subtle versus overt influence attempts upon the tendencies of internals and externals to resist influence, with the hope of exploring this apparent resistance of internals to indirect or subtle coercion. These investigators, however, found no differences as a function of the subtlety of their influence methods. Rather, externals were found to be more accepting of either influence approach in the way they rated the desirability of a given course grading system. Likewise, Hjelle (1970) found that externals manifested greater attitude change than internals when they had been exposed to standard communications advocating positions contrary to their previous attitudes.

Johnson, Ackerman, Frank, and Fionda (1968) have investigated the resistance to temptation as part of a project concerned with moral development and personal adjustments. These authors employed a "complete a story" device in which the story hero experiences social pressure directing him toward the violation of some social norm. Subjects had to complete the stories in which the hero was either at the point of decision making, or had already complied with the pressure and now had to confront the consequences. Among male undergraduates, Johnson et al. found that the more internal the subject, the more likely was he to complete stories in which the hero resisted pressure. In addition, when the transgression had already occurred, internals were more likely to have the hero acknowledge guilt about his having yielded to pressure then were externals. These results did not obtain in the female sample, though I-E was related to a measure of stability among females, the more internal scoring as the more stable on Eysenck's Personality Inventory.

In several later investigations the relationship between I-E and the susceptibility to influence seems to be more complex. Ritchie and Phares (1969) found that externals exhibited more conforming attitude changes regarding governmental budgeting than internals only when the influence arguments were attributed to a high-status individual. When arguments were attributed to prominent figures, externals yielded more than did internals. However, internals were not immune to the arguments presented, showing some shift in the direction of the influencer's commentary. However, internals did not vary with influencer status. Thus, neither internals nor externals could be described as uniformly resistant or susceptible.

That internals are not simply steadfast and unsusceptible to influence is evident in research concerning cigarette smoking. James, Woodruff, and Werner (1965) found that subsequent to the U.S.P.H.S. Surgeon General's report linking cancer with cigarette smoking, among male smokers, those who quit for a specified length of time were more internal than those who believed the report but did not quit smoking. More recently, E. S. Platt (1969) has reported more success at influencing the smoking behavior of internals than of externals. Platt used the role-playing procedures of Janis and Mann (1965) in which subjects perform as physician, patient, or observer during a medical examination report containing bad medical news for the patient regarding cancer and smoking. Platt found that the greatest changes in smoking behavior occurred among individuals who also believed that there were harmful effects from smoking. In this experiment, the combination of active participation procedures and specific beliefs about the criterion behavior created a reversal of the more customary findings regarding the susceptibility to influence and the locus of control.

A series of experiments by this author and his colleagues, not specifically designed to evaluate the response to influence by internals and externals, nevertheless, contributes to that body of information. In one study, contrasting the level of aspiration performance of internals and externals with instructions, varying the degree to which achievement reinforcements were stressed, Lefcourt (1967) found that externals performed in accord with directions, while internals did not. Achievement-oriented patterns of performance were obtained from 91% of external subjects when task directions emphasized the achievement-relevance of the task; when achievement characteristics were not so emphasized, only 18% of external subjects responded in an achievement-oriented fashion. Internals, on the other hand, exhibited little variability with directions. In brief, externals were highly responsive to external definitions of the task, whereas internals seemed to be more largely moved by their own lights, varying little with the experimenter's suggestions.

In another study using the level of aspiration technique, Lefcourt, Lewis, and Silverman (1968) initially found no performance differences between internals and externals in response to skill versus chance directions given with the task. However, when examining the subjects' own reports as to whether they actually perceived the task as skill or chance-determined, differences were noted between the groups. Internals were less likely than externals to have accepted directions which stressed chance determination of the level of aspiration task, and they were more likely to have accepted skill directions. It was concluded, therefore, that internals are somewhat more responsive to directions that concur with their own impressions and less likely to be influenced by those which challenge their own perceptions of the task at hand.

A similar finding in regard to the way in which externals respond to experimenter's directions was reported by Lefcourt and Wine (1969). Part of this experiment concerned the effect of the experimenter's stated purposes on the subjects' attentiveness. The number of observations of things unique to an experimental room were recalled by internals and externals in two conditions: one in which the purpose of the experiment was not defined for the subjects, and another which was described as an experiment focusing upon attention. All subjects then completed irrelevant tasks while in the experimental room. The number of observations that subjects could make of the experimental room itself was obtained after subjects had left that room and were seated in a second room. Unique to the first room was a series of "planted items": an erotic Shakespearian sonnet on the blackboard, signs advertising various events, TV sets on but without sound, etc. The number of unique stimuli recalled increased significantly with the "attention experiment" condition, and this increase was marked for the external group in particular. Internals had observed somewhat more unique stimuli than externals in the noninstructed condition, though not significantly so. With the instructions focusing upon attention, however, externals recalled significantly more unique stimuli than internals and more than their external counterparts in the uninstructed condition. Internals hardly changed at all between conditions.

In this experiment, then, the directions which simply alerted subjects as to what processes the experimenter was to focus on had the effect of altering externals' perceptual behavior. Since subjects had not been aware that the immediate room was to be the target of their attentions, it was as if externals simply began using their eyes when they knew that the experimenters were concerned with attention. In contrast, internals seemed unresponsive to the experimenter's interests insofar as their momentary behaviors were concerned.

In a reaction time study designed to replicate previously reported differences between internals and externals with self- *versus* experimenter-controlled conditions (Cromwell, Rosenthal, Shakow, & Zahn, 1961), Lefcourt and Siegel (1970a) were unable to find similar results with a university student sample. In order to increase the value of the task for a subsequent group of subjects, these investigators provided a detailed explanation regarding the importance of the results. Where Lefcourt and Siegel anticipated that the embellished directions would elicit the originally predicted superiority of internals with self-administered reaction time trials, the results proved to be the opposite. All subjects were quicker with the embellished directions, though externals improved even more than the internals. Again, externals shifted more with experimenter directions than did internals.

In the larger number of studies, then, evidence is found to support the contention that persons holding an internal locus of control can withstand pressures directing them to behave in a certain circumscribed manner. This is not true in all instances, although the exceptions to this generalization are revealing in themselves. Internals do yield to pressures, but not to the same pressures as externals. When acted upon as a subject in an experiment, internals appear to be almost playfully negativistic, as in the verbal conditioning experiments. Likewise, statements presented by authorities do not seem to captivate them. However, internals do respond to reasoned arguments regardless of the status of the source, readily respond to directives that are in agreement with their own perceptions, and shift their own attitudes and behavior when allowed more active participation, as in role playing which engenders internal self-directives. Externals appear to be responsive to more prestigious sources of influence, readily accepting experimenters' suggestions and directions. The merits of the arguments presented seem to be secondary to the prominence of the influencer, and, as reported in the study by Johnson *et al.* (1968), the desire for affiliation and dependence may be more important to externals than the maintenance of moral standards.

The latter point brings us back to the reason for our initial concern with the resistance to influence. It would seem from the data reported thus far that an internal locus of control is associated with a tendency to be circumspect in the face of pressure to yield to influence. However, as of yet, there have been no investigations linking locus of control with the kinds of influence resistance investigated by Milgram, and this sort of research would seem to be necessary if locus of control is to be further implicated with the concerns of freedom, morality, and the resistance to malevolent influences. Internals do seem to be more able to resist external direction than externals. But whether such resistance would persist against heightened pressure or increased inducements to acquiesce are questions requiring further empirical test.

One recent investigation, however, does provide some indirect evidence regarding internals "moral" behavior under pressure. If helping another person despite discomfort can be equated with the refusal to comply in hurting another despite pressure to do so, then a study by Midlarski (1971) indicates that internals may indeed prove resistant even to heightened pressure. In this investigation, subjects found themselves in a position where it was possible to help a confederate finish a sorting task. Each item that subject and confederate lifted would generate a shock from a grid upon which the items had been placed. In other words, each time that a subject helped the confederate, it was at the price of a shock. A shorter form of the I-E scale produced an $r = .54$, $p < .001$, $N = 80$. The more internal an individual, the more likely he was to help his confederate despite, his receiving a not very mild shock.

III. Cognitive Activity

One explanation for the greater resistance to directions among persons with internal control expectancies is that internals are more curious about the situations in which they find themselves than are persons with more external control expectancies. Common sense would dictate that persons holding internal control expectancies be more cautious and calculating about their choices, involvements, and personal entanglements than persons maintaining external control expectancies. Otherwise, the probability of their being able to perceive opportunities for success experiences and to avoid inevitable defeats would be lessened, which in turn would diminish the degree to which they perceive themselves as actors rather than pawns of fate. In brief, to maintain a generalized expectancy of internal control should require some modicum of success at steering oneself around obstacles and toward desired ends. A number of invalidations, or negative reinforcements, should serve to increase self-doubts and consequently lead to increasing external control expectancies. Such self-direction should entail more active cognitive processing of information relevant to the attainment of valued ends, and should be reflected in the types of cognitive strategies that come to characterize the person.

Two of the earliest reported investigations providing information in regard to cognitive activity as a function of locus of control were those by Seeman and Evans (1962) and Seeman (1963). Both studies, previously reviewed, reported the fact that internals had more information relevant to their personal conditions than did externals. Among tuberculosis patients, internals had come to know more about their own conditions than had externals (Seeman & Evans, 1962); and among reformatory inmates, internals exhibited greater learning about the attainment of parole than had externals (Seeman, 1963). Internals did not differ from externals, however, when the information presented for learning was less personally relevant. Differences were prominent only when the learning concerned means toward a valued end.

Since these early publications a series of investigations have been reported that bear further upon the hypothesized cognitive differences between persons with internal *versus* external control orientations. In one study, Davis and Phares (1967) gave their subjects the task of attempting to influence another subject's attitudes toward the Viet Nam war. Subjects were led to believe that the experimenters had a file of data available about each prospective influencee. The main dependent measure consisted of the number of questions that subjects asked of the experimenter about their specific influencees. The authors had hypothesized that internals would be more likely to seek information than externals, so as to become more prepared for their task. Davis and Phares also instructed their subjects as to the likelihood of their being effective. One group received skill directions, another luck directions, and a third were offered no special instructions regarding their likelihood of successful persuasion. In the group receiving the luck instructions, no differences in information-seeking were found. However, internals did request more information than externals about their influencees in both the "skill" and no-instruction groups. The results indicate that internals engage more in the preliminary steps of data gathering than externals which, in turn, might increase their probability of success were the task actually to transpire. That this difference did not obtain when subjects were instructed that there was less likelihood of them being able to influence change in attitudes adds to the credibility of the results.

In another study reported by Phares (1968), internals and externals were compared in their tendencies to use information for decision-making, which all subjects had learned to a similar criterion level. Subjects had learned 10 bits of information about each of four males to errorless recall. A week later subjects had to guess which of eight girls, and which of 10 occupations were most suited to each of the four men. Financial rewards were offered for correct matchings, and subjects had to list reasons for each of their matchings. Information utilization was measured by the number of reasons given for the matches made, as well as the correctness (from previous information) of those reasons. Internals were found to give more reasons, and more correct reasons at that, than externals. This led Phares to conclude that internals are more likely to make use of information that externals are equally aware of, and that, therefore, internals should have a greater potential for effectiveness in their social environment.

Lefcourt and Wine (1969) have also reported some data about the manner in which internals and externals attend to social cues while attempting to learn about another person. In this study, subjects interviewed two target persons, one of whom behaved in a somewhat quizzical fashion, avoiding eye contact with the subject throughout the interview. The second target person, on the other hand, behaved in a more conventional manner with regard to eye contact. It was hypothesized that the uncertainty caused by the behavior of the quizzical target person would engender more curiosity and attentiveness among internal subjects, and that such attention would be evident in their looking behavior, as well as in the number of observations they could make of the target people. Lefcourt and Wine did find that internals looked at the eye-contact-avoidant person more often than they looked at the conventional target person, and looked at him more often than did external subjects. Internals also made more observations than externals of both target persons. The number of observations of the eye-contact-avoidant target person was related to the frequency with which the subject observed that person's facial areas. These authors concluded, then, that internal subjects are more likely than externals to attend to cues providing information which can help to resolve uncertainties.

In another study focusing upon attentiveness, Lefcourt et al. (1968) found that internal and external subjects varied considerably in their attention-related responses, depending upon whether they viewed the level of aspiration task in which they were engaged as skill or chance determined. Internals who perceived the task as skill determined exhibited less inattentiveness, and they reported that they had engaged in more task-relevant and less task-irrelevant thoughts than did internals who believed that the task was more chance determined. Differences among externals as a function of perceived controllability of the task were nowhere as pronounced. These findings were supported by results with decision time. Internals took more time to decide upon each subsequent expectancy statement when they had perceived the task as skill determined. Externals, to the contrary, were more deliberate when they perceived the task as chance determined.

These results, indicating that internals spend more time deliberating about decisions in skill-demanding tasks than chance-determined tasks, while externals tend to show opposite reactions, have been reported in other investigations. Rotter and Mulry (1965) found internals exhibiting longer delays in decision times with skill as opposed to chance directions. Externals did not differ as extensively in that study. Likewise, Julian and Katz (1968) found that internals required longer decision times when the difficulty of decision making increased. Externals, as in the Rotter and Mulry study, did not differ as extensively, revealing little decision time differences between easy and difficult choices. That skill and chance tasks have different meaning for internal and external subjects is evident in the study by Watson and Baumal (1967). In that investigation, internals were found to make more errors in preparation for a task said to be chance determined. Externals showed a similar error proneness when anticipating a skill-determined task. These authors interpreted their results in terms of anxiety engendered by tasks that offer challenges which are incongruent with subjects' habitual orientations.

Pursuing the concern with attention differences, Lefcourt and Siegel (1970a) examined reaction time performance of internal and external subjects administered under various conditions. While no differences were obtained in reaction time performance as a function of I-E, the same investigators (Lefcourt & Siegel, 1970b) did find some success in predicting performance with a measure of field dependence: field-independent subjects had shorter reaction times (greater attentiveness) with subject as opposed to experimenter control of stimulus onset during the reaction time procedure. More important for the present purposes, however, was the reasoning for the use of the field dependence variable in this experiment. Witkin and his colleagues (Witkin, Dyk, Faterson, Goodenough, & Karp, 1962) have expanded upon their earlier research with perceptual field dependence, describing a concept referred to as psychological differentiation. These writers speak of differentiation and identity in such terms that the overlap with the locus of control construct becomes apparent:

> With respect to relations with the surrounding field, a high level of differentiation implies clear separation of what is identified as external to the self. The self is experienced as having definite limits or boundaries. Segregation of the self helps make possible greater determination of functioning from within, as opposed to a more or less enforced reliance on external nurturance and support for maintenance typical of the relatively undifferentiated state [p. 10].

Some relationship between I-E and differentiation, or at least a similar pattern of relationships for these variables with different criterion behaviors, could be anticipated, then, on the basis of the apparent similarities between the locus of control and differentiation constructs. Rotter (1966) had previously reported that no empirical relationship had been found between the I-E scale and the Gottschalk Figures Test (one measure of differentiation). Chance and Goldstein (1967) likewise found an insignificant relationship between I-E and performance on the Embedded Figures Test, though these latter investigators did find that internals improved steadily from trial to trial as they progressed through the Embedded Figures Test. In addition, Deever (1968) and Lefcourt and Telegdi (1971) have found no relationship between the rod and frame, block design, and embedded figures measures of differentiation, and the locus of control. Nevertheless, the constructs bear theoretical similarity in predicting to assertiveness, the experiencing of oneself as a distinct source of causation, and the tendency to be self-reliant rather than acquiescent and conforming. That these variables might prove complementary to each other in predicting to such criteria has received some support. Bax (1966) found significant correlations between I-E and TAT measures of differentiation ($r = .37$, $p < .001$, $N = 96$), and lack of assertiveness ($r = .35$, $p < .001$, $N = 96$) in the expected directions. Dies (1968) has reported similar results. Deever (1968) found that high differentiation and internal control both predicted a greater reliance upon one's own reinforcement history than on group norms for the prediction of performance.

In this latter experiment, subjects had to state how sure they were of success for each trial in which they were to compare the length of two similar lines. The procedure was a typical level of aspiration task with two additional elements: correctness feedback was rigged beforehand; and subjects were provided with norms of peer performance for each trial. Both differentiation as measured by the Embedded Figures Test and the locus of control generated main effects, the former significant at the .001 level, the latter at the .01 level. Internals and highly differentiated subjects expressed greater confidence of success and greater differences from the provided norms than externals and less differentiated subjects. Despite the similar relationship with the criterion, I-E and performance with the embedded figures test was unrelated ($r = .02$).

Lefcourt and Telegdi (1971) have used both I-E and the rod and frame measurement of differentiation in an attempt to predict scores on measures reflecting cognitive activity. The dependent measures consisted of performance on Mednicks' Remote Associates Test, Barron's Human Movement Threshold Inkblot Test, and an incomplete sentences test. As predicted, internal–highly differentiated subjects surpassed all other subjects on each measure. However, external–low-differentiated subjects proved to be second, and the incongruent groups (internal–low-differentiated, external–high-differentiated) were the poorest on each measure. In this study, neither I-E nor differentiation alone produced a significant main effect in the prediction of cognitive activity. Only in combination were significant results obtained. This supports the positions advanced by Schimek (1968) and Crego (1970) advocating the investigation of these convergent concepts of cognitive styles and defense structures simultaneously.

One other set of studies has included measures of I-E and differentiation as predictors of cognitive activity (Lefcourt, Gronnerud, & MacDonald, 1971a; Lefcourt, Sordoni, & Sordoni, 1971b). The former investigators predicted that internal–highly differentiated individuals would be the earliest to recognize that something untoward was occurring as a word-association test, (see Table I) nominally given to check on verbal facility presented a gradually increasing number of sexual double entendres. Internals exhibited excessive time delay earlier in the list than externals,

TABLE I
STIMULUS WORDS IN THE DOUBLE-ENTENDRE WORD-ASSOCIATION LIST[a]

1 fly	11 light	21 sugar	31 measure	41 *HUMP*
2 face	12 work	22 *NUTS*	32 *BLOW*	42 *PET*
3 plant	13 *RUBBER*	23 cross	33 garden	43 *TOOL*
4 voice	14 health	24 *MAKE*	34 *COCK*	44 *SUCK*
5 earth	15 ocean	25 carpet	35 stove	45 *BANG*
6 miss	16 *BUST*	26 *CRACK*	36 *MOUNT*	46 *ASS*
7 door	17 fire	27 lamp	37 city	47 *BALLS*
8 alone	18 watch	28 *SCREW*	38 *QUEER*	48 *PUSSY*
9 good	19 *SNATCH*	29 paper	39 water	49 *BOX*
10 ride	20 drink	30 *PRICK*	40 *PIECE*	50 *LAY*

[a] From Lefcourt *et al.* (1971a).

indicating an earlier development of awareness. External–low-differentiated subjects, on the other hand, were the last to show an increase in length of response time. The first sex response made to the double entendres came earliest from the internal–highly differentiated subjects ($M = 3.08$, or at about the third double entendre). However, it was not the external but internal–low-differentiated subjects who were the last to respond with sex words ($M = 16.33$). Externals had $Ms = 7.08$ and 10.42. The resulting interaction between I-E and differentiation was highly significant ($F = 8.30$, $p < .001$, $1/44$). Videotaped facial expressions indicated that the internal–low-differentiated group also showed more signs of puzzlement throughout the test. In brief, internal–highly differentiated subjects seemed to be more cognitively alert and active than other subjects in that they perceived the nature of the stimulus list early in the task, tested out their hypothesis about same, and gave some visual indication of "knowing" what was happening sooner than did other subjects. Again, the combination of I-E and differentiation offered better prediction of a series of responses than either variable by itself.

A second analysis of the videotaped word-association study was conducted with a focus upon the incidence of humor. Lefcourt *et al.* (1971b) rated three different kinds of humor: cognitive, social, and tension-relief. Cognitive humor was scored when "knowing" smiles and laughs were accompanied by challenging looks, narrowed eyes, and "prideful" appearance. Throughout the double entendre list, internals tended to display more cognitive humor than externals ($F = 3.65$, $p < .10$, $1/44$). In addition, an interaction with the period of the list (it had been divided into five periods of 10 words apiece) was obtained ($F = 2.33$, $p < .06$, $4/176$). This interaction derived from the fact that internals and externals did not differ during the first two periods or first 20 words when double entendres had only begun to be introduced. During periods three and four, internals began exhibiting more cognitive humor than externals ($p < .01$ in both cases), and this difference became most marked during the last period ($p < .001$) when all words presented were double entendres. In terms of total mirth, all smiles and laughter regardless of humor type, internals well exceeded externals. Main effects for laughter ($F = 5.21$, $p < .05$, 1/44) and smiles ($F = 5.79$, $p < .025$, 1/44) indicated that internals were more perceptive of and responsive to the ludicrous situation in which they found themselves.

As in the analyses with decision time, verbal responses, and facial expressions, the incidence of humor indicates that internals are more cognitively alert and active than external subjects. On the other hand, differentiation did not contribute much in predicting the humor response.

Overall, the research regarding cognitive activity and I-E lends some support to the contention that persons with internal control expectancies tend to be more cognitively active than those with external control expectancies. Internals seem to know more about what is important to them, and seem more eager to gain information that would help increase their probabilities for success experiences. In skill tasks, where control is possible, internals look decidedly more deliberate and cautious than externals. Externals, on the other hand, seem more involved in chance tasks, expending time and effort at decisions which seem of little concern to internals. Nevertheless, I-E itself explains only a limited percentage of the variance in cognitive tasks. As evidenced in a recent overview and replication of his own work, Seeman (1967) found support, albeit weak support, for his linkage between locus of control and knowledge of valued information. The latter studies reviewed above indicate that the power of prediction of cognitive activity is often greatly increased when I-E and differentiation are used in concert. Perhaps, as Deever (1968) suggested, a battery of divergent techniques relevant to autonomy is advisable if we are to improve in our prediction of behavior reflecting upon self-reliance.

To add to this point, several investigators have presented information to the effect that the I-E scale, presented in detail in Rotter's (1966) monograph, has certain weaknesses. P. Gurin, Gurin, Lao, and Beattie (1969), Lao (1970), and Mirels (1970) have each presented theoretical and empirical evidence which advances the position that the I-E scale is not unidimensional, but can be meaningfully defined as two relevant but separate measures: one concerning perceived personal control, the other, perceived control of broader social events. Personal *versus* ideological beliefs are apt descriptions of these two factors. Perhaps, the events of the day have created more cynicism about the ability of controlling world as opposed to personal events, such that what was once a more homogeneous orientation has become a more fragmented and finely discriminated set of expectancies. In addition, I-E continues to show a low but reliable relationship with the need for approval (Lefcourt & Wine, 1969), with the Edwards Social Desirability Scale (Cone, 1971), and with the general denial of psychopathology (Goss & Morosko, 1970). Hamsher, Geller, and Rotter (1968) have also reported on what they refer to as "defensive-externality," when behaviorally defined internal males describe themselves as externals. As conceptualized by these investigators, defensive externals are suspicious individuals who believe that authority figures are bent on thwarting their attempts at mastery and control.

In short, the I-E scale itself can only be a weak predictor without considering other variables with which it interacts. In view of its limitations, the growing list of positive results described above and in the 1966 reviews must be viewed as nothing less than remarkable. In no study has I-E accounted for very much of the differences obtained; but the reliability of the contribution toward prediction attests to its value.

IV. Deferred Gratification, Achievement Behavior, and the Response to Success and Failure

A. DEFERRED GRATIFICATION

Another research area of relevance to locus of control concerns the preference for immediate *versus* delayed reinforcements. It would seem plausible that a person who views himself as an effective controller of reinforcements would be one who is accustomed to planning and prolonged work efforts. Long time delays between the expression of desires and their satisfaction should be commonplace for internals, whereas externals should be more impulsive and should prefer more easily obtainable and immediate goals.

In the earlier reviews one investigation was cited in which a correlation between I-E and delayed reinforcement preference was noted. Bialer (1961) found that the more internal the subject, the more likely he was to prefer a delayed larger reinforcement to a smaller immediate reinforcement. Subsequent replications of this finding have been reported. Unfortunately, the methodology employed in these studies concerned with immediate *versus* delayed reinforcement has been limited. The most commonly employed technique has been to offer youngsters a small prize immediately or the option to wait for a larger gift to be delivered after some period of time. This method of testing delay capacity, reviewed in some detail by Mischel (1966), is clever in demonstrating the value of the immediate-delayed reinforcement dimension. However, it suffers in comparison to real decision making about valued goals. For instance, the reinforcements have more often been undeserved, fortuitous, and of only slight value so that the generalization from such choice activity to choices made about real life goals would seem tenuous at best. Despite the limitations of this research, some interesting findings have been reported. Zytkoskee, Strickland, and Watson (1971) found that locus of control and self-imposed delay of gratification were both related to similar demographic variables. Blacks were found to be more external and more likely to choose immediate reinforcements than were whites, and these findings were the most pronounced between the females of the black and white samples. However, the direct correlations between these variables were insignificant, though the experimental design, which also contained an examiner status manipulation, may have confounded these correlations. In a subsequent study, in which Strickland (1972) contrasted results obtained from black and white experimenters, delayed reinforcement preference was found to be related to an internal locus of control within the sample of white subjects. Blacks, on the other hand, were significantly more external, as has been reported previously, and their choice between immediate and delayed reinforcement was unrelated to locus of control.

Walls and Smith (1970) have found I-E to be correlated significantly with the choice of a slightly larger but delayed reinforcement (7 as to 5 pennies), internals choosing to wait for the larger amount. These writers also found I-E to be related to a measure of time perspective: internals judged more accurately the lapse of a minute. Correctness of time judgment was, in turn, related to the preference for delayed reinforcements, replicating previously reported results (Mischel, 1961; Spivack, Levine, & Sprigle, 1959).

In contrast, Walls and Miller (1970) found I-E unrelated to delayed reinforcement choice or time perspective in another study with a small sample of vocational rehabilitation and welfare clients. However, both locus of control and delayed reinforcement preference were related to grade school level; the more educated persons were more internal and more likely to prefer delayed reinforcement.

J. J. Platt and Eisenman (1968) correlated six measures of time perspective with Rotter's I-E scale, and found that internals surpassed externals on each index of time perspective, though only two correlations reached statistical significance (personal future and impersonal past extension). These extension measures were obtained by presenting 10 events to a subject to which he had to indicate the number of years from the present that the event would or had occurred. The more accurate perception of longer expanses of time by internals should be related to the willingness to defer gratification.

In a study concerned largely with the prediction of school achievement,

Lessing (1969) found that Strodtbeck's Personal Control Scale (Strodt-beck, 1958) and a delay of gratification measure were both related to grade-point average. Negro children were more external and less willing to delay gratification than white children, and they achieved less than their white counterparts. From the account of the studies above, it is evident that there is some empirical support for assuming that there is a relationship between one's perception of control and one's willingness to defer gratification. However, it is equally obvious that there are large gaps of missing information, and some uncertainties about results already reported. In a few studies, direct correlations between I-E and delay preferences have been reported; in others there has been a coincidence of internality and preferences for delayed reinforcements among the better educated, more achievement-oriented and less deprived racial groups; and in still others, I-E has been related to measures of time perspective which are, in turn, related to delay preferences. Despite these convergent positive findings, conclusions are problematic because of the lack of sampling of reinforcement preference techniques, the overuse of samples that are atypical or extremes in regard to the measures in question, and the general lack of information linking I-E and "real-life" decisions involving delayed reinforcement. Nevertheless, it would seem unlikely that these variables would not be related to each other. The experience of successes that are contingent upon one's efforts, without which a sense of competence and control would be impossible, require the very prolonged activity and persistence over time that are inherent in working for delayed reinforcements. Perhaps a major reason for the relatively weak findings reported thus far derives from the use of "empty time" in most delay of reinforcement studies. That is, subjects have more often been asked to simply wait rather than to persist in some effort directed toward a valued end. Such waiting for what are often undeserved rewards may be more related to the ability to restrain one's momentary impulses than to the willingness to commit oneself to long-term efforts directed at distant goals.

Overall, the studies reported do suggest that locus of control and reinforcement preference are related. The challenge now would seem to be in the expansion upon these limited findings, testing the relevance of I-E to the making of long-range goal commitments that require tolerance of immediate frustrations and deprivations.

B. Achievement Behavior

Research in the area of achievement behavior contains similar short-comings as does the research with deferred gratification. There has been sparse research into achievement activity of a long-sustained nature. The largest number of studies have linked I-E with grade-point average, achievement test scores, and school room achievement behavior among grade-school children.

Lessing (1969) has reported that a sense of personal control predicted grade-point level of students even when IQ scores were partialled out. The most publicized of the locus of control achievement studies, however, has been the Coleman report (Coleman, Campbell, Hobson, McPartland, Mood, Weinfeld, & York, 1966). Both of the above, as well as studies by Chance (1965), Crandall, Katkovsky, and Preston (1962), Harrison (1968), McGhee and Crandall (1968), and Nowicki and Roundtree (1971) have found that an internal locus of control generally accompanies various aspects of childrens' successful academic achievement. One exception to the rule favoring internality has been reported by Katz (1967) who found little relationship between achievement and scores on the Intellectual Achievement Responsibility Scale (Crandall et al., 1965) among Negro children. The overwhelming majority of studies, however, do report positive association between internality and achievement behavior, and do so despite a wide range of measuring devices for the locus of control.

The strength of this association is exemplified in the study by Harrison (1968), who employed his "View of the Environment Test" and found that a sense of personal control characterized successful students regardless of the socioeconomic status of the home. That is, an internal orientation predicted to academic success among both advantaged and disadvantaged children. This result reflects a rather fine discriminative prediction in view of the fact that less advantaged children are usually found at the more external end of the I-E continuum and at the low end of the achievement spectrum.

Chance (1965) found that the Crandall's Intellectual Achievement Responsibility Scale was related to several school achievement criteria among boys and girls. Correlations with IQ ($r = .34$, $p < .01$ and $.33$, $p < .05$ for each sex respectively), reading skills ($rs = .50$, $p < .01$ and $.45$, $p < .01$), arithmetic performance ($rs = .46$, $p < .01$ and $.51$, $p < .01$), and with spelling test performance ($rs = .56$, $p < .01$ and $.35$, $p < .01$) were all highly significant.

In contrast to these almost uniform results, Nowicki and Roundtree (1971), using the Nowicki-Strickland measure of I-E, found that achievement, as measured by the California Achievement Test, was associated with I-E for males ($r = -.44$, $p < .01$) though not for females ($r = .13$, ns). Intelligence, as assessed by the Otis-Lennon Mental Abilities Test, was not significantly related to I-E for males ($r = .32$, ns) or females ($r = .09$, ns).

Despite some consistency of findings in this area, there is again a notable absence of research concerned with more prolonged achievement activity as might be indicated by types of careers and adult pursuits which require persistence and the willingness to defer gratification. In short, investigations of achievement behavior beyond the limits of a grade-school year and single administrations of achievement tests are necessary to test the generality of the assumed link between I-E and achievement.

C. The Response to Success and Failure

One area of achievement-related research has been explored in some depth: the response to success and failure experiences. If a person were too easily satisfied with small or singular indications of success, or too responsive to impending failures, the likelihood of his engaging in prolonged and continued achievement behavior would be minimal. The maintenance of achievement behavior would seem to require a more measured response to the outcomes of achievement strivings reflecting awareness and growth from experience, without an overresponse leading to the termination of effort.

The earliest studies linking I-E to the coping with success and failure employed the level of aspiration paradigm, in which subjects stated their expectancies for success throughout a series of trials in which they experienced failures and successes. Phares (1955) and James (1957) both studied the effect of skill and chance directions upon the expectancies of subjects who had been designated internals and externals on the basis of scores on the earliest forms of the I-E scale. Externals were found to behave similarly to subjects who had received chance directions, exhibiting less expectancy shifts reflecting their successes and failures, and producing more unusual shifts (raising expectancies after a failure to accomplish lesser levels of achievement, or lowering expectancies after attaining success on higher levels of performance). The occurrence of unusual shifts among more external subjects has been found with some consistency (Battle & Rotter, 1963; Lefcourt & Ladwig, 1965a), as have other level of aspiration variables such as abnormal expectancy shifting frequencies and failure-avoidant patterns (Rotter, 1954). The unusual shift, perhaps, best exemplifies the failure to develop a measured response to one's success and failure experiences. To make such expectancy shifts indicates that a person is not using his prior experiences as a basis for predictions. It is as if one's fortunes were random and one's experiences discrete and unrelated. Investigators concerned with achievement motivation have also used the unusual shift as an indication of withdrawal from achievement challenge, finding that those who fear failure more than they hope for success are more likely to produce unusual shifts of expectancies (Moulton, 1965).

Since the report of the earlier studies, there have been a few investigations published which have replicated some of their findings. Lefcourt *et al.* (1968) found that failure-avoidant patterns and abnormal amounts of expectancy shifting made during performance on Rotter's level of aspiration board characterized the subject who believed that performance on that task was chance determined. These investigators also found that unusual shifts were more common among internals who believed the task to be chance determined than among those who perceived it as a skill task, while the reverse tendency was found among externals. Lefcourt (1967) used the level of aspiration board in another study in which the instructions differed in the degree to which achievement characteristics of the task were emphasized. Internals produced fewer failure-avoidant patterns than externals when instructions were vague in regard to achievement. However, as the directions became more achievement-oriented, significantly fewer externals showed abnormal amounts of shifting and failure-avoidance patterns than other externals who had received nonachievement-stressing instructions. In fact, these achievement-instructed externals surpassed internals in indications of success striving.

Feather (1968) has found that internals make more typical changes of confidence statements (up after success and down after failure) than externals during a series of trials with anagrams. Likewise, Ryckman, Gold, and Rodda (1971) found more typical changes in confidence throughout a series of anagrams among internals who were also high in self-esteem. In contrast, this same research group (Ryckman & Rodda, 1971) found the reverse in a task that was obviously less skill-determined than the anagrams test; internals made less typical confidence shifts than externals.

Lefcourt and Steffy (1970a) have investigated the manner in which level of aspiration performance such as that noted above is related to performance in other tasks. These investigators found that subjects who made a greater number of unusual shifts when performing on the level of aspiration board also shifted about more in their levels of risk-taking during a gambling task, and were less likely to write TAT-like stories containing sexual themes despite the presence of stimuli relevant to sex in the pictures presented to them. These results were interpreted as reflecting inadequate behavior across three disparate tasks (excessive shifting in risk choices is said to be a less strategic approach to the gambling task). At the same time, these authors found no relationships between performances on these tasks and the I-E scale, which they attempted to explain in terms of the testing conditions that may have helped to generate "defensive internality." As a point of interest, these same authors found in a follow-up investigation (Lefcourt & Steffy, 1970b) that the more adequate or success-striving behavior each subject demonstrated on each task, the less well was she rated as a student nurse in a training program that required deference to authority.

In general, the level-of-aspiration type research indicates that internals seem to adjust their behavior more appropriately to their accumulating experiences than do externals. However, when the task seems to be more chance- than skill-determined, it is the more external individual who exhibits experience-contingent expectancies, whereas internals seem to become more random. This reversal with chance-determined tasks is found with expressions of confidence as well as in performance measures such as decision time (as exemplified in Rotter & Mulry, 1965). Internals, then, do seem to be more measured in their responses to success and failure than externals insofar as expectancy statements made during skill-determined level of aspiration tasks are concerned. However, a few studies have presented data which raise questions as to the manner in which internals cope with failure experiences. The earliest of such studies (Efran, 1963) reported that internal high-school students were more likely to have forgotten failure experiences than externals. Rotter (1966) interpreted these results as indicating a lesser need to "repress" by externals who were not as likely to blame themselves for their failures as were internals. Lipp, Kolstoe, James, and Randall (1968) reported a related finding that handicapped externals exhibited lower recognition thresholds for tachistoscopically presented pictures of handicapped persons than more internal handicapped subjects. Externals were said to have a lesser tendency to deny "threatening" stimuli, while internals were seen as more threatened because of the challenge to control that a handicap represents. Phares, Ritchie, and Davis (1968) found a similar kind of result in that externals were able to recall more negative though spurious information that had been presented to them as feedback from their "personality assessments" than were internals. Nevertheless, internals subsequently expressed more interest in making arrangements to confront their assumed personal difficulties than externals. MacDonald and Hall (1969, 1971) have examined the perception of disabilities among internals and externals with results suggesting that, contrary to the study by Lipp et al. (1968), externals fear the difficulties associated with handicaps significantly more than internals. Only with regard to "emotional difficulties" do internals register more anticipation of trouble for maintaining successful role fulfillments, though even then they do not exceed externals in their degree of anticipated difficulty. In regard to the ability to recall completed *versus* incomplete tasks, Butterfield (1965) found no differences between internals and externals. This lack of recall difference was surprising in view of the fact that when subjects were given the opportunity to return to the battery of tasks, internals chose to return to incompleted tasks more than did externals when directions had emphasized the skilled nature of the tasks. In other words, recall and task behavior were independent, which is similar to the finding of Phares *et al.* (1968) whose internals, while recalling less information, were more ready to engage in ameliorative action. In one exception to this data regarding I-E and recall of failures, Borer (1969) found that internals recalled more incompleted than completed tasks, whereas the reverse was true of externals. Internals had a higher ratio of recall of interrupted to completed tasks ($M = 2.36$) than externals ($M = .65$), which produced a highly significant main effect for locus of control ($F = 17.37, p < .001, 1/20$).

While some of the writers mentioned above have advanced the position that internals are more defensive in the face of threat than externals, the larger group of studies concerning cognitive activity, the willingness to defer gratification, and the response to success and failure experiences argue against the interpretation emphasizing defensiveness. Rather, in view of the fact that internals are usually more ready to take action to confront their difficulties, the results indicating more recall and perception of threat-related stimuli may be more aptly interpreted as ruminative tendencies, or the cognitive overworking of negative details which may help to confirm the sense of helplessness that should be common to externals. In other words, the internal may dwell less upon his deficits, forgetting, and perhaps becoming inattentive to cues related to them as he assumes an active stance toward his problems. The external, on the other hand, who has repeatedly described himself as being more anxious (Feather, 1967; Goss & Morosko, 1970; Hountras & Scharf, 1970; J. J. Platt & Eisenman, 1968; Ray & Katahn, 1968; Watson, 1967), lower in self-esteem (Fitch, 1970), and higher in neuroticism and maladjustment (Hersch & Scheibe, 1967) than internals would be more likely to be ruminative about his failures which, in turn, helps to maintain his own self-perception as an inactive pawn of fate.

V. Sources of Control Expectancies

A. FAMILIAL ORIGINS

In the early reviews (Lefcourt, 1966b; Rotter, 1966) there was a notable absence of information regarding familial sources of locus of control, though the latter author had offered suggestions regarding the possible role that inconsistent parental discipline might play in shaping a child's perception of control. The undertaking of research in the area of expectancy development has been limited, though there are indications of increasing interest as in the symposium entitled "Developmental Aspects of Locus of Control Expectancies" presented at the 1971 APA Convention.

Among the earliest studies concerned with the development of control expectancies was that by Chance (1965) who matched childrens' scores on the Crandalls' Intellectual Achievement Responsibility Questionnaire with their mothers' attitudes toward child rearing obtained from interviews and the Parent Attitude Research Inventory. Among boys, internal control expectancies were related to permissive and flexible maternal attitudes, and to maternal expectations of early independence. A weak tendency was also found for birth order; the earlier born child (male or female) was somewhat more internal than later born children. This finding was also reported by Crandall *et al.* (1965) who interpreted this result favoring first-born children as reflecting upon the fact that the first born are often given more responsibilities in their families, whereas the later born are often in the position of being helped. MacDonald (1971a) recently obtained a similar result when restricting his analysis to one- and two-child families. Later-born children tended to be more external than first-born children, and were decidedly more external than only children. The only negative data reported thus far with regard to birth order is in a study by Eisenman and Platt (1968) who found higher external control expectancies among first-born males. Despite the relative consistency of birth-order data, however, the results have been of a small magnitude, rarely accounting for a sizeable percentage of variance.

Four different studies have been reported bearing some similarities, in that each reveals children's locus of control to be less related to parental attitudes than to children's or observers' perceptions of parental behavior. Katkovsky, Crandall, and Good (1967) compared childrens' scores on the Intellectual Achievement Responsibility Questionnaire with home observations of parental behavior, as well as parental attitudes expressed in interviews and on questionnaires. The overall findings indicated that internal control expectancies are related to parental protectiveness, nurturance, and the tendencies to be approving and nonrejecting. As noted above, the largest number of significant results were obtained with the observed behavior measures and not with expressed parental attitudes. Consequently, these investigators raised the question as to the usefulness of parental self-report information.

Davis and Phares (1969) have drawn comparisons between extreme groups of internals and externals on the Children's Reports of Parental Behaviors Inventory. Similar to the preceding investigation, these authors found that parents of internals were judged as being more accepting, having greater positive involvement, and being less rejecting and exercising of hostile control than parents of externals. In addition, parents of internals were perceived as being more consistent disciplinarians than were parents of externals, as Rotter had suggested. On the other hand, these same researchers found no significant differences between parents of internals and externals when parents' attitudes were assessed on the Maryland Parent Attitude Survey. Some interactions were noted, however, that were too complex to interpret, though they were suggestive of differential effects of husbands' and wives' attitudes toward children. Internal children had fathers who advocated indulgence, independence, and self-reliance more than did their mothers, whereas mothers of externals more strongly advocated these child-rearing goals than did their fathers. While it is tempting to draw inferences from such differences, it will suffice to suggest that the evaluation of parent interactions would seem to be a valuable avenue for further exploration.

Shore (1968) used two measures of I-E (Bialer and Battle-Rotter) and the Children's Report of Parent Behavior Inventory with grade-school boys, and had parents complete Rotter's I-E scale, a special scale assessing parental expectations of personal control in child rearing, and two measures of parental attitudes. Among parental attitudes, only the fathers' internality regarding child rearing was related to children's I-E measures: the more internal the father, the more internal the boy ($r = .21, p < .01$). Children who perceived their parents as exerting more psychological control ($r = -.22, p < .01$) and as being less warm ($r = .43, p < .01$) and intrinsically accepting ($r = .46, p < .01$) were more external. Again, childrens' perceptions of parental behavior were more strongly related to children's locus of control than were parental attitudes, and children's perceptions of adult behavior and parental attitudes were unrelated.

MacDonald (1971b) used large samples of college students who completed Rotter's I-E scale along with a Perceived Parenting Questionnaire. Again, perceived parental nurturance was positively related to internality on the I-E scale as was parental consistency in maintaining standards for children's behavior.

One other study employing a somewhat differing methodology has been reported by Epstein and Komorita (1971). These investigators found that Negro children who described their parents as using excessively hostile control, and as being inconsistent disciplinarians on the Children's Report of Parent Behavior, attributed successes in a matching task to external causes. The use of causality attribution during the execution of a task is relatively novel in locus of control research and offers an interesting approach for assessing I-E orientation *in vivo*.

As is evident, the empirical data regarding child-rearing antecedents of locus of control has tended to be somewhat consistent. A warm, accepting home with predictable, consistent standards is more commonly reported by internal children and adolescents than their external counterparts, though expressions of parental attitudes about the same elements seem unrelated to the child's locus of control. Further investigation would, therefore, seem necessary to discover what elements contribute to the child's perception of a warm home, in contrast to parental perceptions of the same. It is noteworthy that in the one investigation in which parental behavior was observed, there was some successful prediction of children's I-E scores. Perhaps, parental behavior and children's perceptions of home atmosphere could prove to be effective multiple predictors of the development of a child's perception of control. In short, good inroads have been made in research conducted thus far which may offer valuable information if pursued and expanded.

B. SOCIAL ORIGINS

Information regarding social origins of control expectancies other than familial has been somewhat more plentiful. Research summarized in earlier reviews had led to the conclusion that class- and caste-related disadvantages result in the development of external control expectancies. A number of more recent investigations have provided support for this position with respect to comparisons between black and white Americans. With the exception of two studies in which the Intellectual Achievement Responsibility Scale was employed (Katz, 1967; Solomon, Houlihan, & Parelius, 1969) and one with Rotter's I-E scale (Kiehlbauch, 1968), most studies continue to show that blacks score in a more external direction than whites (Lessing, 1969; Owens, 1969; Shaw & Uhl, 1969; Strickland, 1972; Zytkoskee et al., 1971). Solomon et al. and Katz both interpreted this failure to find differences between racial groups as being due to the nature of the tests employed. The Intellectual Achievement Responsibility Questionnaire is viewed as the most specific of the I-E measures, concerned primarily with the sense of personal control over reinforcements in the intellectual achievement area. In contrast, the Bialer, Rotter, Nowicki-Strickland measures concern a more generalized sense of control, pertaining to several areas of reinforcement, which may seem less potentially controllable to blacks than academic achievement. The Kiehlbauch finding with Rotter's I-E scale, on the other hand, which failed to discover differences between black and white reformatory inmates, may reflect a real change in black's self-perception occurring as a function of civil rights and black power movements. Lefcourt and Ladwig (1965a) had made a hypothesis that such movements could shift black I-E scores in a more internal direction, thus eliminating the significant differences which had formerly been obtained.

In regard to class-related differences, Gruen and Ottinger (1969) have found that middle-class children are more internal than lower class children, and Walls and Miller (1970) have found educational level to be directly related to internality. Jessor *et al.* (1968) have found that internal control expectancies are positively associated with socioeconomic status, and that objective access to opportunities in a community is positively related to perceived control. These same authors also reported ethnic group differences: Anglo-Americans were more internal than Spanish Americans, with mean I-E scores for Indians falling midway between others. On the basis of their respective cultural histories, Hsieh, Shybut, and Lotsof (1969) successfully predicted I-E scores of Anglo-Americans, American-born Chinese, and Chinese living on Formosa. The results indicated that externality increased significantly from the first to the last-named groups.

In view of the general results indicating that groups with less objective access to reinforcements are more external control in orientation, P. Gurin *et al.* (1969) have raised serious questions as to whether it would be functional for such groups to become more internal. These writers have isolated two elements through a factor analysis of Rotter's I-E scale which they refer to as personal control and system blame. The former factor was found to be unrelated, whereas the latter measure was positively related to the choosing of nontraditional Negro careers, which these authors termed innovative behavior. Likewise, system blame was related to the readiness to join with others for social action. In contrast to previous experiments, then, externality in the sense of blaming the system for one's failures was associated with more aspiring ambitions, and a concern with social action. Consequently, these writers have argued that internality creates support for the status quo among groups that are subject to social injustice, shielding them from the perception of obstacles that can only be overcome through group action. Lao (1970) subsequently reported that these two factors do operate independently, personal control allowing prediction of academic achievement-related behavior, system blame predicting civil rights activity, and the preferred mode of social action (participation in collective movements in preference to a concern with individual improvement).

Whether the compelling arguments of Gurin *et al.* with regard to the value of holding external control beliefs is valid will require more empirical study. The choice of highly ambitious careers among blacks was once assumed to be an indication of unrealistic fantasy (Frazier, 1962; Katz, 1967), especially in view of the fact that the person who was least likely to succeed was often the one who stated the highest aspirations. In addition, some investigators (Escoffery, 1968) have found that internal black college students are more likely to belong to civil rights organizations than their external counterparts, although others have found no relationship between I-E and civil rights activities (Evans & Alexander, 1970).

While many questions may be raised from these data regarding social sources of control expectancies, there is little doubt that locus of control is linked to social learning within given groups. However, as the two factor advocates have argued, the predictions of behavior would be immeasurably improved if I-E for specific sorts of reinforcements could be differentiated from one another. Measures of generalized expectancies of control have been criticized as ignoring the fact that among black people, for instance, there may be considerable variability in control expectancies in one reinforcement area as opposed to another. The need for refinement in the measurement of I-E receives its greatest impetus in this area of social group differences. Perhaps the fact that other investigators have been coupling I-E with other measures to improve predictions—trust (Hamsher, Geller, & Rotter, 1968); field dependence (Lefcourt et al., 1971a; Lefcourt & Telegdi, 1971); and self-esteem (Ryckman et al., 1971)—argues the same point: that I-E often seems relevant but rarely accounts for a sufficiently high proportion of variance to allow for solid behavior prediction.

VI. Changes in Locus of Control

This writer, as well as others, has advanced the position that an internal locus of control, with its assumed correlates of competence and the hope of success, is a common goal of psychotherapy (Lefcourt, 1966a). If one needs to alter his mode of behavior, then an external locus of control is a decided obstacle, and therefore, a target for change.

Two studies with relevance to changing expectancies had been reported in the earlier reviews: One demonstrated that explicit directions has salutary impact upon the control-related behavior of externals (Lefcourt, 1967); the other illustrated how expectancies in a new challenging situation could be increased when a new task was linked with others in which the subjects had already enjoyed some success (Lefcourt & Ladwig, 1965b).

Since the report of these findings, a small number of investigations have been published, some of which have focused upon locus of control changes occurring as a result of natural events, and others as a result of some deliberate effort such as psychotherapy. Among the simplest of natural events, age change alone has been found to influence I-E scores, older children being more internal than younger children (Penk, 1969). Time passage of a smaller span has also been found to be related to control expectancies during a period of incarceration. Kiehlbauch (1968) found that reformatory inmates acknowledged higher externality upon admission, and shortly before release, than during the middle period of their internment. This same finding has been obtained previously by Mastellone.[2] Kiehlbauch also found that manifest anxiety scores covaried with I-E scores. The initial stage of commitment, then, seems to be a time of anxiety and helplessness, whereas the intermediate period of internment with its relative stability offers less anxiety and more opportunity for successful coping behavior. As the time for release approaches, however, uncertainties with regard to coping "on the streets" becomes more vivid and is reflected in the resurgence of a sense of helplessness and anxiety.

Some change studies have examined the effect of specific public events upon I-E scores. Gorman (1968) found that undergraduates scored in a more external direction than Rotter's norms for university students on the day after the 1968 Democratic Party convention. A large proportion of Gorman's student sample had been McCarthy supporters for whom the convention was a severely disillusioning experience. Another national event, the draft lottery, was also found to produce certain predictable effects upon the locus of control scores of college students. McArthur (1970) reported that students who had had the good fortune of becoming less draft eligible through the draft lottery scored as significantly more external on the I-E scale than those whose fates were unchanged by the lottery drawing.

From each of these studies it is possible to infer a mechanism of change. The Kiehlbauch investigation suggests that uncertainty, with its implicit challenge to one's coping ability, can increase one's sense of external control. However, this investigation also indicates that with a stable routine there is some likelihood that a person will regain his sense of control. Gorman's findings may be a simple case of expectancy invalidation. Youthful students who found that their activities on behalf of political goals had been fruitless no doubt experienced a sharp decline in their optimism and belief in control. McArthur's results, on the other hand, illustrate the effect of sudden good fortune, much as it might occur to a gambler with a "big hit." Unanticipated good fortune perhaps makes the reliance upon fate less unacceptable. In short, unanticipated events may invalidate a person's preconceptions for better or for worse and leave him with greater uncertainty about future events. It is unfortunate, however, that such studies have not reported upon the two separate I-E factors discussed by P. Gurin et al. (1969), since the above events would probably have differentially effected the factors of person *versus* system control.

A study by Smith (1970) bears somewhat upon the changing contin-

---

[2] Personal communication, 1969.

gencies principle. This investigation compared I-E scores of clinic clients who requested help in resolving crises with those intending to become engaged in long-term psychotherapy. The crisis client was defined as a person suffering with temporary but acute feelings of being overwhelmed such that self-confidence was at a low ebb. With 5 weeks of therapy designed to help clients adopt more effective coping techniques, crisis patients reported a significant decrease in externality, whereas regular therapy cases remained at the same level, despite a near equivalent number of therapy sessions.

Smith's findings, in a sense, begin where the previous studies leave off. Crisis clients are most often persons who are suffering with extreme uncertainties that have developed after some unforeseen changes in their lives. The crisis intervention, in which the client learns to cope with the acute problems confronting him, apparently restores his sense of control. This process of active coping with problems engendering greater internality has been reported in another therapy study (Dua, 1970). This investigator contrasted the effects of action oriented with reeducative therapy directed at improving interpersonal skills upon the locus of control. The action-oriented treatment involved the planning of specific behaviors for improving relationships with given persons, whereas the reeducative approach was directed toward influencing the clients' attitudes toward those persons. With both approaches, Dua found decreases in externality in comparison to an untreated control group. However, it was the more action-oriented training which produced the most change; clients with action training became more internal than controls and those receiving reeducative procedures.

Prolonged active involvement in problem confrontation has also been found to produce I-E changes in nontherapy investigations. Gottesfield and Dozier (1966) found that the length of participation in a community action program among slum-dwelling poor people was related to the expression of internal control expectancies.

A few investigations have examined the effects of formal therapeutic procedures upon locus of control. Lesyk (1969) evaluated the impact of a token economy, operant conditioning ward upon the behavior of female schizophrenics. Patients received tokens for behaving appropriately and cooperatively each day, and they were asked to estimate the number of tokens they anticipated earning on each subsequent day. I-E-related level of aspiration indices, the Bialer scale, and interview assessments of control expectancy were obtained pre- and postoperant training. After 5 weeks, patients made less expectancy shifts, fewer unusual shifts, and higher internal scores on the Bialer measure. In addition, those subjects with the highest ratings of positive behavior had the most internal Bialer scores, higher internal ratings derived from the interview, and fewer unusual shifts in their expectancies.

With more conventional therapy administered to a small sample of hospitalized psychiatric patients, Gillis and Jessor (1970) found that among patients judged by their therapists as being improved, there was more of an increase in internality than among a sample of untreated patients. Those patients, on the other hand, who were not judged as being improved did not shift in an internal direction.

Masters (1970) has presented a case report involving a successful therapeutic intervention in which his primary strategy involved altering the patient's perception of control. Reinterpretation consisted of analysis of the behavioral sequences which resulted in conflict, and suggesting actions for exerting control over the sources of conflict. While this case is singular, it demonstrates again how a sense of personal control can be an integral component of therapy procedures.

Nowicki and Barnes (in press) employed effectance training during a summer camp experience in an attempt to effect locus of control scores of deprived inner-city adolescents. The camp was described as being highly structured, with emphasis placed on contingent reinforcement for good and poor performance. As indicated in Table II, five out of eight groups showed significant increases in internality from pre- to post-camp testing; all groups but one increased in internality, the one exception exhibiting

TABLE II

SUMMARY OF t TESTS FOR PRE- AND POST-NOWICKI-STRICKLAND LOCUS OF CONTROL SCORES FOR EACH WEEKLY SESSION[a]

Week	N_1	X_1	X_2	t[b]
1	28	16.678	15.285	2.437[c]
2	35	16.228	15.257	1.528
3	54	17.278	15.370	4.341[d]
4	54	16.277	14.888	2.768[e]
5	31	18.226	17.548	1.103
6	27	17.037	17.111	−.130
7	32	16.312	14.125	2.051[f]
8	30	13.700	12.633	2.049[f]
Total	291	16.481	15.254	5.936[d]

[a] From Nowicki and Barnes (in press).
[b] One-tailed test.
[c] Significant at .01.
[d] Significant at .0015.
[e] Significant at .005.
[f] Significant at .05.

no noticeable change at all. This investigation is rather convincing in that it contained eight separate replications of the basic experiment, and produced an overall difference of $t = 5.94$, $p < .002$. In addition, these authors were able to observe a cumulative effect for the youngsters who returned for an extra week's camp experience. Children who returned for a second week in camp had a beginning M of 16.23 on the Nowicki-Strickland I-E measure (the higher the score on this scale, the more external). At the end of the first week, the group M was 14.07, which differed significantly from the initial scores. At the start of the second week, the group M of 14.11 did not differ from scores at the end of the first week. At the end of the second week, the group M was 12.65, again decreasing with a week's camp experience. These overall changes produced a highly significant effect ($F = 21.56$, $p < .001$, 3/75).

While some of these change studies are a bit sketchy and in need of clarification, the consistency of results showing covariation between I-E and therapy improvement is impressive. Nevertheless, it is appropriate to conclude this section with criticisms raised by G. Gurin and Gurin (1970). These writers have argued that personal expectancies of control often do not increase with changes in objective probabilities, as some of the above investigations might suggest. The culture of poverty, for instance, is said to have its own "secondary gains" such that expectancy changes may not be readily welcomed by the impoverished. Secondly, the Gurins suggest that the typical measures of expectancy change employed in research thus far are probably not very stable, and may be unrepresentative of changes in a person's more basic sense of self-confidence. In short, the Gurins seem to advocate more detailed examination of persons who are undergoing change to assess the ramifications and components of change and their impact on the individual's self-image.

While these criticisms offered by the Gurins are meaningful, the research summarized here, especially with regard to therapy of a problem-confronting nature offers confirmation of a theoretically probable relationship between increased effectiveness and increased perception of personal control. As persons successfully cope with immediate difficulties, they do seem to experience an increase in perceived control. Whether this increased sense of control generalized to enable one to face other obstacles without further external prods is questionable, and is perhaps at the core of the concern expressed by the Gurins in their critique of expectancy research.

VII. Conclusion

As it had been stated in the Introduction, research with the I-E dimension has been bounteous. Enough evidence has accumulated to confirm early expectations that the I-E dimension would contribute to the comprehension of certain goal-directed behaviors. However, as also suggested in the Introduction, high-magnitude predictions with a single variable removed from its theoretical network were not expected. The foregoing review well illustrates this point. With occasional exceptions, I-E is found to be a relevant predictor of resistance to influence, cognitive activity, and achievement-related behaviors. However, in almost all investigations discussed, there was considerable room for improvement in the prediction of criteria. In total, there is considerable room for increased information about the details of relationship between I-E and each area reviewed. It is obvious that when I-E is paired with other related but distinct variables such as self-esteem and differentiation, more powerful prediction of the criteria under investigation becomes possible.

In addition, those studies which have examined the psychometric properties of I-E measures provide consistent evidence that among many diverse samples the unidimensional character of I-E no longer obtains. A rather recent investigation that involved a series of factor analytic studies with the I-E scale has offered the suggestion that reliable subscales of the I-E measure have been isolated and should be used in making multiple regression predictions. Reid and Ware (1971) contend that multiple regression research can now be conducted with a series of I-E subscales such as fatalism and social system control, which they have found to be orthogonal to each other. It should become possible, according to these investigators, to make differential predictions of highly specific types of behavior as subareas of perceived control are identified, and the reliability of the related subscales are increased through the refinement of the assessment device. For instance, belief in personal control and low expectancy of social system control could prove to be decisive interactive predictors of the likelihood that a person will join militant movements, whereas each factor by itself might allow for only a small degree of prediction.

In overview, it may be concluded that I-E has already proved to be a fruitful research area. But of even more importance, it seems to have stimulated enough interest among investigators of diverse persuasions that research revolving around problems related to perceived control is growing in new and different directions. In turn, many refinements in assessment techniques and theoretical interpretations of locus of control–related phenomena have been, and hopefully will continue to be advanced.

References

Adorno, T., Frenkel-Brunswik, E., Levinson, D., & Sanford, R. *The authoritarian personality.* New York: Harper, 1950.

Arendt, H. *Adolph Eichmann in Jeruselum: A report on the banality of evil*. New York: Viking Press, 1963.

Aronfreed, J. *Conduct and conscience: The socialization of internalized control over behavior*. New York: Academic Press, 1968.

Battle, E., & Rotter, J. B. Children's feelings of personal control as related to social class and ethnic groups. *Journal of Personality*, 1963, 31, 482–490.

Bax, J. C. Internal-external control and field dependence. Unpublished honor's thesis, University of Waterloo, 1966.

Berg, I., & Bass, B. *Conformity and deviation*. New York: Harper, 1961.

Bialer, I. Conceptualization of success and failure in mentally retarded and normal children. *Journal of Personality*, 1961, 29, 303–320.

Biondo, J., & MacDonald, A. P. Internal-external locus of control and response to influence attempts. *Journal of Personality*, 1971, 39, 407–419.

Borer, A. Internal-external locus of control and the recall of interrupted tasks. Paper presented at the meeting of the Eastern Psychological Association, Philadelphia, April 1969.

Butterfield, E. C. The role of competence motivation in interrupted task recall and repetition choice. *Journal of Experimental Child Psychology*, 1965, 2, 354–370.

Chance, J. E. Internal control of reinforcements and the school learning process. Paper presented at the meeting of the Society for Research in Child Development, Minneapolis, March 1965.

Chance, J. E., & Goldstein, A. G. Locus of control and performance on embedded figures. Paper presented at the meeting of the Midwestern Psychological Association, Chicago, May 1967.

Coleman, J. S., Campbell, E. Q., Hobson, C. J., McPartland, J., Mood, A. M., Weinfeld, F. D., & York, R. L. *Equality of educational opportunity*. Washington, D. C.: US Govt. Printing Office, 1966. (Report from Office of Education.)

Cone, J. D. Locus of control and social desirability. *Journal of Consulting and Clinical Psychology*, 1971, 36, 449.

Crandall, V. C., Katkovsky, W., & Crandall, V. J. Children's beliefs in their control of reinforcements in intellectual-academic achievement behaviors. *Child Development*, 1965, 36, 91–109.

Crandall, V. C., Katkovsky, W., & Preston, A. Motivational and ability determinants of young children's intellectual-academic achievement situations. *Child Development*, 1962, 36, 91–109.

Crego, C. A. A pattern analytic approach to the measure of modes of expression of psychological differentiation. *Journal of Abnormal Psychology*, 1970, **76**, 194–198.

Cromwell, R. L., Rosenthal, D., Shakow, D., & Zahn, T. P. Reaction time, locus of control, choice behavior, and descriptions of parental behavior in schizophrenic and normal subjects. *Journal of Personality*, 1961, 29, 363–379.

Crowne, D. P., & Liverant, S. Conformity under varying conditions of personal commitment. *Journal of Abnormal and Social Psychology*, 1963, **66**, 547–555.

Davis, W. L., & Phares, E. J. Internal-external control as a determinant of information-seeking in a social influence situation. *Journal of Personality*, 1967, **35**, 547–561.

Davis, W. L., & Phares, E. J. Parental antecedents of internal-external control of reinforcement. *Psychological Reports*, 1969, 24, 427–436.

Dean, D. G. Alienation: Its meaning and measurement. *American Sociological Review*, 1961, **26**, 753–758.

deCharms, R. *Personal causation: The internal affective determinants of behavior.* New York: Academic Press, 1968.

Deever, S. G. Ratings of task-oriented expectancy for success as a function of internal control and field independence. *Dissertation Abstracts, Section B,* 1968, **29**(1), 365.

Dies, R. R. Development of a projective measure of perceived locus of control. *Journal of Projective Techniques & Personality Assessment,* 1968, **32**, 487–490.

Dua, P. S. Comparison of the effects of behaviorally oriented action and psychotherapy reeducation on intraversion-extraversion, emotionality, and internal-external control. *Journal of Counseling Psychology,* 1970, **17**, 567–572.

Efran, J. Some personality determinants of memory for success and failure. Unpublished doctoral dissertation, Ohio State University, 1963.

Eisenman, R., & Platt, J. J. Birth order and sex differences in academic achievement and internal-external control. *Journal of General Psychology,* 1968, **78**, 279–285.

Epstein, R., & Komorita, S. S. Self-esteem, success-failure, and locus of control in Negro children. *Developmental Psychology,* 1971, **4**, 2–8.

Escoffery, A. S. Personality and behavior correlates of Negro-American belief in "fate-control." *Dissertation Abstracts, Section A,* 1968, **28**(8), 3261–3262.

Evans, D. A., & Alexander, S. Some psychological correlates of civil rights activity. *Psychological Reports,* 1970, **26**, 889–906.

Feather, N. T. Some personality correlates of external control. *Australian Journal of Psychology,* 1967, **19**, 253–260.

Feather, N. T. Valence of outcome and expectation of success in relation to task difficulty and perceived locus of control. *Journal of Personality and Social Psychology,* 1968, **7**, 372–386.

Fitch, G. Effects of self-esteem, perceived performance, and choice on causal attributions. *Journal of Personality and Social Psychology,* 1970, **16**, 311–315.

Frazier, E. F. *Black bourgeoise.* Glencoe, Ill.: Free Press, 1962.

Fromm, E. *Escape from freedom.* New York: Rinehart, 1941.

Getter, H. A personality determinant of verbal conditioning. *Journal of Personality,* 1966, **34**, 397–405.

Gillis, J. S., & Jessor, R. Effects of brief psychotherapy on belief in internal control: An exploratory study. *Psychotherapy: Theory, Research and Practice,* 1970, **7**, 135–137.

Gore, P. M. Individual differences in the prediction of subject compliance to experimenter bias. *Dissertation Abstracts,* 1963, **24**(1), 390.

Gorman, B. S. An observation of altered locus of control following political disappointment. *Psychological Reports,* 1968, **23**, 1094.

Goss, A., & Morosko, T. E. Relation between a dimension of internal-external control and the MMPI with an alcoholic population. *Journal of Consulting and Clinical Psychology,* 1970, **34**, 189–192.

Gottesfield, H., & Dozier, G. Changes in feelings of powerlessness in a community action program. *Psychological Reports,* 1966, **19**, 978.

Gozali, J., & Bialer, I. Children's locus of control scale: independence from response set bias among retardates. *American Journal of Mental Deficiency,* 1968, **72**, 622–625.

Gruen, G. F., & Ottinger, D. R. Skill and chance orientations as determiners of problem-solving behavior in lower and middle-class children. *Psychological Reports,* 1969, **24**, 207–214.

Gurin, G., & Gurin, P. Expectancy theory in the study of poverty. *Journal of Social Issues*, 1970, **26**, 83–104.

Gurin, P., Gurin, G., Lao, R. C., & Beattie, M. Internal-external control in the motivational dynamics of Negro youth. *Journal of Social Issues*, 1969, **25**, 29–53.

Hamsher, J. H., Geller, J. D., & Rotter, J. B. Interpersonal trust, internal-external control, and the Warren Commission Report. *Journal of Personality and Social Psychology*, 1968, 9, 210–215.

Harrison, F. I. Relationship between home background, school success, and adolescent attitudes. *Merrill-Palmer Quarterly*, 1968, **14**, 331–344.

Hersch, P. D., & Scheibe, K. E. On the reliability and validity of internal-external control as a personality dimension. *Journal of Consulting Psychology*, 1967, **31**, 609–613.

Hjelle, L. A. Susceptibility to attitude change as a function of internal-external control. Paper presented at the convention of the Eastern Psychological Association, Atlantic City, April, 1970.

Hountras, P. T., & Scharf, M. C. Manifest anxiety and locus of control of low-achieving college males. *Journal of Psychology*, 1970, **74**, 95–100.

Hovland, C. I., & Janis, I. L. *Personality and persuasibility*. New Haven: Yale University Press, 1959.

Hsieh, T. T., Shybut, J., & Lotsof, E. J. Internal versus external control and ethnic group membership. *Journal of Consulting and Clinical Psychology*, 1969, **33**, 122–124.

James, W. H. Internal versus external control of reinforcement as a basic variable in learning theory. Unpublished doctoral dissertation, Ohio State University, 1957.

James, W. H., Woodruff, A. B., & Werner, W. Effect of internal and external control upon changes in smoking behavior. *Journal of Consulting Psychology*, 1965, **29**, 127–129.

Janis, I. L., & Mann, L. Effectiveness of emotional role-playing in modifying smoking habits and attitudes. *Journal of Experimental Research in Personality*, 1965, 1, 84–90.

Jessor, R., Graves, T., Hanson, R., & Jessor, S. *Society, personality, and deviant behavior*. New York: Holt, 1968.

Joe, V. C. Review of the internal-external control construct as a personality variable. *Psychological Reports*, 1971, **28**, 619–640.

Johnson, R. C., Ackerman, J. M., Frank, H., & Fionda, A. J. Resistance to temptation and guilt following yielding and psychotherapy. *Journal of Consulting and Clinical Psychology*, 1968, **32**, 169–175.

Julian, J. W., & Katz, S. B. Internal versus external control and the value of reinforcement. *Journal of Personality and Social Psychology*, 1968, **76**, 43–48.

Katkovsky, W., Crandall, V. C., & Good, S. Parental antecedents of children's beliefs in internal-external control of reinforcement in intellectual achievement situations. *Child Development*, 1967, **28**, 765–776.

Katz, I. The socialization of academic motivation in minority group children. In D. Levine (Ed.), *Nebraska symposium on motivation*. Lincoln: University of Nebraska Press, 1967. Pp. 133–191.

Kiehlbauch, J. B. Selected changes over time in internal-external control expectancies in a reformatory population. *Dissertation Abstracts, Section B*, 1968, **29**(1), 371–372.

Lao, R. C. Internal-external control and competent and innovative behavior among

Negro college students. *Journal of Personality and Social Psychology*, 1970, 14, 263–270.

Lefcourt, H. M. Belief in personal control: Research and implications. *Journal of Individual Psychology*, 1966, 22, 185–195. (a)

Lefcourt, H. M. Internal versus external control of reinforcement: A review. *Psychological Bulletin*, 1966, 65, 206–220. (b)

Lefcourt, H. M. Effects of cue explication upon persons maintaining external control expectancies. *Journal of Personality and Social Psychology*, 1967, 5, 372–378.

Lefcourt, H. M., Gronnerud, P., & McDonald, P. Cognitive activity and hypothesis formation during a double entendre word association test as a function of locus of control and field dependence. Unpublished manuscript, University of Waterloo, 1971. (a)

Lefcourt, H. M., & Ladwig, G. W. The American Negro: A problem in expectancies. *Journal of Personality and Social Psychology*, 1965, 1, 377–380. (a)

Lefcourt, H. M., & Ladwig, G. W. The effect of reference group upon Negroes task persistence in a biracial competitive game. *Journal of Personality and Social Psychology*, 1965, 1, 668–671. (b)

Lefcourt, H. M., Lewis, L., & Silverman, I. W. Internal versus external control of reinforcement and attention in a decision making task. *Journal of Personality*, 1968, 36, 663–682.

Lefcourt, H. M., & Siegel, J. M. Reaction time behavior as a function of internal-external control of reinforcement and control of test administration. *Canadian Journal of Behavioral Science*, 1970, 2, 253–266. (a)

Lefcourt, H. M., & Siegel, J. M. Reaction time performance as a function of field dependence and autonomy in test administration. *Journal of Abnormal Psychology*, 1970, 76, 475–481. (b)

Lefcourt, H. M., Sordoni, C., & Sordoni, C. Locus of control, field dependence and the expression of humor. Unpublished manuscript, University of Waterloo, 1971. (b)

Lefcourt, H. M., & Steffy, R. A. Level of aspiration, risk-taking behavior, and projective test performance: A search for coherence. *Journal of Consulting and Clinical Psychology*, 1970, 34, 193–198. (a)

Lefcourt, H. M., & Steffy, R. A. One man's adequacy is another man's failure. *Psychological Reports*, 1970, 26, 689–690. (b)

Lefcourt, H. M., & Telegdi, M. Perceived locus of control and field dependence as predictors of cognitive activity. *Journal of Consulting and Clinical Psychology*, 1971, 37, 53–56.

Lefcourt, H. M., & Wine, J. Internal versus external control of reinforcement and the deployment of attention in experimental situations. *Canadian Journal of Behavioral Science*, 1969, 1, 167–181.

Lessing, E. E. Racial differences in indices of ego functioning relevant to academic achievement. *Journal of Genetic Psychology*, 1969, 115, 153–167.

Lesyk, J. J. Effects of intensive operant conditioning on belief in personal control in schizophrenic women. *Dissertation Abstracts, Section B*, 1969, 29(12), 4849.

Lipp, L., Kolstoe, R., James, W., & Randall, H. Denial of disability and internal control of reinforcement: A study using a perceptual defense paradigm. *Journal of Consulting and Clinical Psychology*, 1968, 32, 72–75.

MacDonald, A. P. Birth order and personality. *Journal of Consulting and Clinical Psychology*, 1971, 36, 171–176. (a)

MacDonald, A. P. Internal-external locus of control: Parental antecedents. *Journal of Consulting and Clinical Psychology*, 1971, 37, 141–147. (b)

MacDonald, A. P., & Hall, J. Perception of disability by the disabled. *Journal of Consulting and Clinical Psychology*, 1969, 33, 654–660.

MacDonald, A. P., & Hall, J. Internal-external locus of control and perception of disability. *Journal of Consulting and Clinical Psychology*, 1971, 36, 338–345.

Masters, J. C. Treatment of adolescent rebellion by the reconstrual of stimuli. *Journal of Consulting Psychology*, 1970, 35, 213–216.

McArthur, L. A. Luck is alive and well in New Haven. *Journal of Personality and Social Psychology*, 1970, 16, 316–318.

McGhee, P. E., & Crandall, V. C. Beliefs in internal-external control of reinforcement and academic performance. *Child Development*, 1968, 39, 91–102.

Midlarski, E. Aiding under stress: The effects of competence, dependency, visibility, and fatalism. *Journal of Personality*, 1971, 39, 132–149.

Milgram, S. Behavioral study of obedience. *Journal of Abnormal and Social Psychology*, 1963, 67, 371–378.

Minton, H. L. Power as a personality construct. In B. A. Maher (Ed.), *Progress in experimental personality research*. Vol. 4. New York: Academic Press, 1967. Pp. 229–267.

Mirels, H. L. Dimensions of internal versus external control. *Journal of Consulting and Clinical Psychology*, 1970, 34, 226–228.

Mischel, W. Preference for delayed reinforcement and social responsibility. *Journal of Abnormal and Social Psychology*, 1961, 62, 1–7.

Mischel, W. Theory and research on the antecedents of self-improved delay of reward. In B. A. Maher (Ed.), *Progress in experimental personality research*. Vol. 3. New York: Academic Press, 1966.

Moulton, R. W. Effects of success and failure on level of aspiration as related to achievement motives. *Journal of Personality and Social Psychology*, 1965, 1, 399–406.

Nowicki, S., & Barnes, J. Effects of a structured camp experience on locus of control orientation. *Journal of Genetic Psychology*, in press.

Nowicki, S., & Roundtree, J. Correlates of locus of control in secondary school age students. Unpublished manuscript, Emory University, 1971.

Nowicki, S., & Strickland, B. R. A locus of control scale for children. *Journal of Consulting and Clinical Psychology*, in press.

Odell, M. Personality correlates of independence and conformity. Unpublished master's thesis, Ohio State University, 1959.

Owens, M. W. Disability-minority and social learning. Unpublished master's thesis, West Virginia University, 1969.

Penk, W. Age changes and correlates of internal-external locus of control scale. *Psychological Reports*, 1969, 25, 856.

Phares, E. J. Changes in expectancy in skill and chance situations. Unpublished doctoral dissertation, Ohio State University, 1955.

Phares, E. J. Differential utilization of information as a function of internal-external control. *Journal of Personality*, 1968, 36, 649–662.

Phares, E. J., Ritchie, D. E., & Davis, W. L. Internal-external control and reaction to threat. *Journal of Personality and Social Psychology*, 1968, 10, 402–405.

Platt, E. S. Internal-external control and changes in expected utility as predictors of the change in cigarette smoking following role playing. Paper presented at the meeting of the Eastern Psychological Association, Philadelphia, April 1969.

Platt, J. J., & Eisenman, R. Internal-external control of reinforcement, time perspective, adjustment, and anxiety. *Journal of General Psychology,* 1968, **79,** 121–128.

Ray, W. J., & Katahn, M. Relation of anxiety to locus of control. *Psychological Reports,* 1968, **23,** 1196.

Reid, D., & Ware, E. E. Multidimensionality of internal-external control: Implications for research. Unpublished manuscript, University of Waterloo, 1971.

Ritchie, E., & Phares, E. J. Attitude change as a function of internal-external control and communicator status. *Journal of Personality,* 1969, **37,** 429–443.

Rotter, J. B. *Social learning and clinical psychology.* New York: Prentice-Hall, 1954.

Rotter, J. B. Generalized expectancies for internal versus external control of reinforcement. *Psychological Monographs,* 1966, **80**(1, Whole No. 609).

Rotter, J. B., & Mulry, R. C. Internal versus external control of reinforcement and decision time. *Journal of Personality and Social Psychology,* 1965, **2,** 598–604.

Ryckman, R. M., Gold, J. A., & Rodda, W. C. Confidence rating shifts and performance as a function of locus of control, self-esteem, and initial task experience. *Journal of Personality and Social Psychology,* 1971, **18,** 305–310.

Ryckman, R. M., & Rodda, W. C. Locus of control and initial task experience as determinants of confidence changes in a chance situation. *Journal of Personality and Social Psychology,* 1971, **18,** 116–119.

Schimek, J. G. Cognitive styles and defenses. *Journal of Abnormal Psychology,* 1968, **73,** 575–580.

Seeman, M. Alienation and social learning in a reformatory. *American Journal of Sociology,* 1963, **69,** 270–284.

Seeman, M. Powerlessness and knowledge: A comparative study of alienation and learning. *Sociometry,* 1967, **30,** 105–123.

Seeman, M., & Evans, J. W. Alienation and learning in a hospital setting. *American Sociological Review,* 1962, **27,** 772–783.

Shaw, R. L., & Uhl, N. P. Relationship between locus of control scores and reading achievement of black and white second-grade children from two socioeconomic levels. Paper presented at the meeting of the Southeastern Psychological Association, New Orleans, May 1969.

Shore, R. E. Some parental correlates of boy's locus of control. Paper presented at the meeting of the Eastern Psychological Association, Washington, D. C., April 1968.

Smith, R. E. Changes in locus of control as a function of life crisis resolution. *Journal of Abnormal Psychology,* 1970, 3, 328–332.

Solomon, D., Houlihan, K. A., & Parelius, R. J. Intellectual achievement responsibility in Negro and white children. *Psychological Reports,* 1969, **24,** 479–483.

Spivack, G., Levine, M., & Sprigle, H. Intelligence test performance and the delay function of the ego. *Journal of Consulting Psychology,* 1959, **23,** 428–431.

Stotland, E. *The psychology of hope.* San Francisco: Jossey-Bass, 1969.

Strickland, B. R. Individual differences in verbal conditioning, extinction and awareness. *Journal of Personality,* 1970, 38, 364–378.

Strickland, B. R. Delay of gratification as a function of race of the experimenter. *Journal of Personality and Social Psychology,* 1972, **22,** in press.

Strodtbeck, F. L. Family interaction, values and achievement. In D. McClelland (Ed.), *Talent and society.* New York: Van Nostrand, 1958.

Throop, W. F., & MacDonald, A. P. Internal-external locus of control: A bibliography. *Psychological Reports,* 1971, **28,** 175–190.

Walls, R. T., & Miller, J. J. Delay of gratification in welfare and rehabilitation clients. *Journal of Counseling Psychology,* 1970, 4, 383–384.

Walls, R. T., & Smith, T. S. Development of preference for delayed reinforcement in disadvantaged children. *Journal of Educational Psychology,* 1970, **61,** 118–123.

Watson, D. Relationship between locus of control and anxiety. *Journal of Personality and Social Psychology,* 1967, **6,** 91–92.

Watson, D., & Baumal, E. Effects of locus of control and expectation of future control upon present performance. *Journal of Personality and Social Psychology,* 1967, **6,** 212–215.

Witkin, H., Dyk, R. B., Faterson, G. E., Goodenough, D. R., & Karp, S. A. *Psychological differentiation.* New York: Wiley, 1962.

Zytkoskee, A., Strickland, B. R., & Watson, J. Delay of gratification and internal versus external control among adolescents of low socioeconomic status. *Developmental Psychology,* 1971, 4, 93–98.

THE EFFECTS OF MODELING, ROLEPLAYING, AND PARTICIPATION ON BEHAVIOR CHANGE[1]

Philip H. Friedman[2]

FAMILY PSYCHIATRY DIVISION,
EASTERN PENNSYLVANIA PSYCHIATRIC INSTITUTE,
PHILADELPHIA, PENNSYLVANIA

[1] This paper was written while the author was on an NIMH postdoctoral research fellowship (No. F02 MH24138-01) at the Department of Behavioral Science, Temple University Medical School, 1968–1969. Thus, the paper was supported in part by the U. S. Public Health Service. Except for the author's own research the review includes research published through August 1969.

The author would like to thank Ross Buck, Barry Miller, and Arnold Lazarus for their valuable criticisms and suggestions in the preparation of the first draft of this paper, and to L. Krasner, A. Goldstein, L. Ullmann, I. Sarason, C. Franks, and Teresa Friedman for their comments and suggestions on the second draft of this paper.

[2] The author's full address is Family Psychiatry Division, Eastern Pennsylvania Psychiatric Institute, Henry Avenue and Abbottsford Road, Philadelphia, Pennsylvania 19129.

I. Introduction

A careful look at the research and theory of psychotherapy and behavior change indicates that some variables and techniques are studied more thoroughly than others (e.g., desensitization, aversion therapy, operant conditioning, modeling, empathy, warmth, genuineness). Moreover, these techniques are rarely studied in relation to other procedures with which they are usually combined in the clinical field. In this review, research into the effects of modeling on behavior change will be integrated with research into the effects of roleplaying and participation on behavior change. The focus will be on changes in maladaptive behavior. Similarities and differences between the theoretical mechanisms hypothesized to account for the changes produced by these procedures will be discussed. The relative contributions of each of these procedures when used conjointly toward effective behavior change will be evaluated. The discussion of modeling and roleplaying will be organized under four subsections representing different theoretical mechanisms used to explain the behavioral changes produced by these procedures: information; rehearsal; motivational variables; cognitive variables. Theoretical mechanisms to account for participation procedures will also be mentioned.

II. Modeling

A. INFORMATION

One of the primary advantages of modeling procedures is that a person observing a model can be exposed to a large amount of information about behavior. In the case of an interpersonal situation, the observer can learn what type of behavior might be exhibited in a specific social situation. The behavior can be presented dramatically by highlighting visual, vocal, and gestural activity of the models that might enhance the retention of the behavioral information. Bandura has emphasized (1965, 1969b) that information observed by a person from models is converted into covert perceptual-cognitive images and covert rehearsal responses that are retained by the individual and later used by him as symbolic cues to overt behavior.

A study conducted by Bandura, Grusec, and Menlove (1966) was designed to manipulate the strength of symbolic responses occurring during modeling. In this study, subjects were divided into a facilitative symbolization (FS) condition, a passive observation (PO) condition, and a competing symbolization (CS) condition. In all three conditions, children observed filmed models perform a sequence of nonverbal responses. Children in the FS condition verbalized the modeling stimuli as they were presented on the screen. Children in the PO group were told only to watch the film carefully, while children in the CS condition were told to count rapidly while attending closely to the film. Later all subjects were offered candy and social rewards for each matching response that they produced correctly. As predicted, children in the FS condition reproduced significantly more matching responses than subjects in the PO condition, who in turn showed significantly more matching responses than subjects in the CS condition.

Bandura argued that the concurrent verbalization by subjects in the facilitative symbolization condition enhanced the development of covert imaginal and verbal associations for the model's behavior. It is, however, difficult to interpret the Bandura et al. (1966) study in terms of covert imaginal and verbal associations. The reason is that the main experimental condition, FS, manipulated the overt verbal responses of the subject rather than exclusively manipulating the covert responses of the subject. Moreover, since the verbal behavior of the subject was manipulated, there was no evidence for the role of covert imaginal responses as the mediating mechanism.

Bandura (1969a, 1969b) has described a study by Gerst (1968) that emphasized the importance of both verbal and imaginal coding responses in the acquisition and retention of nonverbal behaviors. In this study, college students observed a filmed model perform a series of nonverbal, motor responses. These responses consisted of movements taken from the hand signals of the deaf. After observing each modeled response, subjects were instructed to engage in one of four activities for 1 minute. In one group, subjects transformed the modeled responses into vivid imagery. A second group coded the modeled stimuli by describing the specific responses and their movements in concrete verbal terms. A third group reinstated the basic aspects of the response by the use of concise summary labels. An example of a concise verbal label is a description of a pretzel-shaped response as being like an orchestra conductor moving his baton in an orchestral finale (Bandura, 1969b). In the control group, subjects performed mental calculations designed to impede covert coding of the modeled responses. Immediately after the coding session, subjects reproduced the modeled responses. Subjects then performed a distracting task for 15 minutes which was designed to prevent the symbolic rehearsal of modeled responses. Finally, they were asked once again to reproduce the modeled responses.

The results indicated that, compared to the subjects who performed mental calculations to impede covert coding of the modeled responses, the subjects in the three covert coding conditions enhanced observational learning. Concise verbal labels and imaginal responses were equally effective in aiding immediate retention of responses, and both were superior to concrete verbal descriptions of the modeled response. A subsequent test for delayed retention of modeled responses indicated that concise verbal labels were the best coding system for retention of the nonverbal information. Subjects in this condition retained most of what they learned, while subjects who were in the vivid imagery and concrete verbal description conditions displayed a substantial loss of motor responses previously learned.

Friedman (1968, 1971) conducted a study that was specifically designed to see if the covert perceptual-cognitive images elicited by models were any more effective in changing verbal behavior than the covert verbal responses elicited by the observation of models. In this study, 101 low-assertive male and female college students participated in the experiment. First, subjects were selected for self-reported low-assertiveness by means of a specially constructed test, the Action Situation Inventory or ASI (Friedman, 1968). Subjects then were administered a behavioral test for assertiveness. In this pretreatment assessment, subjects were told to assert themselves when a college sophomore interfered with their performance on a task. The college sophomore then engaged in a series of progressively more irritating and insulting behaviors directed toward the subject. The subjects behavior was scored on 15 verbal categories such as threat, demand, request to stop, mild disagreement, agree, and self-critical remarks. Only subjects who made six or less assertive responses in the pretreatment behavioral situation were administered the treatments. Following the treatment, all subjects were given a posttreatment assessment identical to the pretreatment assessment. Two weeks later, 61 subjects participated in a follow-up assessment similar to the posttreatment assessment.

Three of the six treatment conditions in this study were an assertive modeling (AMOD), assertive script (AS), and a nonassertive script (NAS) condition. In the AS condition, subjects read silently four times from a prepared script. The information on assertiveness in this script was identical to the information conveyed to subjects in the AMOD condition. Excerpts from the script are:

Two students are sitting at a table in a library doing some work (reading a book). The sign on the wall says "Quiet, No Talking."

M1 (Talking out loud to himself). Gee, it's pretty hard to find the book you want in the stacks these days.
M2 . . . Could you please be a little quieter, I'm trying to read this book?
M1 . . . Boy am I tired of reading. (Circles the table mumbling out loud).
M2 Would you obey the sign on the wall and stop making so much noise?
M1 (Walks over to M2, looks over his shoulder and says to him) Tut-tut-let's see how far you've gotten? What chapter are you on?
M2 Stop being such a nuisance.
M1 (Reaches over M2's shoulder, turns a few pages and says) What's that?
M2 Get away from this table—you're acting obnoxious and I don't like it. Act your age.

In the NAS control condition, subjects read silently four times from a script that was neutral in content and behaviors exhibited. Excerpts from this script are:

Two students in a library are doing some work (reading a book). They are alone.

M1 I used to like the Beatles the best, but now I like Simon and Garfunkel.
M2 Oh, I saw them when they were here.
M1 What did you think of them?
M2 They seemed to dislike the Coliseum but other than that they were pretty good.
M1 How did you like Chinatown when you were in San Francisco?
M2 It was very colorful and the food was great. Of course, there were some places that were tourist traps.

Behavioral and self-report measures of change in assertive behavior from pre- to posttesting indicated that both subjects in the AMOD and AS condition increased in assertive behavior significantly more than subjects in the NAS control condition. Subjects in the AS condition read the assertive information from a prepared script. There were no significant differences between the AMOD and AS conditions. This study supported the hypothesis that it is primarily covert verbal responses elicited by models and not covert perceptual-cognitive images elicited by the visual and vocal cues of models that produces verbal behavior change. In light of the experimenter's finding, it is of some interest to the area of behavior change that the cartoon aggressive model in the Bandura, Ross, and Ross (1961, 1963) studies were as effective in increasing aggression with children as the enhanced dramatization provided by live and filmed models.

B. Rehearsal

Another explanation of modeling as a behavior change procedure is that modeling elicits an overt rehearsal of the desired response. Overt rehearsal may be the factor that created the difference between the conditions in the Bandura *et al.* (1966) study. This explanation is consistent with the fact that subjects in the competing symbolization condition repetitively engaged in interfering overt verbal responses which hindered their learning. Berger (1966) has explained imitation as a form of practice which is positively correlated with a measure of observational learning. It follows from this practice or overt rehearsal hypothesis that any procedure, modeling or otherwise, that enhances the amount of overt practice of subjects would increase the learning of new behaviors.

Berger (1966) designed an experiment where subjects observed a model who was learning the hand signals of the alphabet for the deaf. He found that the observer subjects practiced overtly the model's behavior. Furthermore, the subjects level of retention of the hand signals was positively correlated ($r = .47$, $p < .05$) with the number of different signals practiced by the observer. Berger found support for his hypothesis from this study, but he also pointed out that some subjects learned responses not overtly practiced. He felt this gave some support to Bandura's sensory contiguity theory from which the concept of perceptual-cognitive imaginal responses arose. However, it is possible that a hypothesis emphasizing the covert practice of hand signals (a proprioceptive response) could account for this learning without hypothesizing perceptual-cognitive factors.

In order to test the rehearsal hypothesis with its emphasis on the overt practice of responses, the previously cited study (Friedman, 1971) included a condition in which subjects rehearsed out loud the responses from a prepared AS opposite another person, an accomplice of the experimenter's. Subjects in this directed roleplaying (DR) condition did not differ from subjects in the AS or AMOD conditions, although they did become more assertive than control subjects. This suggests that the practice or rehearsal of verbal responses need not be overt for behavior change to occur. It again supports the hypothesis that covert verbal rehearsal mediates verbal behavior change occurring from the observation of models.

C. MOTIVATIONAL VARIABLES

1. Arousal and Anxiety Reduction

Much of the research on modeling indicates that subjects who have been emotionally aroused either by adrenaline injections, threats, or other external stimulation are more likely to be influenced by models (Bandura & Rosenthal, 1966; Schachter & Singer, 1962; Staples & Walters, 1961; Walters, Marshall, & Shooter, 1960).

Some theorists have emphasized the role of anxiety reduction in changing maladaptive behavior (Miller & Dollard, 1941; Wolpe, 1958). This raises the question of the extent to which changes in behavior occurring from the observation of models are mediated by reductions in anxiety or arousal. Three studies by Bandura and his colleagues were designed explicitly to reduce the effects of fear or anxiety. In the first study by Bandura, Grusec, and Menlove (1967), 48 boys and girls between the ages of 3 and 5 years were selected because they were fearful of and avoided a dog in a pretreatment assessment. Children were then exposed to one of two modeling treatments which consisted of exposure to a graduated series in which a 4-year-old, fearless, peer model interacted with a cocker spaniel in a positive or neutral context. In the two other conditions, children were only exposed to the dog plus the positive context but without the fearless model, or they were exposed to the positive context only, i.e., a party. In the modeling condition, the fear-provoking qualities of the modeled interactions were increased over eight, 10-minute treatment sessions conducted on 4 consecutive days. The physical restraints on the dog, the directness and intimacy of the modeled approach responses, and the duration of interaction between the model and the dog were varied. A female experimenter administered the pretreatment and posttreatment assessments. The results indicated that the single-modeling condition (one child interacting with one dog) was successful in reducing the children's avoidance of dogs more than the control conditions. The positive context did not enhance the increase in approach behavior to dogs.

In the second study by Bandura and Menlove (1968), 32 girls and 16 boys ranging in age from 3 to 5 years participated. These subjects, who were markedly fearful of dogs, observed eight, 3-minute movies on 4 alternate days. In the single modeling (SM) condition, subjects observed a fearless, 5-year-old male model display progressively bolder approach responses toward a cocker spaniel. In the multiple modeling (MM) condition, subjects observed several different girls and boys of varying ages interact positively with numerous dogs of different sizes, shapes, and degrees of ferocity. Again the models became progressively bolder in response to increasingly threatening dogs in each film. In the control condition, children were shown movies of Disneyland and Marineland for equivalent amounts of time.

The results showed that both the SM and the MM conditions were more effective in increasing the children's approach responses to dogs than the control condition. Although Bandura argued that reduction of arousal mediated the reduction of instrumental avoidance responses conditioned to it, he presented no evidence in these two studies to support the arousal reduction hypothesis. Moreover, he presented no evidence that arousal reduction was greater in the MM than SM condition.

In the third study by Bandura, Blanchard, and Ritter (1969), adult subjects who were snake-phobic were administered a *symbolic modeling,* (SYM) a modeling plus participation plus physical contact by the experimenter (MPPC, also referred to as contact desensitization), and a control condition. A total of 48 subjects, 43 females and five males, qualified for this study as a result of a behavioral avoidance test. Their ages ranged from 13 to 59 years, with a mean age of 27. In addition to the avoidance test, subjects rated orally the intensity of fear they experienced while they were performing each approach behavior to the snake. Subjects in the SYM condition administered the treatment to themselves by regulating the amount of time they were exposed to various segments of a 35-minute color film. The film depicted a graduated and progressively threatening series of interactions between fearless children, adolescents, and adults and various snakes. Consequently multiple models were used. In addition, subjects in this condition were taught deep muscle relaxation and told to use it to neutralize the anxiety-provoking aspects of the film.

Subjects in the MPPC condition first observed, through a one-way mirror, an experimenter interact with a king snake. The experimenter engaged in progressively more threatening interactions with the snake for approximately 15 minutes. Then the subject was invited into the room and the experimenter again demonstrated each approach behavior to the snake. This time, however, the subject was led gradually by the experimenter to engage in more difficult approach behaviors to the snake. Whenever necessary, the experimenter had the subject place his hand on the experimenter's hand who then touched various parts of the snake's body. Later the experimenter and subject performed the approach responses jointly. Eventually the experimenter reduced his participation while the subject touched and held the snake and let it crawl over his body. Subjects in the control condition did not receive any treatment. A fourth treatment, systematic desensitization was employed, but it is not relevant to this discussion. Both the SYM and MPPC conditions produced substantially greater reductions in avoidance behavior and reported fear than control subjects. However, MPPC subjects displayed significantly greater reductions in avoidant behavior than SYM subjects. SYM subjects demonstrated almost complete reductions in reported fear, but only partial reductions in avoidance behavior. Thus, there was no one-to-one correspondence between reductions in avoidance behavior and anxiety in the SYM condition.

A study by Ritter (1968) found that a live-modeling condition was more effective than a control condition in reducing children's avoidant behavior to snakes. Twenty-eight girls and 16 boys ranging in age from 5 to 11 years served as subjects in this experiment. Subjects were treated in groups of seven or eight. Two 35-minute treatment sessions were held and spaced 1 week apart. Five fearless peer models, boys and girls of similar age, interacted with one snake. The experimenter also participated as a model. Although none of the subjects actually interacted with the snake, the subjects were asked to play the role of a "teacher" during the experiment. The teacher's role was to send selected models out of the room, call them back after a few seconds, and instruct them to perform certain tasks with the snake with prompting from experimenter if necessary.

The findings indicated that although there was an overall reduction of reported fear across conditions in the Ritter (1968) study, the fear ratings of modeling subjects did not decrease significantly more than controls. Another study by Ritter (1969b) revealed that a modeling condition was no more effective for adult subjects than a control condition in reducing both avoidance and reported fear of heights. Friedman (1971) found that modeling subjects increased from pre- to posttesting significantly more in assertive behavior than control subjects. There were no differences between conditions in self-reported measures of anxiety and no evidence for reductions in reported anxiety across conditions.

In summary, the evidence for the hypothesis that behavior changes occurring from the observation of models are mediated by reductions in anxiety or arousal has only weak support. It may be that behavior changes and changes in reported anxiety upon observation of models are under the control of different variables and will only occur together under special circumstances.

D. Cognitive Variables

1. Uncertainty, Expectations, Appropriateness, Justification

Walters (1968) has emphasized that the processes mediating the effects of emotional arousal are likely to be perceptual-cognitive variables. Walters suggests that under some conditions a correlation will exist between an observer's emotional arousal level and the extent to which he imitates a model. However, according to Walters, arousal is likely to be mediated by other variables that actually lead to behavior change. One cognitive variable mediating arousal that Walters has found to be important is the uncertainty of the subject concerning the appropriateness of his behavior. In that study (Walters & Amoroso, 1967) uncertainty appeared to cause subjects to seek out cues that were capable of guiding their behavior in socially appropriate ways.

Most of the research regarding the effects on subjects of positive and negative consequences to models (Bandura, 1965, 1969a; Walters & Parke, 1964a; Walters, Parke, & Cane, 1965) has been interpreted by Walters and Parke (1967) in a cognitive framework which holds that subjects learn expectations about what will be the consequence to them for engaging in certain behaviors. Research by Berkowitz and Rawlings (1963) has indicated that if filmed aggression is portrayed as justified, frustrated subjects will engage in more physical aggression than if filmed aggression is portrayed as unjustified. Thus, cognitions about justification for engaging in certain behaviors appear to release these behaviors in subjects. Many of the types of imitative behaviors classified by Gilmore (1968) point to the importance of expectations learned by a subject from a model on how to obtain a reward, achieve a favorable judgement or avoid punishment, or other negative consequences. Bandura (1968) has noted that positive consequences occurring to a model contribute markedly in making modeling a very powerful therapeutic procedure. Friedman (1968), however, indicated that the expectations of the experimenter, the experimenter's approval and the experimenter's instructional set to the subjects may be equally as potent variables as consequences to the model. In his study, the experimenter expected subjects to learn how to assert themselves even though negative consequences occurred to the assertive model. A strong, socially acceptable positive value was placed on self-assertion by the experimenter.

III. Roleplaying

Roleplaying procedures differ from modeling procedures by emphasizing some kind of overt behavioral response by the subject. Moreover, role-playing is a behavioral change procedure used by people with a wide variety of theoretical orientations. It has been variously called psycho-drama by Moreno (1946), behavior rehearsal by A. Lazarus (1966) and Wolpe and Lazarus (1966), improvisation by Janis and King (1954), role enactment by Sarbin (1954), and method acting by Stanislavski (see Moore, 1965). Moreno, for example, has developed a number of roleplaying procedures for therapeutic purposes which have been recently discussed in a book by Corsini (1966). Among these techniques is straight roleplaying, role reversal, alter ego format, mirror technique, and doubling. One of the differences between roleplaying procedures used by pro-ponents of psychodrama and those used by behavior therapists is that the former tend to focus on acting out conflicts occurring in the present or past, whereas the latter emphasize rehearsing new behaviors to be used in the future. One major dimension along which roleplaying procedures vary is the amount of improvised behavior by the subject and the amount of guidance to his behavior. Thus at one extreme the subject is instructed exactly what to do and rehearses these behaviors, and at the other extreme the subject is provided minimal cues or prompts and must improvise his responses.

A. INFORMATION

As previously mentioned in the discussion of modeling, covert verbal rehearsal by a subject appears to be the main process by which information presented through procedures such as modeling, DR or reading a script can be transformed into changes in verbal behavior. In an improvised roleplaying procedure, however, subjects are given minimal cues and prompts to guide their covert and overt verbal responses. Friedman (1971) included an improvised roleplaying (IR) condition in which subjects were given the same script as the subjects in the DR condition, except that they were required to construct their own assertive responses for one of the characters in the script while roleplaying the script *in vivo* opposite an accomplice of the experimenter. Excerpts from the script are:

Two students are sitting at a table in a library doing some work (reading a book). The sign on the wall says "Quiet, No Talking."

M1 (Talking out loud to himself) "Gee, it's pretty hard to find the book you want in the stacks these days."
M2
M1 . . . "Boy am I tired of reading." (Circles the table mumbling out loud).
M2
M1 (Walks over to M2, looks over his shoulder and says to him) "Tut-tut—let's see how far you've gotten. What chapter are you on?"
M2
M1 (Reaches over M2's shoulder, turns a few pages and says) "What's that?"
M2

In the IR condition, subjects were required to improvise, four times the assertive responses made by the college student, M2, in the script. The subjects in the DR condition read out loud, four times, the same assertive material read by subjects in the AS condition. In the AS condition, subjects read the assertive material silently and not in reply to an accomplice of the experimenter who roleplayed the character M1 out loud. The experimenter found that there were no significant differences between the IR, DR, AMOD, and AS conditions in pre- to posttreatment changes in assertive behavior. The IR subjects did, however, have the greatest mean changes in assertive behavior of these four conditions. This study fails to support the idea that the information conveyed to college subjects must necessarily be externally provided to the subjects for behavior change to occur. Perhaps what is necessary for behavior change is a structured situation in which the college students are provided the opportunity and given instructions to construct their own appropriate responses.

B. REHEARSAL

The major difference between roleplaying procedures and modeling procedures for behavior change is that the subject is usually required to participate actively in overt verbal and gestural behavior during roleplaying and not during modeling. When subjects do engage in overt verbal or gestural behavior during modeling, their performance is enhanced (Bandura *et al.*, 1966; Berger, 1966). On the other hand, Friedman (1971) found that repetitive rehearsal of verbal behavior enhanced the self-assertive performance of his subjects, but that the rehearsal did not have to be overt. His findings showed that a DR condition in which subjects overtly rehearsed assertive responses was no more effective than an AMOD or AS reading condition in changing behavior. All of these groups were significantly greater than an NAS control group in pre- to posttreatment behavioral measures of assertiveness. Thus, his results suggest that an ongoing, covert rehearsal of verbal responses is sufficient for changes in verbal behavior.

It may be that under certain conditions an overt rehearsal of responses enhances behavior change over the covert rehearsal of responses. McGuire (1961) in a related area of research has suggested that overt rehearsal would be more effective than covert rehearsal in motivating disinterested subjects. According to McGuire, the less the intrinsic motivation of subjects and the greater the fear of sanctions for not overtly rehearsing, the more effective overt rehearsal would be over covert rehearsal. McGuire also hypothesized that overt rehearsal would more effectively aid response generalization than covert rehearsal. He reasoned that overt rehearsal was more of an analog to the behavior that ultimately must be performed than covert rehearsal. Furthermore, overt rehearsal would generalize more effectively than covert rehearsal with nonverbal (motor) behaviors than with verbal behaviors. Research specifying the conditions under which overt rehearsal is superior to covert rehearsal in modifying maladaptive behaviors still needs to be done.

One disadvantage of forcing people to engage in an overt rehearsal of a prescribed set of responses, such as in DR, has been discussed by Hovland, Janis, and Kelley (1953). These authors point out that implicit interfering responses might occur such as resentful and negativistic thoughts toward the person requesting the behavior be performed or toward the behavior itself. Hovland and his associates have suggested that this is more likely to occur in groups of subjects who orally read a prepared script (DR) in attitude-change studies. On the other hand, these authors suggest that implicit labeling responses of the type "this is my own idea," or "I arrived at this by myself" is likely to facilitate attitude change because less negativistic behavior is likely to occur. The authors believe that these implicit labeling responses are greater in IR procedures than in procedures where the subject passively observes a communication from another person (modeling) or actively reads a prepared script (DR).

C. MOTIVATIONAL VARIABLES

1. Arousal and Anxiety Reduction

If the hypothesis that an increase in emotional arousal leads to greater behavior change is supported, then roleplaying procedures will probably lead to substantial behavior change. Roleplaying procedures require active participation by the subject, which in itself raises the subject's level of arousal. Ordinarily, IR might be expected to produce more emotional arousal than DR because of the greater demands placed upon the subject. Under certain circumstances, though, emotional arousal may be greater in DR than IR.

In a study by Jansen and Stolurow (1962), DR subjects (labeled the imitation condition in the article) experienced more discomfort than IR subjects, because DR subjects felt they revealed their inadequacies more than IR subjects. The roleplaying by these psychiatric aides was done before an audience of peers and professional people. Modeling by other aides preceded the roleplaying. Semantic differential ratings of job problems and job-related concepts were measured as the dependent variable. The authors found that DR was more effective than improvisation. Self-reports indicated that discomfort seemed to generate a high level of motivation in the aides. In this study, the subjects' perception of the expectations of the observers may have increased their discomfort and raised their level of motivation.

Janis and Mann (1965) designed a study to compare the effects of emotional roleplaying (ER) on heavy cigarette smoking in women. They had one group of subjects improvise a scene between a physician and patient who had just been told she had lung cancer from smoking. The male experimenter played the role of the physician. The subject was required to act out as realistically as possible five different scenes: (1) Soliloquy in the waiting room while awaiting the doctor's diagnosis based on X-rays and other medical tests; (2) Conversation with the physician as he gave the diagnosis; (3) Soliloquy while the physician phoned for a hospital bed; (4) Conversation with the physician concerning arrangements for hospitalization; (5) Conversation with the physician about the causes of lung cancer.

During the dialogue, the experimenter, acting from a standard script, talked about the malignant mass found from the patient's chest X-ray, the moderate chance for a successful surgical operation, the need to contact the patient's family about the 6 weeks she'll be in the hospital, the patient's smoking history, the connection between smoking and cancer, and the urgent need for the patient to stop smoking immediately. In general, the procedure in the ER condition was cleverly arranged to emphasize the importance of pain, physical incapacity, hospitalization, and possible death to the person told she had lung cancer. A second group of subjects listened passively to the roleplayed scenes (a type of modeling).

Two weeks after the treatment, the ER group was found to change significantly more in attitudes and smoking habits than the listening group. A follow-up study conducted by Mann and Janis (1968), 18 months later still showed significant differences between the groups. The authors believed and presented some evidence to show that it was the personal threat or fear of getting lung cancer by roleplaying subjects that created and maintained the difference between the groups. Mann's study (1967) further supported this interpretation.

The notion that increases in anxiety mediate behavior change conflicts with hypotheses such as those proposed by Wolpe (1958, 1966) that behavior change is accompanied by a reduction in anxiety. Wolpe (1966) specifically made this statement in referring to changes produced in assertive behavior. He stated "Such action (expressing resentment outwardly) leads to reciprocal inhibition of the anxiety response [p. 212]." However, in Friedman's roleplaying study (1971), changes in assertive behavior were not accompanied by reductions in reported anxiety. In general, there is some evidence in support of the hypothesis that behavior change resulting from roleplaying is mediated by high levels of emotional arousal. There is no support for the hypothesis that anxiety reduction mediates behavior changes occurring from roleplaying procedures.

2. Satisfaction

Attitude change studies (Hovland et al., 1953; Janis & King, 1954) have demonstrated that IR was more effective in changing attitudes concerned with movie attendance, meat shortages, cold cures, and draftees than an oral reading group or a silent reading group. An oral reading condition is procedurally the same as a DR condition. The attitudes have in all cases been measured by self-reports. The investigators (Hovland et al., 1959; Janis & King, 1954) provided a number of hypotheses to account for their results. One hypothesis is that the subjects in the IR condition are more satisfied with their performance than subjects in the oral or silent reading groups, and that greater satisfaction leads to a greater acceptance of the communication.

A study (King & Janis, 1956) conducted to test the satisfaction hypothesis made the material to be improvised particulary difficult. Despite this and consequent ratings by the subjects showing less satisfaction in the IR condition, this condition showed more attitude change than an oral or silent reading group. Moreover, subjects who received favorable ratings from the experimenter on their improvised talks and a relatively high degree of satisfaction in their self-ratings showed about the same amount of opinion change as subjects who received unfavorable or no ratings. Friedman (1971) found no significant difference in the satisfaction reported by IR, DR, AMOD, AS, or NAS control subjects with their performance.

3. Effort

Another hypothesis that has been recently proposed to account for these results places a primary emphasis on a motivational variable important to cognitive dissonance theory. Zimbardo (1965) has attempted to show that it is not the cognitive-intellectual aspect of improvising new arguments which is crucial to the roleplaying procedure but rather the magnitude of the barriers or aversive stimuli to be overcome in attaining a goal, i.e., effort. The cognitive-intellectual formulation eventually favored by Janis and King stated that during IR, the subject constructs new supporting arguments and cogent illustrations, and reformulates old arguments in his own words. He thus persuades himself that the communication is correct.

Zimbardo (1965) designed a study to compare the motivational hypothesis concerning effort with the cognitive, improvisation hypothesis. In his study subjects had to either improvise or read a script under slightly delayed (SD) or extensively delayed (ED) auditory feedback conditions. The ED feedback was designed to create marked physical effort on the part of his subjects. The results tended to support the hypothesis that greater physical effort leads to greater attitude change but did not support the hypothesis that improvising leads to greater attitude change than reading a prepared script. A supplementary self-report measure showed that subjects in the ED condition experienced more physical and, to a lesser degree, psychological effort in presenting their speech than subjects in the SD condition. There were no differences in reported satisfaction between the two conditions.

Friedman (1971) found that IR subjects reported exerting no more physical effort than subjects in the DR, AMOD, AS, and NAS conditions. On the other hand, IR subjects reported exerting less psychological effort than AMOD subjects, but not less than DR and AS subjects. However, there were no differences in the behavioral change measures between these conditions. His data fail to support the hypothesis that behavior changes occurring from roleplaying procedures are a consequence of the physical or psychological effort exerted by subjects.

4. Improvisation

The improvisation interpretation proposed by Hovland et al. (1953) to account for their roleplaying and attitudes change results claims that the effectiveness of the improvised roleplaying procedure is primarily due to subjects improvising new information, constructing supportive arguments, elaborations, and cogent examples, and reformulating old arguments in support of a given opinion which leads to a greater acceptance of that opinion. According to this cognitive-intellectual hypothesis, a person thus persuades himself that the communication is correct. This interpretation, like the effort and satisfaction interpretations by the authors, was developed to account for opinion or attitude changes, and not necessarily to account for behavior changes.

In order to explore the implications of the improvisation hypothesis, Friedman (1971) attempted to assess how well subjects roleplayed by having the accomplice who roleplayed opposite the subjects rate their performance. For IR subjects, this assessment included how well the subject constructed his own assertive responses and how involved he was in the roleplaying performance: The experimenter found that there were no differences between the accomplice's rating of how well subjects roleplayed in the DR and IR conditions. However, he did find that for IR subjects there was a significant correlation between how well the subjects played the role and changes in assertive behavior ($r = -.78$). The correlation indicated that the better the subject played the role, the greater the change in assertive behavior. This implies that subjects who can improvise responses during a roleplaying procedure can later transfer these responses to another behavioral situation. It also implies that some subjects cannot improvise responses during roleplaying, and that for these subjects the improvised roleplaying procedure is unlikely to lead to marked changes in behavior.

Friedman also found that subjects in the IR condition who felt more capable of asserting themselves following the roleplaying showed the greatest change in assertiveness ($r = .46$, $p < .05$), and that a significant negative correlation existed between a scale of social inhibition developed by Janis-Field and change in assertive behavior ($r = -.50$, $p < .05$). His data suggests that it is the socially inhibited subjects who are incapable of constructing and improvising assertive responses during the roleplaying treatment and thus unable to profit a great deal from the IR procedure.

Data from an experiment by Efran and Korn (1969) on the measurement of social caution further corroborate Friedman's findings. Efran and Korn found that subjects who were designated socially cautious by fellow group members were significantly more inhibited, cautious, and self-conscious when engaging in IR in six different situations than subjects who were nominated as active participants in the group. Furthermore, the socially cautious subjects were rated by the experimenter as being more anxious and by themselves as being more uncomfortable while roleplaying than the active subjects.

In the Efran and Korn study, the subject roleplayed six situations: calling the cleaners about a hole found in his suit; calling his friend's grandmother to offer condolences; calling to make a blind date; calling a friend who had divulged some personal information to others; calling a friend long distance as a birthday surprise; and commenting on a girl's desire to cancel a special date because she had to stay home with her sick brother, when the subject knew she had no brother.

In general, Friedman and Efran and Korn's data support the findings of Zimbardo (1965) and McGuire (1964) that IR is threatening to many subjects because they are ill-prepared from lack of experience to construct new responses. Zimbardo, for example, points out that a large number of subjects in his and King and Janis' (1956) study were unable to improvise any new material. It would thus appear that for socially inhibited subjects who are threatened by an IR procedure, it may be necessary to provide them with explicit information to guide their behavior from AMOD, DR, or AS procedures. These subjects apparently need external cues to guide their covert and overt verbal responses.

D. Cognitive Variables

1. Expectations, Appropriateness, Justification

Janis and King's cognitive-intellectual hypothesis for IR stressing spontaneous elaborations, additions, and reformulations of arguments by a subject has already been discussed. Other cognitive variables that may be important in behavior change through roleplaying procedures are the development of expectations, anticipations, and justifications. Kelman (1961) has pointed out that if a person takes an action discrepant with his previous behavior or attitude, he will be engaging in new experiences which will lead him to new expectations about his capabilities, and the consequences, justifications, and social rewards for behaving in certain ways.

Friedman (1971) found that despite negative consequences occurring to subjects who were roleplaying assertive behavior, marked behavioral changes in assertiveness occurred in subjects from pre- to postassessment. A cognitive expectancy hypothesis similar to Walters and Parke's explanation of the effects of consequences occurring to a model might be partially invoked to explain this finding. According to this hypothesis, the roleplaying subjects learned that the experimenter expected them to assert themselves during roleplaying and to transfer the assertive behavior learned during roleplaying to the posttreatment behavioral assessment. Moreover, the subject may have learned that he could expect a favorable judgement or approval from the experimenter for engaging in assertive behavior.

The results of an experiment by Wagner (1968) on the reinforcement of the expression of anger through roleplaying can be partially explained by a cognitive-expectancy hypothesis and the important role of the experimenter in inducing behavior change. Wagner's subjects talked into a tape recorder and were told to respond as though they were actually present in each situation. The two experimental conditions consisted of having the subject engage in IR in ten anger-eliciting situations. All experimental subjects were encouraged by the experimenter to express anger toward the other person. In one experimental condition, the person roleplaying opposite the experimenter submitted to the subjects' anger and apologized to the subject [positive reinforcement (PR)] condition and in the other experimental condition, the other person retaliated angrily at the subject when he expressed anger [punishment (P)] condition.

Wagner's results indicated, as he predicted, that the subjects in the PR condition increased in anger expressiveness from pre- to posttesting significantly more than subjects in the P and control conditions. Contrary to prediction, the P group did not have a significant decrement in anger expressiveness when compared to the control group. In fact, the P group showed increases in anger expressiveness that fell between the PR and control group.

It seems plausible that the subjects in the P group learned two sets of conflicting expectations. First, that the person they roleplayed opposite would punish their expressions of anger. Second, that the experimenter would approve of their expressing angry feelings. If the latter set of expectations was stronger than the former set of expectations, the subject's tendency to express his anger would be greater than his tendency to inhibit the expression of his anger. Consequently, increases in anger expressiveness would occur, which is in accord with Wagner's findings. According to this interpretation, subjects in the PR condition learned to expect a favorable reaction from the other person for anger expressiveness and approval from the experimenter. Both sets of expectations by the subject would then lead to a maximum increase in anger expressiveness. Further research investigating the role of expectations created in the subject by the experimenter and by the person roleplaying opposite the subject is badly needed.

IV. Modeling, Modeling plus Roleplaying, and Roleplaying

Until recently there has been little research combining modeling with roleplaying into a behavior change procedure. A clinical study by A. Lazarus (1966) attempted to compare behavior rehearsal with nondirective therapy and advice in effecting behavior change. Behavior rehearsal, however, was defined broadly to include role reversal whereby Lazarus played the role of client first and the client played the role of some other person, e.g., employer or mother. To the extent this was done, modeling was combined with roleplaying. This study has the obvious limitations noted by Lazarus of having the therapy and the evaluation conducted by the same person. As A. Lazarus (1966) is well aware, evidence for change must be objective in the sense that a clear-cut behavioral change must be demonstrated in the client's life. However, in his study the client's self-report to the therapist was used as evidence and therefore subject to bias.

For each of the three therapeutic approaches, Lazarus saw 25 patients with problems in assertiveness such as expressing disagreement with a friend's social arrangement, refusing to accede to an unreasonable request, and requesting an increment in salary. The results showed that modeling plus roleplaying (behavior rehearsal) was most successful with 92% change, followed by advice-giving with 44% change and reflection-interpretation with 32% change.

An intriguing and complex study was performed by Sarason (1968) on institutionalized juvenile delinquents who were administered both roleplaying and modeling plus roleplaying procedures.[3] Sarason's study was conducted at the Cascadia Juvenile Reception-Diagnostic Center. The subjects of his study were primarily male first offenders, ages 15–18 years, who were committed to Cascadia by the juvenile courts of Washington. They lived in cottages in which 20–25 boys resided. Sarason conducted a series of studies over the past few years in which groups of juvenile delinquents were directed to either observe graduate psychology students enact 15 different situations, roleplayed the situations themselves from verbal descriptions of the situations, observed models and roleplayed, or

---

[3] Although it is not specifically stated in the article, a personal communication from Sarason indicated that modeling subjects also received the roleplaying procedure.

did not participate in any special procedure. Role playing subjects were given directions on how to enact their roles and what was expected of them, but they were told to improvise upon the information given them.[4] In the modeling plus roleplaying condition, the boys first observed the graduate students enact the situation and then roleplayed the situation with others. The situations were quite carefully developed and were spread out over 15 sessions. Most of the treatment conditions were followed by group discussion by the boys. One study was done in which a modeling plus roleplaying treatment was not followed by group discussion.

The situations roleplayed or modeled fell into four categories. The first set of situations dealt with the problems teenagers have in coping with authority, such as police officers and employers. Of particular concern in these situations was how teenagers could control impulsive behavior. A second set of situations involved the importance of planning ahead, an area in which juvenile offenders generally are extremely deficient. A third set of situations involved recognizing and coping with peer pressure that is potentially destructive to the teenager. The fourth set of situations involved interacting with the other people in a positive, prosocial fashion so that the juvenile could learn to make a good impression without "conning" other people.

An example of one situation used by Sarason in the modeling study is the Handling Anger Scene. In this scene a teenager, Bill, worked in a gas station and was mad at his boss, but he acted like nothing had happened. Excerpts from the scene are:

Bill: The lube room is clean and the oil's put away.
Boss: It's about time. You're going to have to move a little faster around here if you want to keep your job.
Bill: Yes sir. Can I go now? I'm a little overtime.
Boss: Hell no . . . you've got to finish that Chev. That guy was just in here yelling at *me* because it wasn't done.
Bill: Well you know I wanted to leave on time. I told you this morning I had a date.
Boss: That's your problem. I told you that you're going to finish the Chev so you'd better get at it. That's all.
Bill: O.K. . . . well . . . I'm going to call my girl first and tell her I'll be late.
Boss: Yeah, but hurry it up.

Sarason stated that in terms of behavior ratings by the ward staff and attitude changes by the boys, experimental subjects were rated as showing more positive behavior change than control subjects. Sarason indicated that these results were strongest and most positive in the case of modeling

[4] I. Sarason, personal communication, 1969.

plus roleplaying groups, and second in order of potency was the role-playing condition.[5] Sarason has recently indicated that followup data reveal dramatic differences in recidivism between experimental and untreated control groups.[6] It is difficult to establish exactly what determined the changes in Sarason's study, since subjects who roleplayed were administered a combination of DR and IR which was usually followed by group discussion. It is possible that this set of procedures is optimally effective for behavior change.

In the only other experimental study combining modeling and roleplaying procedures Friedman (1971) found that a combination of modeling plus directed roleplaying (MDR) procedures was the most effective method of changing assertive behavior in college students from pre- to posttreatment assessment. In his experiment MDR was significantly more effective in changing assertive behavior than an AMOD, DR, or AS condition.

In explaining these results, the investigator noted that the hypothesized mediating variables to account for the efficacy of MDR over an AS may have summated. Thus cognitive-perceptual images and overt response repetition elicited by an MDR treatment may have fostered greater changes in assertiveness than in either the AMOD or DR condition alone, or in the AS condition. Friedman (1971) has summarized his interpretation by suggesting that when modeling and DR are combined, the subject has available to him (1) assertive information that evokes response rehearsal, (2) a variety of externally presented visual and vocal cues that provide him with covert cognitive-perceptual images which serve as internal cues for assertiveness, and (3) a repertoire of overtly rehearsed responses to emit in the presence of these internal cues. He hypothesized that the combination of these mediating variables produces the greatest increase in assertive behavior from pre- to posttreatment assessment.

V. Participation, Modeling plus Participation

Both a participation procedure and a roleplaying procedure emphasize overt response repetition by the subject. The difference between a roleplaying procedure and a participation (PAR) procedure is that during roleplaying the subject (1) encounters stimuli that resemble but are markedly different from the stimuli he will encounter in the assessment situation, (2) is instructed to act as if he were another person engaging in a specified set of behaviors, (3) usually is immediately exposed to very

[5] See footnote 3.
[6] See footnote 4.

threatening stimuli rather than being gradually exposed to the very threatening stimuli. During a PAR treatment procedure, subjects perform the same overt responses that they are tested on during pre- and posttreatment assessment. Usually subjects engage in these overt responses while confronting the same stimuli, e.g., dog, snake, top of a building, they will be exposed to during testing.

PAR procedures have only been investigated experimentally with non-verbal behaviors. The one experimental study that has investigated the role of a PAR procedure administered alone was conducted by Sherman (1969). In Sherman's study, water-phobic subjects gradually participated in 26 behaviors in the water which were hierarchically arranged. Over the course of three weekly 15–20-minute sessions subjects in this repeated PAR alone condition did as well as subjects in a desensitization (DES) plus PAR condition, and significantly better than a DES alone and no-treatment control condition. In a pilot clinical study, Davison (1965) found that all three subjects in a PAR procedure performed the terminal behavior (allowing a beetle to crawl all over her hand) during treatment. During posttesting, only two of the subjects performed the terminal behavior. Both of the subjects in the relaxation plus PAR procedure and none of the control subjects performed the terminal behavior during treatment and posttesting. Another pilot study by Cooper, Furst, and Bridger (1969) found that both of the subjects in a PAR procedure would perform the terminal behavior of holding the snake in their hands.

Since participation is similar in many ways to roleplaying, it is likely that the mediating variables hypothesized to account for its effectiveness would be quite similar to those used to account for the effectiveness of roleplaying procedures. These mediating variables are cognitive-perceptual images, covert response repetition, overt response repetition, motivational changes such as arousal or anxiety reduction, and cognitive variables such as expectations of what will be the consequence of engaging in certain behaviors.

A number of studies have compared the efficacy of PAR combined with other procedures such as modeling, DES, relaxation, and physical contact. For this review, we are primarily concerned with the PAR and modeling procedures in changing maladaptive behavior. These other procedures, however, may further enhance the behavior changes occurring from modeling and PAR.

Ritter (1968) found that a procedure combining modeling by an experimenter with participation by a subject and physical contact by an experimenter (MPPC) was more effective in increasing children's approach behavior to snakes than a MM condition (also called vicarious desensitization). MM was in turn more effective than a no-treatment control group. The latter finding replicated the results of an earlier study by Bandura *et al.* (1967).

Later a study was done by Ritter (1969a) on adults with a fear of heights in order to isolate the effects of the several variables involved in Ritter's 1968 study. In this study, subjects were run in groups as in the Ritter 1968 study. Ten female and two male adults who were obtained through newspaper advertisements and recommendations served as subjects in the experiment. Only subjects who were unable to climb above the 26-feet point of a 52-foot outdoor concrete staircase were included as subjects. Experimental subjects were administered one 24-minute treatment session. In the MPPC condition (also called contact desensitization) the experimenter first demonstrated walking up to each of nine landings on the staircase and looking down over the railing without looking down. The female experimenter then placed her arm around the waist of each subject and guided her to each landing. After about two repetitions, the experimenter removed her arm. Eventually, the subject walked to each landing alone and tried to stand there for 2 minutes. This procedure was followed for each of nine landings. Subjects who were not working with the experimenter observed or practiced on their own while waiting their turn. At the ninth and highest landing, the three subjects in this group plus the experimenter linked arms and jointly walked several times to the landing. In the modeling plus participation (MP) group, the same procedure was followed except that the experimenter walked alongside the subject without any physical contact.

Ritter (1969a) found that MPPC led to greater increases in approach behavior to heights than MP alone or to a no-treatment control. Surprisingly, MP did not in this study lead to greater changes in approach behavior than the no-treatment control group. Ritter suggested this might have occurred because MP subjects were handicapped by viewing the poor performance of other group members. In a sense, the other group members served as an additional but inadequate live models in this condition.

A later study conducted by Ritter (1969b) was done to further explore these variables but with a greater degree of control over them. Adult acrophobic subjects were individually run in this experiment. In this experiment, 13 females and two adult males who responded to advertisements for severely height phobic volunteers participated. The subjects were first administered a 44-item height-avoidance test on a roof of a seven-story building. The procedure for subjects in the MPPC condition and the MP condition was identical to the Ritter (1969a) study except subjects were run individually. In the modeling (MOD) condition, the female experimenter demonstrated the approach behavior to each height while the subject sat toward the center of the roof and observed the experimenter. Ritter's results showed that MPPC was greater than MP in increasing approach behavior to heights. The MP condition was in turn more effective than a MOD condition in changing approach behavior, but unexpectedly MOD was not more effective than a no-treatment control procedure.

As previously mentioned, Bandura *et al.* (1969) conducted an experiment on children's fear of snakes. In their experiment, an MPPC condition was more effective than both a multiple SYM condition and a DES (imagery plus relaxation) condition in increasing approach behavior to snakes. These two latter conditions were more effective in changing approach behavior to snakes than a no-treatment control condition.

PAR procedures as mentioned above have been shown to add to the efficacy of MOD procedures. Moreover, research by Barlow, Leitenberg, Agras, and Wincze (1969) and Garfield, Darwin, Singer, and McBrearty (1967) has indicated that relaxation is more effective when combined with PAR than with imagery, and DES is more effective when interspersed with PAR than when administered alone. These studies further emphasize that PAR can be an important ingredient in a combined behavior change procedure.

The most common explanation of PAR procedures when combined with modeling are in terms of anxiety reduction and overt nonverbal response repetition. Although changes in reported fear have been shown to occur in two of the studies using PAR procedures (Bandura *et al.,* 1969; Ritter, 1969a), two other studies (Ritter, 1968, 1969b) have failed to find that changes in self-reported fear occurred along with changes in avoidance behavior. Thus, the evidence for fear reduction mediating behavioral change occurring from PAR procedures is equivocal. Possibly fear reduction may or may not accompany behavior change depending on the role of other unspecified variables (e.g., see Walters, 1968).

The research on roleplaying indicated that overt response repetition was not necessary for behavior change to occur at least for verbal responses. It is possible that covert nonverbal motor response repetition accounts for changes in nonverbal behavior occurring from a PAR procedure, just as covert verbal response repetition can account for most of the changes in verbal behavior occurring from a DR procedure. However, it seems unlikely that this is the case because of the difficulty of engaging in many forms of covert nonverbal behavior. Therefore, it is likely that overt rehearsal is an important variable mediating behavioral change occurring from a PAR procedure.

VI. Additional Considerations

A. Interpersonal–Noninterpersonal, Verbal–Nonverbal Behavior

Most of the studies done to date have measured noninterpersonal, non-verbal behaviors such as approach behavior to dogs, snakes, heights, and water, or reductions in cigarette smoking (see Table I). The remaining studies have measured various forms of interpersonal, verbal assertiveness. It is possible that the mediating mechanisms used to change non-verbal behaviors are different from the mediating mechanisms used to change verbal behaviors. Thus, perceptual cognitive-imagery, verbal codes, and overt practice may be relatively more important in changing non-verbal behaviors and covert verbal response repetition may be more important in changing verbal behaviors. In any case, the relative contribution of these variables in changing nonverbal and verbal behavior needs to be further investigated, as well as the role of cognitive expectancies.

If MOD, roleplaying, and PAR procedures for changing behavior are going to be relevant to the wide range of problems seen in the clinic by

TABLE I

Effectiveness of Modeling, Roleplaying, and Participation Studies in Eliciting Criterion Behavior at Posttesting

	Snakes		Heights		
	Bandura et al. (1969)	Geer & Turtletaub (1967)	Ritter (1968)	Ritter (1969a)	Ritter (1969b)
Modeling					
1. Single		67%[c]			20%[e] (20%)[f]
2. Multiple	33%[a,b]	53%			
Modeling plus roleplaying					
Modeling plus participation					
1. Without physical contact				0%[d]	60%[e] (60%)[f]
2. With physical contact	92%[a]	80%			100%[e] (40%)[f]
Roleplaying					
1. Directed					
2. Improvised					
Control	0%[a]	11%[c]	0%		

TABLE I (*Continued*)

	Dogs		Interpersonal		
	Bandura et al. (1967)	Bandura & Menlove (1968)	O'Connor (1969)	Friedman (1971)	A. Lazarus (1966)
Modeling					
1. Single	67%[g] (55%)[g,h]	25%[g]		63%[k] (44%)[l]	
2. Multiple		38%[g]	67%[i] (50%)[j]		
Modeling plus roleplaying				81%[k] (69%)[l]	92%
Modeling plus participation					
1. Without physical contact					
2. With physical contact					
Roleplaying					
1. Directed				53%[k] (53%)[l]	
2. Improvised				50%[k] (50%)[l]	
Control	33%[g] (13%)[g,h]	31%[g]		38%[k,m] (38%)[l,m] 6%[k,n] (6%)[l,n]	44%[o] 32%[p]

Note: Data are presented as percentage of subjects demonstrating criterion behavior. In some studies two sets of criterion behavior were used. The figures for the second criteria are shown in parentheses.

[a] Terminal score = 29.
[b] Plus relaxation.
[c] Terminal score = crossing barrier for first time.
[d] Models were incompetent.
[e] Change score = 8 or more.
[f] Terminal score = 18 or more.
[g] Terminal score = 14.
[h] Highly avoidant subjects. Pretest score = 7 or less.
[i] Change score = 4 or more.
[j] Terminal score = 6 or more.
[k] Change score = 4 or more.
[l] Terminal score = 7 or more.
[m] Read assertive script.
[n] Read nonassertive script.
[o] Advice-giving.
[p] Reflection-interpretation.

psychotherapists, much more research needs to be done on interpersonally oriented behavior problems. A recent study by O'Conner (1969) on withdrawn nursery school children is a good example of research that needs to be done. In O'Conner's study, 13 nursery school children were selected as having exhibited marked withdrawal over an extended period of time as judged by their teachers. In addition, the subjects were measured on behavioral indices such as looking at, and interacting with, as displaying isolate behavior in the classroom over a period of 8 days. These isolates displayed an average of less than two social interactions for the 32 intervals scored compared to a nonisolate group of children who displayed an average of greater than nine social interactions. The children in the symbolic multiple modeling (SYMM) condition saw individually a sound-color film lasting 23 minutes. The film portrayed 11 scenes in which children interacted in a nursery school setting.

In this SYMM treatment by O'Connor, various children of different ages and sexes demonstrated social approach behavior in different scenes. The scenes were roughly graduated from least to most threatening based on the vigor of the social activity and the size of the group. The scenes ranged from mild activities such as two children sharing a book or toy while seated at a table, to six children excitedly throwing play equipment around the room. In all cases, the consequences for social approach behavior by the children were positive, such as smiles, talking, and offers to play by the other children. The positive consequences to the model was aided by a sound track by a woman with a soothing voice who described the social actions of the model and the outcomes. In the control condition, subjects saw a 20-minute film of the acrobatic performances of Marineland dolphins accompanied by a musical soundtrack. The control film did not contain any human characters. The results indicated that the subjects in the SYMM condition showed substantially greater changes in social interaction measured in the classroom immediately afterward than control subjects.

B. ELICITATION OF CRITERION BEHAVIOR

As Patterson (1969) has pointed out, there is a difference between the elicitation of a behavior and the maintenance or persistence of that behavior over time. He has suggested that the value of a technique such as modeling may be in its ability to elicit behavior rapidly. Therefore, it is of value to review how successful MOD, roleplaying, and PAR procedures alone and combined are in rapidly eliciting behavior and the amount or degree of behavior actually elicited by these procedures. In order to do this, published data from a number of studies (O'Connor, 1969; Ritter, 1969a, 1969b) were reanalyzed.

A summary of the available statistics can be found in Table I. The figures in the Table indicate the percentage of subjects in each condition who obtained or surpassed some behavioral criterion. In the reanalysis of the Ritter (1969a, 1969b) studies of acrophobia two criteria were used: either a change score of +8 (the maximum possible score was 44 and subjects were selected who had scores under 18) or a posttest score of 18 or more. In the O'Connor (1969) study two criteria were also used: a change score of +4 social interactions and a posttreatment social interaction score of 6 or more.

The data presented in Table I are grouped according to type of treatment and type of problem. Inspection of the data in Table I indicates that in a SM condition the criterion behavior was elicited at posttesting in 20 to 60% of the subjects. In the MM condition the criterion behavior was elicited in from 33 to 67% of the subjects. The Table indicates that a modeling treatment administered alone was relatively ineffective for at least one third (33%) of subjects. It is interesting to note that in the two studies of interpersonal behavior, the MOD treatment elicited the behavioral criterion in the higher range of percentages, an average of 65% of the subjects.

In the one study comparing the two forms of modeling directly, 38% of the MM subjects engaged in the criterion behavior at posttesting, whereas 24% of SM subjects achieved this criterion. Thirty-one percent of the subjects in the control group also achieved this criterion behavior at posttesting. These differences were not statistically significant. The MM condition presents to a subject a variety of models of different sexes and sizes interacting with a variety of phobic objects of different sizes, shapes, mobility, and degrees of ferocity. In terms of the ability of this procedure to elicit behavior change, the data are not yet sufficient to strongly support the contention that the MM treatment is more effective than a SM procedure in which one model interacts with one phobic object.

The available data on roleplaying procedures indicated that a DR or IR procedure could elicit the criterion behavior in 53 and 50% of the subjects, respectively (Friedman, 1971). There are no experimental data available on what percentage of subjects criterion behavior is elicited in a PAR procedure administered alone. In the Sherman (1969) study, water-phobic subjects gradually participated in 26 behaviors in the water which were hierarchically arranged. Over the course of three 15–20-minute sessions, subjects in this repeated PAR- alone condition increased a mean of 2.56 behaviors. Subjects in a no-treatment control condition increased a mean of .90 behaviors. Unfortunately, data were not presented in terms of the percentage of subjects who engaged in criterion behavior in each treatment. In a pilot clinical study, Davison (1965) found that all three subjects in a PAR procedure performed the criterion behavior during treatment. During posttesting however, only two of the subjects performed the criterion behavior. The available data can only suggest that a PAR procedure administered alone may be moderately effective in eliciting criterion behavior. Much more research on this basic procedure needs to be done.

The studies which combined modeling with other treatment procedures involving overt rehearsal of the subject were able to elicit the criterion behavior in from 60 to 92% of the subjects. These figures excluded the

Ritter (1969a) study in which subjects served as models in addition to the experimenter but behaved incompetently. In general, these data indicate that a marked increase in behavior is possible in a high percentage of subjects participating in this treatment combination. It appears that the addition of overt rehearsal whether it be by PAR, DR, or IR was more effective than an SM or MM treatment alone in eliciting substantial behavior changes. There is evidence to suggest that when physical contact was added to the MOD plus overt rehearsal combination, the treatment procedure could be further enhanced. Thus in an MPPC procedure, the criterion behavior was elicited from 80 to 100% of the subjects. This statement must be qualified, however, when a more stringent set of criteria was applied to the Ritter (1969a) study. When this was done, the figure for the number of subjects engaging in criterion behavior dropped from 100 to 40%.

C. Persistence of Behavioral Changes

Most of the experiments reported in this review have measured behavior occurring immediately before and immediately after the experimental procedures. A few of the studies have also measured the behavior under investigation some weeks or months later. Thus, Friedman (1971) measured assertive behavior 2 weeks after the treatment procedures. Bandura et al. (1967, 1969) and Bandura and Menlove (1968) measured changes in avoidance behavior to animals 1 month after the treatment procedures. Janis and Mann (1965) and Mann and Janis (1968) obtained measurements on their subjects cigarette smoking 2 weeks, 6 months, and 18 months after the treatment was administered.

The main implication of these studies is that behavior changes occurring from MOD, roleplaying, and PAR conditions generally persisted at least for a short period of time (see Table II). Thus between 19 and 55% of MOD subjects demonstrated criterion behavior at short-term follow-up. However, subjects in Friedman's study (1971) who either overtly rehearsed the information provided in the MOD condition (DR) or covertly rehearsed the information (AS) maintained criterion behavior in comparable amounts (44% and 54% respectively) at follow-up. The most effective procedures for maintaining or enhancing behavior change at short-term follow-up were MPPC (primarily female subjects, Bandura et al., 1969), MDR for males (Friedman, 1971), and IR for females (Friedman, 1971; Janis & Mann, 1965).[7] Between 71 and 100% of the subjects demonstrated criterion behavior at follow-up in these conditions.

[7] L. Mann, personal communication, 1969. Two weeks after roleplaying, 3 of 14 subjects had quit smoking, and seven subjects had cut down five or more cigarettes per day.

TABLE II

PERSISTENCE[a] AND GENERALIZATION[b] OF CRITERION BEHAVIOR IN MODELING,
ROLEPLAYING, AND PARTICIPATION STUDIES[c]

	Bandura et al. (1967)	Bandura & Menlove (1968)	Bandura et al. (1969)	Friedman (1971)	Mann & Janis (1968)
Modeling					42%—4.75 cig.[p,s]
1. Single	$\left[\begin{array}{c}42\%^{e}\\(33\%)^{e,f}\end{array}\right]^{d}$	19%[e]		55%[j] (55%)[k]	4.0 cig.[q,s] 5.2 cig.[r,s]
2. Multiple		50%[e]	[33%][g,h]		
Modeling plus roleplaying				100%[j,l] (100%)[k,l] 33%[j,m] (50%)[k,m]	
Modeling plus participation with physical contact			92%[g,i] [42%][g]		
Roleplaying					
1. Directed				44%[j] (44%)[k]	
2. Improvised				0%[j,l] (33%)[k,l] 80%[j,m] (80%)[k,m]	71%—10.50 cig.[t] 9.85 cig.[q] 13.5 cig.[r]
Control	$\left[\begin{array}{c}12\%^{e}\\(0\%)^{e,f}\end{array}\right]^{d}$	25%[e]	[0%][g]	54%[j,n] (54%)[k,n] 30%[j,o] (30%)[k,o]	

[a] Figures not in brackets or parentheses indicate percentage of subjects demonstrating criterion behavior at follow-up.

[b] Figures in brackets indicate percentage of subjects who demonstrated generalized criterion behavior.

[c] Figures in parentheses represent another criterion behavior was also used for that study.

[d] Represents percentage of subjects who demonstrated generalized criterion behavior at follow-up.

[e] Terminal score = 14.

[f] Highly avoidant subjects. Pretest score = 7 or less.

[g] Terminal score = 29.

[h] Plus relaxation.

[i] Actual figure (92%) was not presented but had to be inferred from general discussion of follow-up results.

[j] Change score = 4 or more.

[k] Terminal score = 7 or more.

[l] Males only.

[m] Females only.

[n] Read assertive script.

One study that is consistent with the sex by treatment interaction found at follow-up in the data obtained by Friedman (1971) was the Mann and Janis (1968) study. Their subjects were females who engaged in improvised ER opposite a male roleplayer (the experimenter). This study was a follow-up to the Janis and Mann (1965) experiment. Results indicated that roleplaying subjects changed from an initial reduction after 2 weeks of 10.5 cigarettes, to a reduction of 9.85 cigarettes at 6 months, and 13.5 cigarettes at 18 months. The comparable figures for control subjects who listened to a tape recording of the ER (audio modeling) were 4.75, 4.00, and 5.20 at 2 weeks, 6 months, and 18 months, respectively. Unfortunately, male subjects were not included in this study. The Surgeon General's report intervened between the 6-month and 18-month test dates and may have prevented the decline in the effects of the improvised ER condition between these two test dates.

In general, there still is insufficient evidence to clearly establish the effectiveness of MOD, roleplaying, and PAR in treatments over an extended period of time. This particularly applies if we are interested in the effectiveness of these treatment procedures over a wide range of behavior problems, especially interpersonal behaviors with varied populations. The research to date is promising and should be further extended.

D. Generalization of Behavioral Changes

Less than half of the studies included behavioral measures of generalization. Bandura et al. (1967) and Bandura and Menlove (1968) tested subjects in the laboratory on both the experimental animal, a cocker spaniel, and on an unfamiliar animal, a white mongrel. Bandura et al. (1969) assessed subjects on their approach behavior toward the experimental king snake and an unfamiliar corn snake. Inspection of Table II indicates that from 33 to 42% of the subjects in the MOD treatments demonstrated generalized criterion behavior. This can be compared with the 33–67% of subjects in these studies who performed criterion behavior to the experimental animal alone (Table I). This finding suggests that a MOD procedure is capable of a substantial amount of generalization to a closely related object. Table II also reveals that only 42% of the

---

[o] Read nonassertive script.

[p] Two weeks after the treatment: of 12 subjects, one quit smoking and four cut down five or more cigarettes per day. Mean reduction = 4.75 cigarettes.

[q] 6-month follow-up.

[r] 18-month follow-up.

[s] Subjects who heard a tape recording of emotional roleplaying.

[t] Two weeks after the treatment: of 14 subjects, three quit smoking and seven cut down five or more cigarettes per day. Mean reduction = 10.5 cigarettes.

subjects in MP showed generalized criterion behavior compared with 92% of the subjects who demonstrated criterion behavior to the experimental animal.

Bandura *et al.* (1969) reported that 47% of their subjects reported encounters with snakes outside the laboratory subsequent to the treatments. The experimenters state that in all cases the reduction in fear of snakes achieved in treatment generalized to snakes in naturalistic situations. They did not indicate whether there were any differences among treatment conditions. Two weeks after the behavioral follow-up, Friedman (1968, 1971) administered an assertiveness questionnaire measuring assertion outside the laboratory. He found some generalized effects of the MOD treatment but for females only. Sarason (1968) measured change in the ward behavior of his male juvenile delinquents. Since this was not the behavior modeled or rehearsed during treatment, it could be considered a generalized effect of the procedures. As previously stated, experimental subjects showed more positive changes in ward behavior than control subjects.

The relatively small amount of research done on the generalized effects of MOD, roleplaying, and PAR procedures administered alone and combined suggest moderate, generalized effects of these treatments. Extensive research in this area is needed, particularly on behaviors measured outside the laboratory setting.

E. Number, Duration, Frequency, Spacing of Sessions; Repetition, Sequencing, and Pacing of Behaviors; Group vs. Individual Treatment

The total amount of time the subject participates in MOD, roleplaying, or PAR procedures varies markedly (Table III). Typically, the total exposure to models has occurred within the 20–35-minute or 70–80-minute range. The typical amount of time spent in roleplaying is approximately 60 minutes, while subjects in the one PAR only procedure spent about 30–60 minutes in treatment.

The number of sessions administered to subjects varies considerably and only roughly approximates the total treatment time, because treatment sessions vary in length from 3 minutes to 60 minutes. Moreover, the number of sessions has ranged between one and 15 with a median of two. The frequency of sessions also varies from once per week to twice a day for 4 alternate days (Table III).

In MOD plus overt rehearsal studies, practice by the subject has both followed the complete MOD sequence (Friedman, 1971; Sarason, 1968) and been interspersed throughout the MOD sequence (Ritter, 1968, 1969a, 1969b). In one study (Bandura *et al.,* 1969) the whole MOD sequence was first observed and then segments of the behavior were alternately observed and then practiced.

In some studies the total behavior sequence modeled is observed only once (Bandura *et al.,* 1967; Bandura & Menlove, 1968; O'Connor, 1969). In other studies (Bandura *et al.,* 1969; Friedman, 1971; Ritter, 1968, 1969b), the total behavior sequence modeled is observed more than one time. The subject usually has the opportunity to engage in each behavior more than once in the PAR and MP studies (Bandura *et al.,* 1967; Ritter, 1968, 1969a, 1969b; Sherman, 1969). In the roleplaying and MOD plus roleplaying studies (Friedman, 1971; A. Lazaras, 1966; Sarason, 1968), subjects often have the opportunity to engage in each behavior more than once. In the Janis and Mann (1965) and Wagner (1968) studies, however, subjects only engaged in each behavior or behavior sequence once.

In most of the MOD, PAR, and MP studies, the behavior observed or engaged in has been graded in terms of difficulty or threatening properties to the subject. In the roleplaying and MOD plus roleplaying studies, however, the subject is usually expected to engage immediately in fairly difficult behaviors and the behaviors are usually not graded in difficulty. A few studies (Bandura *et al.,* 1969; Ritter, 1969a, 1969b) have permitted the subject to pace himself through the behavior sequence. The subject can then spend as much time as he wants on each graded behavior item. Some studies run subjects in groups, while the remaining studies run subjects individually (Table III).

Inspection of the outcome data from all the studies indicates no clear-cut effect of the variables of number, duration, frequency, or spacing of sessions, repetition and sequencing of modeled or rehearsed behaviors, pacing or graded sequencing of behaviors, or individual *vs.* group treatment. Most of these learning variables have been shown by Sheffield and Maccoby (1961) and his colleagues (Lumsdaine, 1961; McGuire, 1961) to be important in observational and participatory learning of motoric and nonmotoric tasks. It seems possible that these same variables would be important in the learning of approach behaviors to animals, heights, and people. Consequently, considerable research needs to be done on the role of these variables in facilitating behavior change.

F. SEX OF THE SUBJECT, EXPERIMENTER, MODEL, AND ASSISTANTS

Most of the studies reported in this paper used exclusively or predominantly female subjects (Table III). The only studies that reported analyzing for sex (Friedman, 1971; Ritter, 1968) found no differences at posttesting, although Friedman (1971) found a sex by treatment inter-

TABLE III
Characteristics of Modeling, Roleplaying, and Participation Studies

	Snakes			Heights		Dogs	
	Bandura et al. (1969)	Geer & Turtletaub (1967)	Ritter (1968)	Ritter (1969a)	Ritter (1969b)	Bandura et al. (1967)	Bandura & Menlove (1968)
Subject's age (years)	13–59	College students	5–11	20–55	14–49	3–5	3–5
Sex							
1. Subject	43 F 5 M	32 F	28 F 16 M	10 F 2 M	13 F 2 M	24 F 24 M	32 F 16 M
2. Experimenter	F	M & F	F	F	F	F	F
3. Models or roleplayers	M & F	F	M & F	F	F	M	M & F
Sessions							
1. Number	4–5	1	2	1	1	8	8
2. Length (min/session)	35	5	35	24	35	10	3
3. Frequency	2 per week	Once	1 per week	Once	Once	2 per day, 4 consecutive days	2 per day, 4 alternate days
4. Total time (minutes)	130–166	5	70	24	35	80	24
Individual or group	Individual	Individual	Group	Group	Individual	Group	Group
Graded behavior	Yes	No	Yes	Yes	Yes	Yes	Yes

	Water	Cigarettes		Interpersonal			
	Sherman (1969)	Janis & Mann (1965)	Friedman (1971)	A. Lazarus (1966)	O'Connor (1969)	Sarason (1968)	Wagner (1968)
Subject's age (years)	College students	College students	College students	Adult neurotic clients	Nursery school	Teenage juveniles delinquents	Hospital psychiatric patients, 30–60
Sex							
1. Subject	54 F	26 F	61 F 60 M	Approximately 50 F 25 M	8 F 5 M	All M	29 F
2. Experimenter	M	M	M	M	M	M	M
3. Models or roleplayers	X	M	M	M	M & F	M	Unspecified
Sessions							
1. Number	1	1	1	4	1	15	2
2. Length (min/session)	10–20	60	8	30	23	40	30
3. Frequency	1 per week	Once	Once	1 per week	Once	3 per week	2 consecutive days
4. Total time (minutes)	30–60	60	8	120	23	600	60
Individual or group	Individual	Individual	Individual	Individual	Individual	Group	Individual
Graded behavior	Yes	No	No	No	Yes	No	No

action at follow-up. Inspection of the data in Table III reveals that the models or assistants have been exclusively male or both male and female in all the studies except those conducted by Ritter (1968, 1969a, 1969b) and Geer and Turtletaub (1967). Male and female experimenters have been used about equally often (Table III). In the Ritter (1968, 1969a, 1969b), A. Lazarus (1966), and Janis and Mann (1965) studies, the experimenter served as both the experimenter and as a model or roleplayer.

There have been practically no studies investigating the importance of the sex of experimenter, subjects, models, and roleplayers, especially as they interact with each other. Sex may be an important variable in the effectiveness of these procedures and may account for some of the discrepancy in the results of the various studies reported.

G. AGE OF THE SUBJECT

Much of the research to date has been done on children or college students (Table III). The studies by Bandura *et al.* (1969), A. Lazarus (1966), Ritter (1969a, 1969b), and Wagner (1968) on adults and by Sarason (1968) on adolescents have not used these two population groups. There is no doubt that research on children and college students is important, but much more research needs to be done on other populations if the results found so far are to be generalized to the total age range of the population.

VII. Summary

This article reviewed research and theory on the effects of MOD, roleplaying, and PAR procedures on the change of maladaptive behavior. The importance of information, rehearsal, motivational, and cognitive processes mediating behavioral change were discussed. It was suggested that the mechanisms mediating changes in verbal behavior might be different from the mediating mechanisms used to change nonverbal behavior. Covert verbal rehearsal was found to be the major variable mediating verbal behavior changes occurring from MOD and DR procedures. Perceptual-cognitive imagery, expectations, and verbal codes were hypothesized to be important mediating variables for changes in nonverbal behavior occurring from a MOD procedure. Socially inhibited subjects were unable to engage in an IR procedure and consequently appeared to require explicit cues to guide their behavior. The most effective behavior change procedures were found to combine MOD with either roleplaying or PAR procedures. The effects of these procedures persisted over a short follow-up period and showed moderate generalization to closely related behaviors. The need for more research on maladaptive behaviors and populations typically seen by psychotherapists was emphasized.

VIII. Comments and Suggestions

Since the focus of the article was on changes in maladaptive behavior, no attempt was made to review the extensive literature on behavioral changes occurring from MOD procedures that were not directly related to maladaptive behavior. Recent reviews of this research can be found in Bandura (1969b) and Flanders (1968). Many of the studies evaluating the role of reinforcement variables in MOD procedures were not discussed for three reasons. First, the above authors have focused their reviews on this class of variables. Second, experiments on changes in maladaptive behavior are usually designed to maximize the effects of reinforcement variables. Third, the author was more interested in integrating the MOD research with the exciting research being done on roleplaying and PAR procedures.

A few suggestions that were not mentioned or emphasized sufficiently in the body of the paper should also be discussed. Little research has been done on the role of incentives and cognitive sets or expectancies provided the subject by the experimenter or therapist immediately prior to the treatment procedures. None of the roleplaying or PAR studies evaluated the role of informational feedback to the subject by the experimenter, the therapist, or another source following his enactment of behavior during the treatment. Since therapists of many orientations routinely use a procedure like this with their clients, research in this area is needed. Substantial research has been done on audio-visual models. Very little research has been done on audio or visual models separately to see what independent contribution each of these input variables makes beyond providing verbal information to the subject.

In order to enhance the effectiveness of the treatment procedures, MOD might be combined with IR or MM combined with multiple roleplaying using a variety of situations, responses, and roleplayers. Subjects might be administered a sequence of procedures such as MM, MDR, multiple IR, informational feedback, and PAR procedures. Many of these procedures could probably be administered more rapidly in a group than in an individual setting.

One of the most important considerations in terms of the effectiveness of the treatment procedures is the transfer of training of behavior to situations not directly rehearsed or observed in the laboratory or clinic. In therapeutic practice, this is often done by assigning the client tasks to be undertaken *in vivo* between administrating the treatments. At first these tasks usually closely match the behaviors learned during the treatment. Later the client is encouraged to undertake new tasks not directly rehearsed or observed during the treatment session. In this way the client presumably develops not only a new set of adaptive behaviors, but a generalized ability to cope adaptively with stressful events in his life. Hopefully, research in the future will expand the procedures discussed in this article, so that the development of generalized coping behaviors in client subjects (Friedman, 1970; R. Lazarus, 1966) can be evaluated.

References

Bandura, A. Vicarious processes: A case of no-trial learning. In L. Berkowitz (Ed.), *Advances in experimental social psychology.* Vol. 2. New York: Academic Press, 1965. Pp. 1–55.

Bandura, A. Modeling approaches to the modification of phobic disorders. In R. Porter (Ed.), *The role of learning in psychotherapy.* Boston: Little, Brown, 1968. Pp. 201–216.

Bandura, A. Modeling theory: Some traditions, trends, and disputes. Paper presented at the Walter's Memorial Symposium at the meeting of the Society for Research in Child Development, Santa Monica, California, March, 1969. (a)

Bandura, A. Social-learning theory of identificatory processes. In A. Goslin (Ed.), *Handbook of socialization theory and research.* Chicago: Rand McNally, 1969. Pp. 213–262. (b)

Bandura, A., Blanchard, E., & Ritter, B. The relative efficacy of desensitization and modeling approaches for inducing behavioral, affective and attitudinal changes. *Journal of Personality and Social Psychology,* 1969, 13, 173–199.

Bandura, A., Grusec, J., & Menlove, F. Observational learning as a function of symbolization and incentive set. *Child Development,* 1966, 37, 499–506.

Bandura, A., Grusec, J., & Menlove, F. Vicarious extinction of avoidance behavior. *Journal of Personality and Social Psychology,* 1967, 5, 16–23.

Bandura, A., & Menlove, F. Factors determining vicarious extinction of avoidance behavior through symbolic modeling. *Journal of Personality and Social Psychology,* 1968, 8, 99–109.

Bandura, A., & Rosenthal, T. Vicarious classical conditioning as a function of arousal level. *Journal of Personality and Social Psychology,* 1966, 3, 54–62.

Bandura, A., Ross, D., & Ross, S. A. Transmission of aggression through imitation of aggressive models. *Journal of Abnormal and Social Psychology,* 1961, 63, 575–582.

Bandura, A., Ross, D., & Ross, S. A. Vicarious reinforcement and imitative learning. *Journal of Abnormal and Social Psychology,* 1963, 67, 601–607.

Barlow, D., Leitenberg, H., Agras, W., & Wincze, J. The transfer gap in systematic desensitization: An analogue study. *Behavior Research and Therapy,* 1969, 7, 191–196.

Berger, S. M. Observer practice and learning during exposure to a model. *Journal of Personality and Social Psychology,* 1966, 3, 696–701.

Berkowitz, L., & Rawlings, E. Effects of film violence on inhibitions against subsequent aggression. *Journal of Abnormal and Social Psychology,* 1963, **66,** 504–512.

Cooper, A., Furst, J., & Bridger, W. A brief commentary on the usefulness of studying fears of snakes. *Journal of Abnormal Psychology,* 1969, **74,** 413–414.

Corsini, R. *Roleplaying in psychotherapy.* Chicago: Aldine, 1966.

Davison, G. Relative contributions of differential relaxation and graded exposure to *in vivo* desensitization of a neurotic fear. Paper presented at the convention of the American Psychological Association, Chicago, September, 1965.

Efran, J., & Korn, P. Measurement of social caution: self-appraisal, roleplaying and discussion behavior. *Journal of Consulting and Clinical Psychology,* 1969, **33,** 78–83.

Flanders, J. A review of research on imitative behavior. *Psychological Bulletin,* 1968, **69,** 316–17.

Friedman, P. The effects of modeling and roleplaying on assertive behavior. Unpublished doctoral dissertation, University of Wisconsin, 1968.

Friedman, P. Limitations in the conceptualizations of behavior therapists: Toward a cognitive behavioral model of behavior therapy. *Psychological Reports,* 1970, **27,** 175–178.

Friedman, P. The effects of modeling and roleplaying on assertive behavior. In R. D. Rubin, H. Fensterheim, A. A. Lazarus, & C. M. Franks (Eds.), *Advances in behavior therapy 1969.* New York: Academic Press, 1971. Pp. 149–169.

Garfield, Z., Darwin, P., Singer, B., & McBrearty, J. Effect of *in vivo* training on experimental desensitization of a phobia. *Psychological Reports,* 1967, **20,** 515–519.

Geer, J., & Turtletaub, A. Fear reduction following observation of a model. *Journal of Personality and Social Psychology,* 1967, **6,** 327–331.

Gerst, M. Symbolic coding operations in observational learning. Unpublished doctoral dissertation, Stanford University, 1968.

Gilmore, J. Toward an understanding of imitation. In E. Simmel, R. Hoppe, & G. A. Milton (Eds.), *Social facilitation and imitative behaviors.* Boston: Allyn & Bacon, 1968. Pp. 217–238.

Hovland, C., Janis, I., & Kelley, H. *Communications and persuasion.* New Haven: Yale University Press, 1953.

Janis, I., & King, B. The influence of roleplaying on opinion change. *Journal of Abnormal and Social Psychology,* 1954, **49,** 211–218.

Janis, I., & Mann, L. Effectiveness of emotional roleplaying in modifying smoking habits and attitudes. *Journal of Experimental Research in Personality,* 1965, **1,** 84–90.

Jansen, M. J., & Stolurow, L. An experimental study of roleplaying. *Psychological Monographs,* 1962, **76**(31, Whole No. 550).

Kelman, H. C. The induction of action and attitude change. *Proceedings of the XIV International Congress of Applied Psychology,* 1961, 81–110.

King, B., & Janis, I. Comparison of the effectiveness of improvised versus non-improvised roleplaying in producing opinion changes. *Human Relations,* 1956, **9,** 177–186.

Lazarus, A. Behavioral rehearsal vs. non-directive therapy vs. advice in effecting behavior change. *Behaviour Research and Therapy,* 1966, **4,** 209–212.

Lazarus, R. *Psychological stress and the coping process.* New York: McGraw-Hill, 1966.

Lumsdaine, A. (Ed.) *Student response in programmed instruction: A symposium.*

Washington, D. C.: National Academy of Sciences—National Research Council, 1961.

Mann, L. The effects of emotional roleplaying on smoking attitude and behavior. *Journal of Experimental Social Psychology*, 1967, 3, 334–348.

Mann, L., & Janis, I. A follow-up study of the long-term effects of emotional roleplaying. *Journal of Personality and Social Psychology*, 1968, 8, 339–342.

McGuire, W. Audience participation and audio-visual instructions: overt-covert responding and rate of presentation. In A. Lumsdaine (Ed.), *Student response in programmed instruction: A symposium*. Washington, D. C.: National Academy of Sciences—National Research Council, 1961. Pp. 417–426.

McGuire, W. Inducing resistance to persuasion: Some contemporary approaches. In L. Berkowitz (Ed.), *Advances in experimental social psychology*. Vol. 1. New York: Academic Press, 1964. Pp. 192–231.

Miller, N., & Dollard, J. *Social learning and imitation*. New Haven: Yale University Press, 1941.

Moore, S. *The Stanislavski system*. New York: Viking Press, 1965.

Moreno, J. *Psychodrama*. Vol. 1. New York: Beacon House, 1946.

O'Connor, R. Modification of social withdrawal through symbolic modeling. *Journal of Applied Behavior Analysis*, 1969, 2, 15–22.

Patterson, G. Social learning: an additional base for developing behavior modification technologies. In C. Frank (Ed.), *Assessment and status of the behavior therapies and associated developments*. New York: McGraw-Hill, 1969.

Ritter, B. The group desensitization of children's snake phobias using vicarious and contact desensitization procedures. *Behaviour Research and Therapy*, 1968, 6, 1–6.

Ritter, B. Treatment of acrophobia with contact desensitization. *Behaviour Research and Therapy*, 1969, 7, 41–45. (a)

Ritter, B. The use of contact desensitization, demonstration plus participation and demonstration alone in the treatment of acrophobia. *Behaviour Research and Therapy*, 1969, 7, 157–164. (b)

Sarason, I. Verbal learning, modeling and juvenile delinquency. *American Psychologist*, 1968, 23, 254–266.

Sarbin, T. Role theory. In G. Lindzey (Ed.), *Handbook of social psychology*. Vol. I. Cambridge, Mass.: Addison-Wesley, 1954. Pp. 223–255.

Schachter, S., & Singer, J. Cognitive, social, and physiological determinants of emotional state. *Psychological Review*, 1962, 69, 379–399.

Sheffield, F., & Maccoby, N. Summary and interpretation of research on organizational principles in constructing filmed demonstrations. In A. Lumsdaine (Ed.), *Student response in programmed instruction: A symposium*. Washington, D. C.: National Academy of Sciences—National Research Council, 1961. Pp. 117–131.

Sherman, A. Behavioral approaches to treatment of phobic anxiety. Unpublished doctoral dissertation, Yale University, 1969.

Staples, F., & Walters, R. H. Anxiety, birth order, and susceptibility to social influence. *Journal of Abnormal and Social Psychology*, 1961, 62, 716–719.

Wagner, M. Reinforcement of the expression of anger through roleplaying. *Behaviour Research and Therapy*, 1968, 6, 91–95.

Walters, R. H. The nature of imitative behavior. In E. Simmel, R. Hoppe, & G. Milton (Eds.), *Social facilitation and imitative behaviors*. Boston: Allyn & Bacon, 1968. Pp. 1–30.

Walters, R. H., & Amoroso, D. M. Cognitive and emotional determinants of the occurrence of imitative behavior. *British Journal of Social and Clinical Psychology*, 1967, **6**, 174–185.

Walters, R. H., Marshall, W. E., & Shooter, J. R. Anxiety, isolation and susceptibility to social influence. *Journal of Personality*, 1960, **28**, 518–529.

Walters, R. H., & Parke, R. D. Influence of the response consequences to a social model on resistance to deviation. *Journal of Experimental Child Psychology*, 1964, **1**, 269–280. (a)

Walters, R. H., & Parke, R. D. Social motivation, dependency, and susceptibility to social influence. In L. Berkowitz (Ed.), *Advances in experimental social psychology*. Vol. 1. New York: Academic Press, 1964. Pp. 231–276. (b)

Walters, R. H., & Parke, R. D. The influence of punishment and related disciplinary techniques on the social behavior of children: Theory and empirical findings. In B. A. Maher (Ed.), *Progress in experimental personality research*. Vol. 4. New York: Academic Press, 1967.

Walters, R. H., Parke, R. D., & Cane, V. A. Timing of punishment and the observation of consequences to others as determinants of response inhibition. *Journal of Experimental Child Psychology*, 1965, **2**, 10–30.

Wolpe, J. *Psychotherapy by reciprocal inhibition*. Stanford: Stanford University Press, 1958.

Wolpe, J. Direct behavior modification therapies. In L. Abt & B. Riess (Eds.), *Progress in clinical psychology*. Vol. 7. New York: Grune & Stratton, 1966.

Wolpe, J., & Lazarus, A. *Behavior therapy techniques*. Oxford: Pergamon, 1966.

Zimbardo, P. The effect of effort and improvisation on self-persuasion produced by roleplaying. *Journal of Experimental Social Psychology*, 1965, **1**, 103–120.

THE EFFECT OF VICARIOUS REINFORCEMENT ON IMITATION: A REVIEW OF THE LITERATURE[1]

Mark H. Thelen and David L. Rennie

DEPARTMENT OF PSYCHOLOGY, UNIVERSITY OF MISSOURI, COLUMBIA,
MISSOURI, AND DEPARTMENT OF PSYCHOLOGY, YORK UNIVERSITY,
TORONTO, ONTARIO, CANADA

I. Introduction

Vicarious reinforcement clearly has been a critical concept in the research on imitation. Hill (1960) and Mowrer (1960) have suggested that vicarious reinforcement is necessary to explain some imitative learning. Bandura and Walters (1963), and Berger (1961) were among the first to study vicarious reinforcement as a potentially critical dimension of vicarious learning. Since these earlier reports, a substantial number of studies have been reported which, in part, manipulated some aspect of vicarious reinforcement as an independent variable. These studies have

[1] The authors are grateful to John Akamatsu, Dennis McGuire, and David Simmonds for their constructive comments about the paper.

led various authors to claim that vicarious reinforcement has been demonstrated to have an effect upon the observer's subsequent imitative behavior. These claims may be seen in the writings of Bandura (1965b, 1969, 1971), wherein he writes that vicarious reinforcement effects on an observer have been demonstrated and, furthermore, that vicarious reinforcement is central to the "performance" of imitative behavior.[2] Flanders recently reviewed research on imitative behavior. In his review, Flanders (1968) stated, "It is hypothesized that one vicarious reinforcement effect is increased imitation of M [model] by O [observer]. A large number of studies with human subjects have confirmed this hypothesis . . . [p. 320]." It would appear that at least some writers and researchers in the area of imitation are convinced that vicarious reinforcement leads to a subsequent effect upon imitative behavior. An attempt is made in the present paper to carefully review the literature concerning the effects of vicarious reinforcement on imitation. The review will focus on research in the imitation tradition, usually involving one model and not on research falling in the area of conformity. Following the review of the literature, the authors consider a number of variables which may be critical to the effect of vicarious reinforcement on imitation.

A. Definition of Imitation and Vicarious Reinforcement

Behavior is imitative when it is similar to that of a model as a function of the subject having observed that model. While a definition of imitation is not a clear-cut matter (e.g., Aronfreed, 1969b; Berger, 1961; Flanders, 1968; Gewirtz & Stingle, 1968), the above definition provides an adequate guideline for the purposes of this paper.

For purposes of this review, a definition of vicarious reinforcement suggested by Flanders (1968) will be adopted: "Vicarious reinforcement is defined as the operation of exposing O to a procedure of presenting a reinforcing stimulus to M (i.e., a presumed or confirmed reinforcing stimulus for O) after and contingent upon a certain response by M

---

[2] Bandura's position on vicarious reinforcement (1965b, 1969, 1971) appears to be that vicarious reinforcement is neither necessary nor sufficient for either the acquisition or the performance of modeled behavior. However, vicarious reward may facilitate acquisition, particularly of complex and/or ambiguous modeling cues, by increasing the observer's arousal, which in turn heightens his general attentional processes, and by heightening the observer's attention to modeling and associated situational cues which are discriminative for reinforcement. Furthermore, since it requires more motivation to perform a model's response than it does to simply acquire it, reinforcement is *more* facilitative of performance than of acquisition. It is this notion which is the basis for his proposition that observer's can acquire a response and maintain it in memory storage without performing the response until such time as an incentive condition motivates him to do so.

[p. 312]." A vastly different definition has been given by Bandura (1971): "Vicarious reinforcement is defined as a change in the behavior of observers as a function of witnessing the consequences accompanying the performance of others [p. 230]." Bandura's definition does not allow for the determination of whether vicarious reinforcement in fact does cause a change in behavior. The present authors wish to add a point of clarification to Flanders' definition. It is required that the reinforcing stimulus to the model be presented by a person or agent external to the model. This excludes from immediate consideration the use of anxiety reduction or the absence of aversive consequences, for example, as reinforcing stimuli to the model. The reason for excluding such procedures is that any situation which results in behavior change or imitation in an observer could be attributed to perceived changed states in the model which are construed as reinforcing. It is noted that vicarious reinforcement refers to both vicarious reward and vicarious punishment.

B. THEORETICAL CONSIDERATIONS

A number of investigators have contributed toward the theoretical nature of vicarious reinforcement (Aronfreed, 1969a, 1969b; Bandura, 1965b, 1969, 1971; Berger, 1961, 1962, 1968; Mowrer, 1960). Some theorists (Mowrer, Berger, Aronfreed) have concentrated on demonstrating an affective mechanism underlying vicarious reinforcement, whereas Bandura has presented a mixed model entailing affective and informational components underlying the phenomenon. Gewirtz and Stingle (1968) have proposed that vicarious reinforcement functions as a generalized cue to the observer for a similar reinforcement (reward or punishment) when he imitates.

Berger (1961, 1962, 1968) has introduced *vicarious instigation* as a mechanism underlying vicarious reinforcement in both instrumental and classical conditioning. According to this notion, the model's emotional response, inferred from the model's stimulus or overt response, serves as a stimulus for the observer's emotional response. The observer's emotional response need not be the same as the model's emotional response. In fact Berger advances four paradigms. Empathy occurs when a model's positive or negative emotional response elicits a similar emotional response in an observer. Sadism occurs when a model's negative emotional response results in a positive emotional response in an observer, and envy is the converse of this paradigm. True vicarious instigation occurs only when the observer's emotional response is based on the inferred model's emotional response. Pseudovicarious instigation occurs when (a) the model's stimulus and/or overt response serves as a stimulus for the observer's emotional response independent of the model's inferred emotional response, or (b) the model's emotional response serves as a discriminative stimulus indicating to the observer that he will receive the stimulus being presented to the model.

In the classical conditioning paradigm, incidental cues associated with the model's emotional response become conditioned stimuli of the observer's emotional response. In instrumental conditioning, the observer's emotional response serves as a positive or negative reinforcement of the observer's responses it follows and/or of the observer's cognitive representations of the model's responses.

Bandura (1965b, 1969, 1971) does not adhere to this claim by Berger that the information-imparting functions of vicarious reinforcement cannot be construed as a mechanism underlying the phenomenon. At the same time, he proposes that vicarious reinforcement has affective, motivating effects as well. According to this theory, vicarious reinforcement may (a) increase the saliency of the modeling cues associated with vicarious reinforcement and make them discriminative for probable reinforcement contingencies for the observer; (b) serve a similar function with respect to the environmental cues associated with the modeling responses; (c) increase the model's status which may make his behavior more discriminative for probable reinforcement; (d) increase the observer's motivation and thereby facilitate his acquisition and performance of the modeled responses; and (e) elicit emotional responses in the observer which become conditioned to the modeled responses themselves or to environmental stimuli associated with the responses.

Demonstrations of affective mechanisms underlying vicarious reinforcement have come primarily from studies of vicarious aversive conditioning [Berger's "negative empathy" paradigm (Bandura & Rosenthal, 1966; Berger, 1962; Craig & Weinstein, 1965)]. With the exception of anecdotal data on sadism (Bandura & Rosenthal, 1966), there is little evidence for the other three paradigms described by Berger, and there has been a dearth of evidence of vicarious instigation as a reinforcer in instrumental conditioning. Furthermore, recent work (Craig, 1968; Craig & Lowery, 1969; Craig & Wood, 1969) has shown that (a) there are differences in heart rate responding between subjects undergoing direct aversive stimulation, and subjects undergoing vicarious aversive stimulation, and (b) there are no differences in heart rate responding between subjects undergoing vicarious instigation and subjects undergoing pseudovicarious instigation. Craig and his associates found that direct aversive stimulation produced heart rate acceleration whereas vicarious aversive stimulation produced heart rate deceleration. These findings suggest that when the observer witnesses aversive consequences to the model, the observer does not empathically experience them as much as he is interested in them as a source of information about possible consequences to himself. These findings have led Craig to conclude that

Berger's vicarious-pseudovicarious instigation distinction is not a particularly useful one.

The evidence contributing toward an understanding of the processes underlying vicarious reinforcement has not been impressive, mainly because the requirements for the adequacy of such evidence is extreme indeed. As Berger (1968) points out, and has been underscored by Craig and his co-workers, the methodological problems in sorting out the empathic components from the informational components of vicarious reinforcement are very pronounced. Furthermore, as indicated by Berger, most of the studies in the literature have not been directed toward vicarious reinforcement as an explanatory phenomenon but rather as a descriptive phenomenon, wherein the studies were designed to show that the operation of giving reinforcement to a model alters the response probability of the observer. It is for this reason that the present reviewers have concentrated on vicarious reinforcement as a descriptive phenomenon.

C. GENERAL APPROACH

The focus of the present review is on the empirical and procedural literature concerning the matter of vicarious reinforcement and imitation. This paper will compare studies which supported vicarious reinforcement effects on imitation with studies which failed to demonstrate vicarious reinforcement effects. This will be followed by an appraisal of different types of procedures which have been employed to study vicarious reinforcement.

D. BASIC CONSIDERATIONS

The studies under review may be broadly categorized as follows: (a) research involving the manipulation of one level or percentage of vicarious reinforcement; and (b) research on the effects of different percentages of vicarious reward. Studies of the first type are oriented toward measuring the effects of vicarious reinforcement vis-a-vis no vicarious reinforcement on imitation. Studies of the second type are designed to assess the relative effects of increasing amounts of vicarious reward.

E. ONE-LEVEL VICARIOUS REINFORCEMENT STUDIES

Studies which manipulate a single level or percentage of vicarious reinforcement are essentially of two types. The first type, most commonly used by Bandura and his co-workers, exposes the subject to the entire sequence of modeled behavior before he has an opportunity to respond (i.e., nonalternate-trials design). In the second type, exemplified by the work of Kanfer and Marston (1963), the subject alternates responding with the model during the observation phase (alternate-trials design).

In some studies, subjects in an alternate-trials procedure were given direct reinforcement for imitating the model during acquisition. When all subjects were given direct reinforcement for imitating, any vicarious reinforcement effects could not be generalized to conditions of no direct reinforcement. The subjects in the nonalternate-trials studies, on the other hand, were seldom given direct reinforcement for spontaneous imitation, although they sometimes were given "high incentives" (direct reinforcement) for recall of the modeled behavior following the testing of spontaneous imitation.

Granted that the aim of the one-level studies is to demonstrate the influence of vicarious reinforcement vis-a-vis no vicarious reinforcement on imitation, it is important to look at necessary experimental controls. In the one-level studies, the only suitable control for the effects of observing the model is the inclusion of a model no-consequences or similar control group. [As an example of a similar control, Marlatt, Jacobson, Johnson, and Morrice (1970) used a "neutral" consequence to the model group.] The model no-consequence control is imperative to control for the effect of observation per se on imitation which has been demonstrated in many studies (e.g., Berger, 1966; Phillips, 1968b). Some researchers (e.g., Bandura, Ross, & Ross, 1963) observed differences in imitation between vicarious reward and vicarious punishment subjects. However, when such a study lacks a model no-consequence control group, it is impossible to determine if the effects were a function of vicarious reward, vicarious punishment, or both.

F. PERCENTAGE VICARIOUS REWARD STUDIES

In the percentage vicarious reward studies, some subjects may observe a model rewarded for 100% of the critical responses, other subjects may observe a model rewarded for 67%, and still other subjects may observe a model rewarded for 33% of the critical responses. These studies are typically of an alternate-trials design and often involve direct reinforcement for imitation of the model. However, they do not need a model no-consequences control so long as there is no attempt to use the data as evidence for the effect of vicarious reward as compared with no vicarious reward. Such studies only provide information concerning the effect of different levels of vicarious reward on imitation. Studies involving the partial vicarious reward effect on the extinction of a modeled response are reviewed in Section II,C.

II. Review of the Literature

Table I summarizes critical information from studies reported in the literature. In the first three columns, a *dash* entry signifies that the condition was not present in the study or that appropriate controls were not employed; a *yes* entry means that the condition was present and significant effects were observed; a *no* entry means that the condition was present but significant effects were not observed. The fourth column signifies if the study was of an alternate-trials or nonalternate-trials design.

As suggested by the organization of Table I, it is useful to review the research literature in terms of one-level vicarious reward studies, percentage vicarious reward studies, and vicarious punishment studies. Studies on vicarious reinforcement effects as assessed by high-incentive measures will also be briefly reviewed.

A. ONE-LEVEL VICARIOUS REWARD STUDIES

The first column in Table I depicts those studies which contained a vicarious reward condition and an appropriate control, usually a model no-consequences control. Ten of the studies found increased imitation as a function of vicarious reward. On the other hand, 16 studies failed to obtain vicarious reward effects. This would appear to raise doubts about the unqualified statements of Bandura (1965b) and Flanders (1968) that vicarious reward increases imitation. (While Flanders cites a number of percentage vicarious reward studies in support of this contention, these studies involve different questions and different controls and are presented in a separate section.)

As mentioned earlier, in order to assess the effects of vicarious reward *versus* observation per se on imitation, it is essential to have a model no-consequences control or some other control for simply observing a model. Flanders (1968) cites a number of studies as supporting his contention of vicarious reward effects on imitation, which in fact do not support such a conclusion. Studies by Bandura (1965a), Walters and Parke (1964), Walters, Parke, and Cane (1965) contained a model no-consequences control, but, contrary to Flanders, failed to observe an increase in imitation as a function of vicarious reward. It appears that Flanders included these studies as supportive of vicarious reward effects because the vicarious reward group imitated significantly more than the vicarious punishment group; however, the vicarious reward group did not imitate significantly more than the model no-consequences group. Walters, Leat, and Mezei (1963), also cited by Flanders as demonstrating vicarious reward effects, found that the vicarious reward group imitated significantly more than the vicarious punishment group. Since the study lacked a model no-consequences control, the separate effects of vicarious reward and vicarious punishment could not be assessed. In a study by McDavid (1962), also cited by Flanders, all subjects observed a model who was rewarded for every response. Therefore, the McDavid study did not include a model no-consequences or other appropriate control group. Marston (1965) and Willis (1963) were also cited by Flanders, but neither study contained

TABLE I

Studies on Vicarious Reinforcement

	One-level vicarious reward[a]	Varied % vicarious reward[a]	Vicarious punishment[a]	Alternate trials[b]
Akamatsu & Thelen (1971)	No	—	—	No
Bandura (1962)	No	—	—	No
Bandura (1965a)	No	—	Yes	No
Bandura et al. (1967)	Yes	—	—	No
Bisese (1966)	—	Yes	—	Yes
Chalmers et al. (1963)	—	Yes	—	Yes
Clark (1965)	Yes	—	—	Yes
Ditrichs et al. (1967)	No	—	—	No
Dubanoski (1967)	No	—	Yes	No
Elliott & Vasta (1970)	No	—	—	No
Flanders & Thistlethwaite (1970)	No	—	—	No
D. L. Hamilton et al. (1970)	Yes*	—	—	No
Kanfer & Marston (1963)	Yes	—	—	Yes
Kelly (1966)	Yes	—	Yes[c]	No
Liebert & Fernandez (1970b)	Yes	—	—	No
Liebert & Fernandez (1970a)	Yes	—	Yes	No
Luchins & Luchins (1955)	—	—	Yes	Yes
Marlatt (1970)	Yes	—	Yes	No
Marlatt et al. (1970)	No	—	Yes	No
Marlowe et al. (1964)	Yes*	—	—	No
Marston (1964)	No[d]	—	—	Yes
Marston (1966)	Yes	—	—	Yes
Marston & Kanfer (1963)	—	Yes	—	Yes
Mausner & Block (1957)	—	Yes	—	Yes
Paschke et al. (1967)	—	—	Yes*[e]	No
Phillips (1968b)	No	—	—	Yes
Phillips (1968a)	No	—	—	Yes
Rosenbaum et al. (1962)	—	Yes	—	Yes
Rosenbaum & Tucker (1962)	—	Yes	—	Yes
Rosekrans (1967)	No	—	No	No
Thelen (1969)	No	—	No	No
Thelen & Soltz (1969, E1)	Yes[f]	—	—	No
Thelen & Soltz (1969, E2)	No	—	—	No
Walters & Parke (1964)	No	—	Yes*	No
Walters et al. (1965)	No	—	Yes	No

[a] For the three columns, the entrees are meant as follows: Yes means that such a manipulation was made and with significant results; no means that such a manipulation was made with no significant results; —means that the manipulation was not carried out or a model no-consequences was lacking; an asterisk by a yes means that the manipulation was made but the results were mixed.

[b] A yes entry signifies that the subject responded after the model on each trial. A no entry signifies that the subject was exposed to the entire sequence of modeled behavior before he had an opportunity to respond.

a vicarious reward manipulation. In the Marston study, the modeled behavior was self-reward and there was no vicarious reward contingent upon the modeled behavior. The Willis (1963) study contained a model competence manipulation which occurred prior to the modeled behavior, and again, no vicarious reward was contingent upon the modeled behavior. Thus, seven of the studies cited by Flanders (1968), in support of his contention that vicarious reward increases imitation, either did not provide such support or were not designed to provide directly relevant data.

When Bandura (1965a) failed to obtain vicarious reward effects, he attributed it to disinhibitory processes in the model no-consequences group, because the modeled behavior, aggression, is often negatively socially evaluated. Bandura suggested that the lack of negative consequences to the model following behavior that is often punished may have the same effect on imitation as vicarious reward. A number of other researchers (e.g., Walters & Parke, 1964; Walters et al., 1965) have used modeled behavior which might have involved disinhibition, and which therefore did not provide for a clear assessment of vicarious reward effects. In a later study on the imitation of stringent standards of self-reward, Bandura obtained results which he claimed provided good evidence that vicarious reward increased imitation (Bandura, Grusec, & Menlove, 1967). However, since stringent standards of self-reward are often praised in our society, the model no-consequences manipulation may have had effects similar to punishment to the model (inhibition?)—thus resulting in the greater imitation by the vicarious reward group. A number of studies, especially studies by Akamatsu and Thelen (1971), Bandura (1962), Ditrichs, Simon, and Greene (1967), Dubanoski (1967), and Flanders and Thistlethwaite (1970), are less subject to problems of inhibition or disinhibition and failed to show vicarious reward effects. It is doubtful that the failure of these studies to show vicarious reward effects can be attributed to disinhibition. Considering all of the studies reviewed, it would appear that the effect of vicarious reward on imitation in comparison to the effect of mere observation of the model is equivocal.

---

[c] Subjects, who observed a model criticized for dropping marbles slowly, subsequently dropped marbles in a hole at a faster rate than controls.

[d] The vicarious reward manipulation was during extinction procedures wherein the model made the critical response with decreasing frequency.

[e] Incorrect modeled responses were punished, resulting in greater imitation of correct responses.

[f] The vicarious reward group showed less imitation than a model no-consequences control.

B. Percentage Vicarious Reward Studies

Studies in this group involved manipulation of the percentage of vicarious reward of the critical modeled behavior wherein all subjects received some vicarious reward. These studies are summarized in column two of Table I. Unless otherwise indicated, a *yes* entry signifies more imitation under conditions of high percentage vicarious reward. All six of the studies reviewed reported increased imitation as a function of increased vicarious reward, although Chalmers, Horne, and Rosenbaum (1963) obtained mixed results. It may be concluded that an increased percentage of vicarious reward results in increased imitation.

C. Partial Vicarious Reward Effects on Extinction

This area of research involves presenting the observers with different percentages of vicarious reward and in this respect is similar to Section II,B on percentage vicarious reward. However, there are two distinct differences: (a) Research in this area is concerned with the effect of different percentages of vicarious reward on *extinction;* and (b) except for Bisese (1966) and Thelen and Soltz (1969, E1), research in this area has involved eliciting the simple modeled response by instruction (e.g., dropping a marble in a hole) and assessing the observers' speed or persistence in repeatedly performing the response. The latter procedural feature makes such studies vastly different from those wherein the observer is not instructed to perform the modeled behavior, which is usually a more complex behavior. Therefore, while such studies are briefly reviewed here, they will not be of focus in the remainder of the paper.

Lewis and Duncan (1958) and Thelen and Soltz (1969, E1) found no difference in extinction as a function of percentage vicarious reward. Bisese (1966) and Rosenbaum and Bruning (1966) found that high percentage vicarious reward observers showed more resistance to extinction than low percentage vicarious reward observers. Two studies have demonstrated a partial vicarious reward effect. Berger and Johansson (1968) and M. L. Hamilton (1970) found increased resistance to extinction as a function of decreased (across observers) percentage vicarious reward. In addition, Hamilton obtained similar results on a spontaneous recovery measure obtained 1 week later. Given the divergence of the results, more studies are needed in order to discern the conditions critical to partial vicarious reward effects on extinction.

D. Vicarious Punishment

Column three in Table I depicts studies concerning vicarious punishment. All of the studies in this group, except Paschke, Simon, and Bell

(1967) involved vicarious punishment of the modeled behavior which was assessed during subsequent testing of the subject. The Paschke *et al.* study involved vicarious punishment of "incorrect" modeled responses, whereas the "correct" modeled responses were assessed during subsequent testing of the subject. Paschke *et al.* found that vicarious punishment subjects made more "correct" discriminations during subsequent testing in one of two observation conditions. Kelly (1966) found that subjects, who observed a model criticized for dropping marbles slowly, subsequently dropped marbles in a hole at a faster rate than controls. Excluding Paschke *et al.* (1967) and Kelly (1966), 8 of the 10 studies showed that, as compared with a model no-consequences (or neutral consequences) control, vicarious punishment caused a significant decrement in imitation. Seven of the eight studies contained the nonalternate-trials procedure, although both of the studies reporting no vicarious punishment effects were also of the non-alternate-trials design. In an additional study related to this area, Benton (1967) found that observers imitated a model who played with taboo toys more if the model was punished after he had picked up the toy than if the model was punished as he approached the toy. Generally, these experiments suggest that vicarious punishment of modeled behavior has a suppressive or inhibitory effect on imitation, i.e., the subsequent reproduction of that behavior.

E. Vicarious Reinforcement and High-Incentive Testing Conditions

Some researchers have investigated the effects of vicarious reinforcement on the acquisition of the modeled behavior as measured by high-incentive conditions. This usually takes the form of directly asking the subject to demonstrate or recall the model's behavior and then confirming or rewarding an imitative response. The purpose of the high-incentive recall measure is to assess, to the fullest extent possible, how much of the modeled behavior the subject has learned. While such research is not of central interest in the present review, brief mention will be made of these studies. All but two of these studies (Fernandez & Liebert, 1970; Liebert & Fernandez, 1969) are cited in Table I because they also included a measure of spontaneous imitation.

Research has shown that the same results were obtained for vicarious reward effects under high-incentive conditions as were obtained under conditions of spontaneous imitation (Akamatsu & Thelen, 1971; Flanders & Thistlethwaite, 1970; Liebert & Fernandez, 1970a, 1970b; Walters *et al.*, 1965). On the other hand, vicarious punishment does not have the same effect under high-incentive conditions as under conditions of spontaneous imitation. Liebert and Fernandez (1970b) found that subjects who observed a model punished showed less spontaneous imitation but more high-incentive recall than model no-consequences subjects. Bandura (1965a) found that the effects of vicarious punishment on spontaneous imitation did not obtain under high-incentive test conditions. Walters and Parke (1964) and Walters *et al.* (1965) found that the subjects in a vicarious punishment condition were not significantly different from model no-consequences subjects as they were under spontaneous imitation conditions.

Liebert and Fernandez (1969) and Fernandez and Liebert (1970) did not obtain a measure of spontaneous imitation, and therefore these studies are not reported in Table I. Under conditions of direct reward for matching responses, Liebert and Fernandez (1969) found that among first-grade girls, vicarious reward led to a significant increment with a high-complexity task but not with a low-complexity task. However, a similar study with preschoolers revealed no significant effects of vicarious reward with a high- or low-complexity task (Fernandez & Liebert, 1970).

Overall, these studies show that the effects of vicarious reward on elicited imitation are similar to the effects of vicarious reward on spontaneous imitation, but the effects of vicarious punishment on spontaneous and elicited imitation are often different. The subjects are likely to show appreciably more elicited imitation than spontaneous imitation following vicarious punishment. This is consistent with research on vicarious punishment (reviewed in Section II,D), and suggests that vicarious punishment has a suppressive effect on spontaneous imitation.

III. Discussion

Based on the review of the literature concerning the effects of vicarious reinforcement on imitation, the authors suggest that the support for such effects is much more equivocal than has been suggested by Bandura (1965b) and Flanders (1968). One of the glaring problems has been the failure of many studies to control for the effect of observation per se on imitation by neglecting to include a model no-consequences group. Other researchers have concluded that vicarious reward increases imitation because that group imitated more than a vicarious punishment group. Again, a model no-consequences control is needed. A second problem has been the reliance upon disinhibition as an explanation for the lack of differences between the model no-consequences group and the vicarious reward group. A third design problem has been the direct reinforcement of subjects for making the modeled response during testing. When all subjects receive direct reinforcement, it is, of course, impossible to be sure that any vicarious reinforcement effects are independent of direct reinforcement conditions. Most studies having direct reinforcement as a part of the procedure were of the alternate-trials design. Studies by Bisese (1966), Clark (1965), Paschke *et al.* (1967), Rosenbaum, Chalmers, and Horne (1962), and Rosenbaum and Tucker (1962) were especially vulnerable to this point, since all subjects in these studies received at least some direct reinforcement. Other studies (Ditrichs *et al.,* 1967; Kanfer & Marston, 1963; Marston & Kanfer, 1963; Phillips, 1968a) contained direct reinforcement manipulations, but not for all subjects, so that an assessment of vicarious reinforcement effects, independent of direct reinforcement, could be made. Generally, the studies which contained direct reinforcement for all subjects are not in sufficient number to detract from or restrict the general observations made in the review of Table I nor from the comments to be made in the present section.

In the next two sections (III,A and B), vicarious reward and vicarious punishment are discussed in further detail. As will be seen, vicarious reward receives most of the attention because the research is more substantial and the results more equivocal.

A. Vicarious Reward

As discussed earlier, two distinctively different experimental procedures have been used to study the effect of vicarious reward on imitation—the alternate trials- and the nonalternate-trials procedures. The fourth column in Table I indicates whether each study contained an alternate-trials or nonalternate-trials design. Only 7 of the 20 studies with a nonalternate-trials procedure demonstrated that, as compared with a model no-consequences or neutral consequences condition, vicarious reward increased imitation (Thelen & Soltz, 1969, E1 and E2 are counted as one study). On the other hand, three of the six studies with an alternate-trials procedure demonstrated positive vicarious reward effects as compared with a model no-consequences control. The three alternate trials studies which did not show vicarious reward effects are Marston (1964) and Phillips (1968a, 1968b). In the Marston study, all subjects observed the model receive the same frequency of reward during acquisition. The subjects continued to alternate responding with the model during an extinction phase which contained the vicarious reward manipulations. Extinction was determined by the model making the critical response with *decreasing* frequency. During this phase, some subjects observed the model but with no consequences. This is the only study which manipulated vicarious reward under conditions of modeled extinction. Although there appear to be no vicarious reward effects under such conditions, this study is qualitatively different from the other alternate-trials studies. Phillips

(1968b) used a 30% rate of vicarious reward in Experiment I and a 60% rate of vicarious reward in Experiment 2. In contrast, all three of the alternate-trials studies which contained a model no-consequences control and showed vicarious reward effects (Clark, 1965; Kanfer & Marston, 1963; Marston, 1966) involved a 100% rate of vicarious reward. The third study in question (Phillips, 1968a) involved the subject responding alternately with the model for 270 trials. In the Clark, Kanfer, and Marston, and Marston studies, the subject responded 50 times or less during the acquisition phase (although in the Marston study there was a group of nine models). It may be that, when a large number of acquisition trials are used, the effect of observing the model is so great that it precludes a possible vicarious reward effect. It may be concluded that an alternate-trial procedure with a 100% vicarious reward manipulation is more likely to result in increased imitation than when vicarious reward is manipulated within a nonalternate-trials procedure.

The above is consistent with the research on the effects of percentage vicarious reward. All six of the studies demonstrated that a model who received a high percentage of vicarious reward was imitated more than a model who received a lower percentage of vicarious reward (although Chalmers et al., 1963, obtained mixed results). Each of these studies was of the alternate-trials type.[3]

Overall, it appears that researchers using an alternate-trials procedure have demonstrated that vicarious reward increases imitation, whereas, those using a nonalternate-trials procedure have not regularly demonstrated such effects.

Given this distinctive pattern among the various studies on vicarious reward, it might be useful to consider the critical features of an alternate-trials design as a pivotal point from which to develop clues regarding the effect of vicarious reward on imitation. These critical features may be most fruitfully discussed in comparison with the essential features of the non-alternate-trials procedure. First, it is important to note that the alternate-trials procedure is not a pure vicarious learning situation in the sense of no-trial learning as described by Bandura (1965b). In the alternate-trials procedures, by definition, the subject responds alternately with the model, thereby precluding a completely vicarious situation. Essentially, the procedure is one wherein vicarious observation and participation are both present. Also, in contrast with the nonalternate-trials studies, which necessarily involve an extinction measure of imitation, the alternate trials

---

[3] Most of the percentage vicarious reward studies also involve a communication that the modeled responses which are not correct are incorrect. Such studies are manipulating more than vicarious reward.

studies usually contain an acquisition measure of imitation.[4] Another feature of the alternate-trials design is that, as has been pointed out by Waxler and Yarrow (1970), the modeled behavior is an inherent part of the stimulus situation for the observer. The temporal contiguity between the modeled behavior and the observer's response is quite close in the alternate-trials design, whereas in the nonalternate-trials procedure, much of the modeled behavior has occurred some time before the imitation measure is obtained. The failure to differentiate these two lines of research may have introduced much confusion to the literature on vicarious reinforcement and imitation. For example, Bandura (1965b) and Flanders (1968) reviewed both lines of research as though there were no critical differences between them.

We will now compare the alternate-trials and nonalternate-trials procedures with an eye to other variables which might further clarify the effect of vicarious reward on imitation.

1. Model Presumed to Be Observing the Subject during Testing

The studies reviewed varied with respect to whether or not the subject presumed that he was observed by the model during testing, or if he was led to believe that he was not being observed by the model. Unfortunately, a number of articles (e.g., Phillips, 1968b) do not contain sufficient information to determine if the subjects presumed the model to be present during testing. Generally speaking, the nonalternate-trials studies involved procedures such that the subject did not expect or believe that he was observed by the model. The alternate-trial design, on the other hand, often involved procedures wherein the subject probably construed that the model was informed of his responses. Marlatt (1969) found model presence effects on imitation, but his study did not contain vicarious reinforcement manipulations. However, Bandura *et al.* (1967), Marlatt (1970), and Marlowe, Breecher, Cook, and Doob (1964) used the nonalternate-trials procedure and observed vicarious reward effects. These studies were such that the subject probably did not presume the model to be observing.

[4] All of the nonalternate-trials studies involved an extinction measure of imitation, that is, the model's behavior was not part of the immediate situation. The alternate-trials studies, with the exception of Marston (1964), and possibly Mausner and Block (1957), contained an acquisition measure of imitation, that is, the measure was taken in the course of observing the model and model reward. Some of the alternate-trials studies contained an acquisition and extinction measure of imitation, in which case the results for acquisition are reported in Table I. In most of these studies, extinction involved continuation of the modeled behavior but without vicarious consequences. All of the studies except Clark (1965) showed similar results as regards vicarious reinforcement and imitation under acquisition and extinction testing conditions.

Furthermore, Marston (1966) reported vicarious reward effects in an alternate-trials study even though the subjects were told that the "modeled" voice was on tape. Liebert and Fernandez (1970b) found that model presence or absence had no differential influence on the effect of vicarious reward on imitation. The conclusion is that model presence is not critical for vicarious reward to increase imitation.

2. Experimenter and/or Model Reinforcer Presumed to Be Observing the Subject

It is possible that the presence of the experimenter and/or the model reinforcer during the test for imitation could facilitate the effect of vicarious reward on imitation. Unfortunately, the experimenter was usually the person who rewarded the model; thus, the two variables were confounded. In the typical alternate-trials study, the experimenter and/or the model reinforcer were observing or presumed to be observing the subjects. Such was also the case in many of the nonalternate-trials studies, but in some the subject was led to believe that he was not being observed. Excepting Dubanoski (1967), where no determination of experimenter presence could be made, the experimenter was not present or not presumed to be observing in six of the nonalternate-trials studies (Bandura, 1965a; Bandura et al., 1967; Elliot & Vasta, 1970; Thelen & Soltz, 1969; Walters & Parke, 1964; Walters et al., 1965). Each of these studies, except for Bandura et al. (1967), failed to demonstrate vicarious reward effects. Of the 13 nonalternate-trials studies in which the experimenter was present or presumed to be present, six studies (D. L. Hamilton, Thompson, & White, 1970; Kelly, 1966; Liebert & Fernandez, 1970a, 1970b; Marlatt, 1970; Marlowe et al., 1964) demonstrated vicarious reward effects. Similarly, excepting for Dubanoski (1967), where no determination could be made, the model reinforcer was not present or not presumed to be observing during testing in seven of the nonalternate-trials studies (Bandura, 1965a; Bandura et al., 1967; Elliott & Vasta, 1970; Rosekrans, 1967; Thelen & Soltz, 1969; Walters & Parke, 1964; Walters et al., 1965). Each of these studies, except for Bandura et al. (1967) failed to demonstrate vicarious reward effects. Of the 12 studies in which the model reinforcer was present or presumed to be observing, six (the same studies cited for experimenter presence) demonstrated vicarious reward effects. It appears that the likelihood of vicarious reward effects is increased if the experimenter and/or model reinforcer are present during testing.

Hicks (1968) found that positive evaluative statements made by an "incidental" coobserver to the subject about the taped model's behavior increased ($p < .10$) imitation only when the coobserver was present during testing. The positive evaluative statements had no effect when the coobserver was not present during testing. Although the evaluative statements were not made to the model, the Hicks' study offers some support for the inference that the presence of the model reinforcer during testing increases the probability of vicarious reward effects on imitation.

The results of a study by Kobisigawa (1968) also suggest that experimenter presence may be important. He found that the latency of boys' touching feminine toys was significantly less for model-rewarded than no-model control observers when the experimenter was present during testing. The effects of vicarious reward were less clear-cut in the experimenter absent condition.

A possible reason for the importance of the presence of the experimenter or model-reinforcer is that he may be seen as the person who directs the situation and evaluates the model's behavior. Furthermore, if the observer is seeking information to maximize positive consequences for his subsequent behavior, the presence of the model rewarder would be essential for him to obtain positive consequences.

3. Continuous or Intermittent Vicarious Reward vs. Reward Given at the End of the Modeled Behavior

Some of the studies reviewed gave the vicarious reward only after the model had completed the entire sequence of behavior, whereas a number of other studies involved vicarious reward on a continuous or at least intermittent basis. The alternate-trials studies invariably involved vicarious reward on a continuous or intermittent basis. The nonalternate-trials procedure was mixed over the various studies, that is, some involved continuous vicarious reward and others involved vicarious reward given only at the end. Since the alternate-trials studies, which include the percentage vicarious reward studies, necessarily contained continuous or intermittent vicarious reward, they will be excluded from the discussion in this section. Eight of the 14 studies with a nonalternate-trials procedure, which contained a continuous or intermittent vicarious reward manipulation, failed to show vicarious reward effects. However, six of the seven nonalternate-trials studies, which showed increased imitation as a function of vicarious reward, contained continuous or intermittent vicarious reward. Only one of the seven nonalternate-trials studies, wherein the vicarious reward was given at the end of the modeled behavior, demonstrated vicarious reward effects. In a study especially designed to assess this question, Thelen and Soltz (1969) found that subjects who observed a model receive continuous reward imitated that model more than subjects who observed a model rewarded only at the end of the sequence. While not sufficient to assure increased imitation, the use of continuous or intermittent vicarious reward increases the probability of demonstrating vicarious reward effects.

Continuous or intermittent vicarious reward might be expected to result in greater imitation because it involves more total reward than does reward given only at the end of the modeled behavior. Furthermore, as Bandura (1965b) has suggested, the former procedure may increase the acquisition of modeled behavior by increasing the attention of the observer to the modeling cues associated with the reinforcement.

4. Age

The nonalternate-trials studies, with the exception of Bandura (1962), Ditrichs *et al.* (1967), D. L. Hamilton *et al.* (1970), Marlatt (1970), and Marlowe *et al.* (1964), employed subjects under 14 years of age. Most of these studies utilized children under 10 years of age. On the other hand, the alternate-trials studies, with the exception of Clark (1965) who employed 9- to 11-years-olds, utilized college students or adults as subjects. However, Bandura *et al.* (1967), Kelly (1966), and Liebert and Fernandez (1970a, 1970b) obtained vicarious reward effects utilizing children, and Phillips (1968a, 1968b) utilized adults and failed to obtain such effects. The age of the subjects appears not to be critical to whether vicarious reward increases imitation.

5. The Structure of the Modeling Task

The studies also may be viewed in terms of whether they were designed to function on a trials basis with a clearly defined stimulus delimiting the beginning of each trial and calling for a discrete response, or on a less structured basis wherein the subject was not told to attend to particular stimuli. By definition, the alternate-trials procedures are more structured in this respect and may be similar to imitative discrimination learning. The nonalternate-trials studies may be more or less structured, depending upon the particular procedure. The structured studies with a nonalternate-trials procedure consist of a number of delineated trials with appropriate instructions to induce the model (and, after the modeling sequence, the subject) to respond. The less structured studies did not proceed on a trials basis. The nonalternate-trials studies fall about 50/50 in the less structured and more structured categories. It is noteworthy that, of the seven nonalternate-trials studies which demonstrated vicarious reward effects, five were of the more structured type (Bandura *et al.*, 1967; D. L. Hamilton *et al.*, 1970; Liebert & Fernandez, 1970a, 1970b; Marlowe *et al.*, 1964). A study by Kelly (1966), which involved a simple marble-dropping task, and a study by Marlatt (1970), which dealt with interview behavior, were the only less structured studies with a nonalternate-trials design which demonstrated vicarious reward effects. Eight of the less structured studies, including Bandura (1965a), Elliott and Vasta (1970), Marlatt *et al.* (1970), and Walters *et al.* (1965) failed to show vicarious reward effects. It is conceivable that an imitation situation designed with the structure provided by a trials situation permits for a clearer association between the critical stimuli, the modeled behavior, and the vicarious reward. This inference is supported by D. L. Hamilton *et al.* (1970), who found that vicarious reward increased imitation only among subjects who were aware of the contingency between the model's responses and the vicarious reward. Even though four studies (Akamatsu & Thelen, 1971; Bandura, 1962; Flanders & Thistlethwaite, 1970; Thelen, 1969) utilized a trials procedure and failed to observe vicarious reward effects, it appears to be a potentially significant factor in determining the effect of vicarious reward on imitation.

6. Nature of the Reward to the Model

Most of the nonalternate-trials studies, including the seven studies with a vicarious reward effect on imitation, contained praise as the vicarious reward. Only three studies used tangible rewards, and two of these also used praise. Similarly, a majority of the alternate-trials studies also utilized praise. This includes the Marston studies and the Phillips studies (see Table I). The nature of the reward to the model has been too similar in nearly all the studies to likely account for the differing results concerning vicarious reward and imitation.

Related to the nature of the reward to the model is the expressiveness with which the model is rewarded and the model's emotional reaction to the reward. As mentioned, nearly all of the studies used praise as reward to the model, and few of the studies reflected concern with the expressiveness of the model rewarder or the model's emotional reaction. However, Berger and Johansson (1968) found increased resistance to extinction when the subjects observed a model who showed emotional reactions to the reward, and Berger and Ellsbury (1969) found increased recall of the model's behavior when the verbal rewards to the model were given in an expressive manner. Perhaps the emotional tone of the vicarious reward and the model's emotional reaction are more important than the particular reward given.

7. Expectancy to Perform

A consideration, which is clearly not independent of some of the above mentioned variables, is the subject's expectancies concerning the experimental situation, especially whether or not he expects to perform after observing the model. This expectancy might involve performing some task but perhaps not the same task performed by the model. Or the subject may expect to perform exactly the same task as he observed the model perform. Marlowe *et al.* (1964) have suggested that subject's expectancy to perform may be critical to the demonstration of vicarious reward effects on imitation. A subject who expects to perform, especially the same task which he observed the model perform, is likely to be more vigilant with respect to relevant cues, including vicarious reward. It is clear that the alternate-trials studies, by their very nature, lead the subject to expect to perform. In fact, after the first trial he does perform. This, then, is consistent with the observation that the alternate-trials studies have generally demonstrated vicarious reward effects. The nonalternate-trials procedure does not necessarily lead to such an expectancy. In some of the nonalternate-trials studies, for example Akamatsu and Thelen (1971), the subject was told nothing about what he might do after observing the model. In other studies, such as Bandura (1965a), the subject was advised that he would play a game after watching the film, but again, he was not explicitly told what he would do. In still other studies (Thelen, 1969) the subject expected to perform a similar task but was not instructed so as to be oriented toward the critical modeled behavior. Perhaps the best test of this hypothesis, aside from additional research, is to review the seven nonalternate-trials studies which obtained vicarious reward effects.

Bandura *et al.* (1967) led the subject to believe the model was a subject like himself, and he was simply to let the model take his turn first. There was a clear expectancy to perform. Liebert and Fernandez (1970a, 1970b) also utilized a nonalternate-trials design and observed vicarious reward effects on imitation. Their studies were also designed in such a way that the subject knew, almost beyond doubt, that he would perform the task, a two-choice discrimination task of preferences, following the model. In the Kelly (1966) study the subjects were told that the other person (model) would go first and then it would be their turn. Marlatt (1970) told the subjects that they would be asked to talk to an interviewer but, in order to get some idea of what to expect, they would first listen to a tape-recorded interview of a previous subject (the model). D. L. Hamilton *et al.* (1970) obtained vicarious reward effects in one of two conditions, but it is not clear if the subjects expected to perform the same task. Marlowe *et al.* (1964) found that only subjects with a high need for approval showed vicarious reward effects. In this study, there was no clear expectancy to perform the same task as they had observed the model perform—thus, the Marlowe *et al.* findings are not clearly consistent with the hypothesis. However, they obtained equivocal results. Given the literature, as reviewed here, the authors suggest that expectancy to perform may be one of the most critical variables determining the effect of vicarious reward on imitation. A study which contained expectancy to perform manipulations along with vicarious reward manipulations has recently been completed by the authors. The study supported the prediction that expectancy to perform is a critical condition for vicarious reward effects.

B. VICARIOUS PUNISHMENT

The literature on vicarious punishment is substantially less than that on vicarious reward; however, the results are much more consistent. As reviewed in Table I, most of the studies show that vicarious punishment leads to significantly less imitation than observing a no-consequences model.

Vicarious punishment effects cannot be explained in terms of the variables discussed in Section III,A. In fact, many of the studies contained procedural features which, if present in vicarious reward studies, would reduce the chance of significant effects. For example, Bandura (1965a), Dubanoski (1967), Walters and Parke (1964), and Walters et al. (1965) used a nonalternate-trials procedure (see fourth column of Table I), gave the vicarious punishment at the end of the modeled behavior, and did not employ a structured-trials procedure. Yet in these studies vicarious punishment effects were demonstrated.

Until a greater body of literature is developed concerning the effects of vicarious punishment on imitation, it may be difficult to discern the critical variables and comprehend the processess involved. It certainly appears that vicarious punishment effects are more easily demonstrated than vicarious reward effects. The possible informational value of vicarious reward has been discussed by a number of writers (e.g., Bandura, 1965b, 1971). Perhaps vicarious punishment carries more information concerning the modeled behavior than does vicarious reward. Another possibility is that vicarious punishment is much more salient than vicarious reward. It may be argued that, in a variety of situations, the careful attention of an observer to the contingencies and the consequences is more likely if the model is punished than if he is rewarded. The reader may recall the study by Kelly (1966) in which vicarious punishment (criticism) of the rate of performance led the subject to perform at a faster rate than vicarious reward (praise). Kelly suggested that an informational or motivational explanation could account for the "potency" of vicarious punishment. Of course, these explanations are not mutually exclusive, and only more carefully controlled research will help to clarify the influence of these variables.

IV. Summary and Conclusions

A review of the literature concerning the effects of vicarious reinforcement on imitation has shown that a substantial number of studies failed to demonstrate an increase in imitation as a function of vicarious reward. Based on the present review, the likelihood of demonstrating vicarious reward effects is greatly increased if the experimenter is present during testing (and probably also the person who rewarded the model), if the task proceeds on an alternate-trials basis, and if the subject has an expectancy to perform the modeled task after observing the model. Providing the reward to the model on a continuous or intermittent basis may also increase imitation. It is likely that no one of the variables is the sole factor determining the effect of vicarious reward on imitation. In more general terms, vicarious reward effects are most likely to occur when the subject believes he will have to perform the modeled task, and when the task has definable properties permitting a clear association between the *relevant* task stimuli, the critical modeled behavior, and the vicarious reward.

The research on vicarious punishment is much less equivocal than that on vicarious reward. In most of the relevant studies, vicarious punishment has led to a reduction in imitation. Variables which may be important to the effect of vicarious reward on imitation are insignificant as regards the effect of vicarious punishment on imitation.

The procedures and operations of the alternate-trials and nonalternate-trials studies were compared. The differences are so profound that a comparison of the data from two such studies should be done with utmost caution.

References

Akamatsu, T. J., & Thelen, M. H. The acquisition and performance of a socially neutral response as a function of vicarious reward. *Developmental Psychology,* 1971, **5,** 440–445.

Aronfreed, J. The concept of internalization. In D. A. Goslin (Ed.), *Handbook of socialization theory and research.* Chicago: Rand McNally, 1969. (a)

Aronfreed, J. The problem of imitation. In L. P. Lipsitt & H. W. Reese (Eds.), *Advances in child development and behavior.* Vol. 4. New York: Academic Press, 1969. (b)

Bandura, A. Social learning through imitation. In M. R. Jones (Ed.), *Nebraska symposium on motivation.* Vol. 10. Lincoln: University of Nebraska Press, 1962. Pp. 211–269.

Bandura, A. Influence of models' reinforcement contingences on the acquisition of imitative responses. *Journal of Personality and Social Psychology,* 1965, **1,** 589–595. (a)

Bandura, A. Vicarious processes: A case of no-trial learning. In L. Berkowitz (Ed.), *Advances in experimental social psychology.* Vol. 2. New York: Academic Press, 1965. (b)

Bandura, A. Social learning theory of identificatory processes. In D. A. Goslin (Ed.), *Handbook of socialization theory and research*. Chicago: Rand McNally, 1969.

Bandura, A. Vicarious and self-reinforcement processes. In R. Glaser (Ed.), *The nature of reinforcement*. New York: Academic Press, 1971.

Bandura, A., Grusec, J. E., & Menlove, F. L. Some social determinants of self-monitoring reinforcement systems. *Journal of Personality and Social Psychology*, 1967, **5**, 449–455.

Bandura, A., & Rosenthal, T. L. Vicarious classical conditioning as a function of arousal level. *Journal of Personality and Social Psychology*, 1966, **3**, 54–62.

Bandura, A., Ross, D., & Ross, S. A. Vicarious reinforcement and imitative learning. *Journal of Abnormal and Social Psychology*, 1963, **67**, 601–607.

Bandura, A., & Walters, R. H. *Social learning and personality development*. New York: Holt, 1963.

Benton, A. A. Effects of timing of negative response consequences on the observational learning of resistance to temptation in children. *Dissertation Abstracts, Section A*, 1967, **27**, 2153–2154.

Berger, S. M. Incidental learning through vicarious reinforcement. *Psychological Reports*, 1961, **9**, 477–491.

Berger, S. M. Conditioning through vicarious instigation. *Psychological Review*, 1962, **69**, 450–466.

Berger, S. M. Observer practice and learning during exposure to a model. *Journal of Personality and Social Psychology*, 1966, **3**, 696–701.

Berger, S. M. Vicarious aspects of matched-dependent behavior. In E. C. Simmel, R. A. Hoppe, & G. A. Milton (Eds.), *Social facilitation and imitative behavior*. Boston: Allyn & Bacon, 1968.

Berger, S. M., & Ellsbury, S. W. The effect of expressive verbal reinforcements on incidental learning by models and observers. *American Journal of Psychology*, 1969, **82**, 333–341.

Berger, S. M., & Johansson, S. L. Effect of model's expressed emotions on an observer's resistance to extinction. *Journal of Personality and Social Psychology*, 1968, **10**, 53–58.

Bisese, V. S. Imitation behavior as a function of direct and vicarious reinforcement. *Dissertation Abstracts*, 1966, **26**, 6155. (Abstract)

Chalmers, D. K., Horne, W. C., & Rosenbaum, M. E. Social agreement and the learning of matching behavior. *Journal of Abnormal and Social Psychology*, 1963, **66**, 556–561.

Clark, B. S. The acquisition and extinction of peer imitation in children. *Psychonomic Science*, 1965, **2**, 147–148.

Craig, K. Physiological arousal as a function of imagined, vicarious and direct stress experiences. *Journal of Abnormal Psychology*, 1968, **73**, 513–520.

Craig, K., & Lowery, H. J. Heat-rate components and conditioned vicarious autonomic responses. *Journal of Personality and Social Psychology*, 1969, **11**, 381–387.

Craig, K., & Weinstein, M. Conditioning and vicarious affective arousal. *Psychological Reports*, 1965, **17**, 955–963.

Craig, K., & Wood, K. Physiological differentiation of direct and vicarious affective arousal. *Canadian Journal of Behavioral Science*, 1969, **1**, 98–105.

Ditrichs, R., Simon, S., & Greene, B. Effect of vicarious scheduling on the verbal conditioning of hostility in children. *Journal of Personality and Social Psychology*, 1967, **6**, 71–78.

Dubanoski, R. A. Imitation as a function of role appropriateness of behavior and response consequences to the model. *Dissertation Abstracts, Section A*, 1967, **27**, 2613–2614.

Elliott, R., & Vasta, R. The modeling of sharing: Effects associated with vicarious reinforcement symbolization, age, and generalization. *Journal of Experimental Child Psychology*, 1970, **10**, 8–15.

Fernandez, L. E., & Liebert, R. M. Vicarious reward and task complexity as determinants of imitative learning: A modified replication. *Psychological Reports*, 1970, **26**, 473–474.

Flanders, J. P. A review of research on imitative behavior. *Psychological Bulletin*, 1968, **69**, 316–337.

Flanders, J. P., & Thistlethwaite, D. L. Effects of informative and justificatory variables upon imitation. *Journal of Experimental Social Psychology*, 1970, **6**, 316–328.

Gewirtz, J. L., & Stingle, K. G. Learning of generalized imitation as the basis for identification. *Psychological Review*, 1968, **75**, 374–397.

Hamilton, D. L., Thompson, J. J., & White, A. M. Role of awareness and intentions in observational learning. *Journal of Personality and Social Psychology*, 1970, **16**, 689–694.

Hamilton, M. L. Vicarious reinforcement effects on extinction. *Journal of Experimental Child Psychology*, 1970, **9**, 108–114.

Hicks, D. J. Effects of co-observer's sanctions and adult presence on imitative aggression. *Child Development*, 1968, **39**, 303–309.

Hill, W. F. Learning theory and the acquisition of values. *Psychological Review*, 1960, **67**, 317–331.

Kanfer, F. H., & Marston, A. R. Human reinforcement: Vicarious and direct. *Journal of Experimental Psychology*, 1963, **65**, 292–296.

Kelly, R. Comparison of the effects of positive and negative vicarious reinforcement in an operant learning task. *Journal of Educational Psychology*, 1966, **57**, 307–310.

Kobasigawa, A. Inhibitory and disinhibitory effects of models on sex-inappropriate behavior in children. *Psychologia*, 1968, **11**, 86–96.

Lewis, D. J., & Duncan, C. P. Vicarious experience and partial reinforcement. *Journal of Abnormal and Social Psychology*, 1958, **57**, 321–326.

Liebert, R. M., & Fernandez, L. E. Vicarious reward and task complexity as determinants of imitative learning. *Psychological Reports*, 1969, **25**, 531–534.

Liebert, R. M., & Fernandez, L. E. Effects of vicarious consequences on imitative performance. *Child Development*, 1970, **41**, 847–852. (a)

Liebert, R. M., & Fernandez, L. E. Imitation as a function of vicarious and direct reward. *Developmental Psychology*, 1970, **2**, 230–232. (b)

Luchins, A. S., & Luchins, E. H. On conformity with true and false communications. *Journal of Social Psychology*, 1955, **42**, 283–303.

Marlatt, G. A. Comparison of direct and vicarious reinforcement control of interview behavior. Paper presented at the meeting of the Western Psychological Association, Vancouver, 1969.

Marlatt, G. A. A comparison of vicarious and direct reinforcement control of verbal behavior in an interview setting. *Journal of Personality and Social Psychology*, 1970, **16**, 695–703.

Marlatt, G. A., Jacobson, E. A., Johnson, D. L., & Morrice, D. J. Effect of exposure to a model receiving evaluative feedback upon subsequent behavior in an interview. *Journal of Consulting and Clinical Psychology,* 1970, **34,** 104–112.

Marlowe, D., Breecher, R. S., Cook, J. B., & Doob, A. N. The approval motive, vicarious reinforcement, and verbal conditioning. *Perceptual and Motor Skills,* 1964, **19,** 523–530.

Marston, A. R. Variables in extinction following acquisition with vicarious reinforcement. *Journal of Experimental Psychology,* 1964, **68,** 312–315.

Marston, A. R. Imitation, self-reinforcement, and reinforcement of another person. *Journal of Personality and Social Psychology,* 1965, **2,** 255–261.

Marston, A. R. Determinants of the effects of vicarious reinforcement. *Journal of Experimental Psychology,* 1966, **71,** 550–558.

Marston, A. R., & Kanfer, F. H. Group size and number of vicarious reinforcements in verbal learning. *Journal of Experimental Psychology,* 1963, **65,** 593–596.

Mausner, B., & Block, B. L. A study of the additivity of variables affecting social interaction. *Journal of Abnormal and Social Psychology,* 1957, **54,** 250–256.

McDavid, J. W. Effects of ambiguity of environmental cues upon learning to imitate. *Journal of Abnormal and Social Psychology,* 1962, **65,** 381–386.

Mowrer, O. H. *Learning theory and the symbolic processes.* New York: Wiley, 1960.

Paschke, R. E., Simon, S., & Bell, R. W. Vicarious discrimination learning in retardates. *Journal of Abnormal Psychology,* 1967, **72,** 536–542.

Phillips, R. E. Comparison of direct and vicarious reinforcement and an investigation of methodological variables. *Journal of Experimental Psychology,* 1968, **78,** 666–669. (a)

Phillips, R. E. Vicarious reinforcement and imitation in a verbal learning situation. *Journal of Experimental Psychology,* 1968, **76,** 669–670. (b)

Rosekrans, M. A. Imitation in children as a function of perceived similarity to a social model and vicarious reinforcement. *Journal of Personality and Social Psychology,* 1967, **7,** 307–315.

Rosenbaum, M. E., & Bruning, J. L. Direct and vicarious experience of variations in percentage of reinforcement. *Child Development,* 1966, **37,** 959–966.

Rosenbaum, M. E., Chalmers, D. K., & Horne, W. C. Effects of success and failure and the competence of the model on the acquisition and reversal of a matching behavior. *Journal of Psychology,* 1962, **54,** 251–258.

Rosenbaum, M. E., & Tucker, I. F. The competence of the model and the learning of imitation and nonimitation. *Journal of Experimental Psychology,* 1962, **63,** 183–190.

Thelen, M. H. The modeling of verbal reactions to failure. *Developmental Psychology,* 1969, **1,** 297.

Thelen, M. H., & Soltz, W. The effect of vicarious reinforcement on imitation in two social-racial groups. *Child Development,* 1969, **40,** 879–887.

Walters, R. H., Leat, M., & Mezei, L. Inhibition and disinhibition of response through emphathic learning. *Canadian Journal of Psychology,* 1963, **17,** 235–243.

Walters, R. H., & Parke, R. D. Influences of response consequences to a social model on resistance to deviation. *Journal of Experimental Child Psychology,* 1964, **1,** 269–280.

Walters, R. H., Parke, R. D., & Cane, V. A. Timing of punishment and the observation of consequences to others as determinants of response inhibition. *Journal of Experimental Child Psychology,* 1965, **2**, 10–30.

Waxler (Zahn), C., & Yarrow, M. R. Factors influencing imitative learning in preschool children. *Journal of Experimental Child Psychology,* 1970, **9**, 115–130.

Willis, R. H. Two dimensions of conformity-nonconformity. *Sociometry,* 1963, **26**, 499–513.

ANXIETY, DRIVE THEORY, AND COMPUTER-ASSISTED LEARNING

Charles D. Spielberger, Harold F. O'Neil, Jr., and Duncan N. Hansen

PSYCHOLOGY DEPARTMENT AND COMPUTER ASSISTED INSTRUCTION CENTER,
FLORIDA STATE UNIVERSITY, TALLAHASSEE, FLORIDA

I. Introduction

The major goals of this article are to formulate hypotheses about the effects of individual differences in anxiety on the learning process, and to test these in experiments on computer-assisted learning. However, in order to study the effects of anxiety on learning, it is necessary first to specify the conditions under which anxiety is aroused, and then to delineate the complex effects of anxiety on performance. The latter will require a theory of learning that takes into account both the drive characteristics and the interfering response properties of anxiety.

Research on anxiety and learning has suffered from ambiguity with regard to the status of anxiety as a theoretical concept. The results of recent investigations suggest that an adequate theory of anxiety must distinguish conceptually and operationally between anxiety as a transitory state and as a relatively stable personality trait. According to Spielberger (1966b):

Anxiety states (A-States) are characterized by subjective, consciously perceived feelings of apprehension and tension, accompanied by or associated with activation or arousal of the autonomic nervous system. Anxiety as a personality trait (A-Trait) would seem to imply a motive or acquired behavioral disposition that predisposes an individual to perceive a wide range of objectively nondangerous circumstances as threatening, and to respond to these with A-State reactions disproportionate in intensity to the magnitude of the objective danger [pp. 16–17].

A comprehensive theory of anxiety must differentiate between anxiety states, the stimulus conditions that evoke these states, and the defenses that serve to avoid or ameliorate them (Spielberger, 1972). In Section II of this article, a trait-state conception of anxiety will be discussed, and methods of measuring trait and state anxiety will be described.

Spence-Taylor Drive Theory and the empirical evidence supporting it will be briefly reviewed in Section III. This theory emphasizes the complex effects of the motivational component of anxiety on the learning process. In Section IV, research on the effects of anxiety in programmed instruction (PI) will be evaluated from the standpoint of Trait-State Anxiety Theory and Drive Theory. Finally, in Section V, studies of anxiety and computer-assisted learning that have been carried out in the Florida State University CAI Center will be reported. The concepts and methods that are used in computer-assisted instruction (CAI) will also be discussed.

II. Trait-State Anxiety Theory

A. INTRODUCTION

The conception of anxiety presented in Fig. 1 assumes that the arousal of A-State involves a process or sequence of temporally ordered events. This process may be initiated by an external stimulus that is appraised by an individual as dangerous, such as the imminent threat of injury or death faced by a soldier in combat. Or it may be aroused by situations that involve psychological stress, such as the threat to self-esteem that is encountered in performing on a competitive task. Internal stimuli which cause an individual to anticipate danger may also evoke higher levels of A-State. Situations or circumstances in which personal adequacy is evaluated are likely to be perceived as more threatening by high A-Trait individuals than by persons who are low in A-Trait.

Once a stimulus situation is appraised as threatening, Trait-State Anxiety Theory (Spielberger, 1972) posits that: (1) an A-State reaction will be evoked; (2) the *intensity* of the A-State reaction will be proportional to the amount of threat the situation poses for the individual;

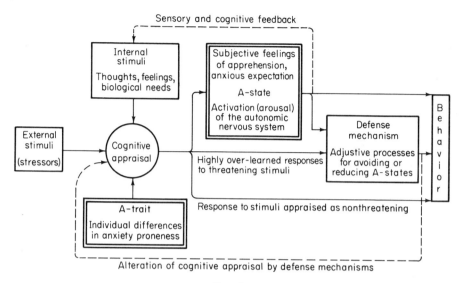

Fig. 1.

and (3) the *duration* of the reaction will depend upon the persistence of the evoking stimuli and the individual's previous experience in dealing with similar circumstances. The theory further assumes that through sensory and cognitive feedback mechanisms, high levels of A-State intensity will be experienced as unpleasant, and may serve to initiate cognitive or motoric defensive processes that have effectively reduced A-States in the past. Stressful situations that are encountered frequently may lead an individual to develop effective coping responses that quickly alleviate or minimize the danger, thereby reducing the intensity of the A-State reaction. A person may also respond directly to situations that are appraised as threatening with defensive processes that serve to reduce the intensity of A-States.

In summary, the schematic diagram in Fig. 1 provides a cross-sectional analysis of anxiety phenomena. Two different anxiety constructs, A-State and A-Trait, are posited and distinguished from the stimulus conditions which evoke A-States and the defenses that help individuals to avoid or reduce them. The classes of variables that we believe to be most significant in anxiety research are: (a) the characteristics of the stimuli, both external and internal, that evoke A-States; (b) the nature of the cognitive processes that are involved in appraising various stimuli as dangerous or threatening; and (c) the defense mechanisms that are employed to avoid A-States, or to reduce the intensity of these states once they are experienced.

A major task for a trait-state theory of anxiety is to specify the characteristics of stimuli that evoke differential levels of A-State in persons who differ in A-Trait. According to Atkinson (1964), a "fear of failure" motive is reflected in measures of A-Trait which suggests that situations that involve the risk of failure may have greater impact on high A-Trait individuals than on low A-Trait persons. On the basis of a comprehensive review of research findings with anxiety scales, I. G. Sarason (1960) has noted that the performance of persons with high scores on various measures of anxiety was more adversely affected by ego-involving or failure instructions than was the performance of individuals who scored low on such measures.

Experimental investigations of anxiety phenomena have produced findings that are generally consistent with Atkinson's view that fear of failure is a major characteristic of high A-Trait people, and with Sarason's conclusion that ego-involving instructions are more detrimental to the performance of high A-Trait individuals than persons with low A-Trait. In general, the experimental literature on anxiety appears to indicate that situations which pose direct or implied threats to self-esteem produce differential levels of A-State in persons who differ in A-Trait (Spielberger, 1966b; Spielberger, 1972).

Although failure or ego-involving instructions evoke higher levels of A-State intensity in high A-Trait subjects than in low A-Trait subjects, whether or not a particular high A-Trait individual will show an elevation in A-State will depend upon the extent to which he perceives a specific situation as dangerous or threatening, and this will be greatly influenced by his aptitude and skills, and by his past experience. While a difficult task may evoke high levels of A-State in most individuals with high A-Trait, a particular high A-Trait person who has the requisite skills and experience to do well on this task is not likely to regard it as threatening. Conversely, a task that most people find nonthreatening might be regarded as extremely dangerous by a low A-Trait individual for whom it had special traumatic significance. Thus, while measures of A-Trait provide useful information regarding the probability that high levels of A-State will be aroused, the stressful impact of any given situation can be ascertained only by taking actual A-State measurements in that situation.

B. THE STATE-TRAIT ANXIETY INVENTORY

The State-Trait Anxiety Inventory (STAI) was developed to provide reliable, relatively brief, self-report measures of both state and trait anxiety. Item selection procedures and the item validation process for the STAI are described in detail by Spielberger and Gorsuch (1966) and Spielberger, Gorsuch, and Lushene (1970). The STAI A-State scale consists of 20 statements that ask people to describe how they feel at a particular moment in time; subjects respond to each scale item (e.g., "I feel tense") by rating themselves on the following 4-point scale: (1) not at all; (2) somewhat; (3) moderately so; (4) very much so. The A-Trait scale consists of 20 statements that ask people to describe how they generally feel; subjects respond to each scale item (e.g., "I lack self-confidence") by checking one of the following: (1) almost never; (2) sometimes; (3) often; (4) almost always.

The STAI A-State scale evaluates subjective feelings of tension, nervousness, worry, and apprehension, and defines a continuum of increasing levels of A-State intensity. Low scores indicate moderate levels of tension and apprehensiveness, and high scores reflect states of intense apprehension and fearfulness that approach panic. It has been demonstrated that scores on the STAI A-State scale increase in response to various kinds of stress and decrease as a result of relaxation training (Spielberger *et al.,* 1970). Further evidence bearing on the construct validity of the STAI A-State scale may be found in recent studies by Hodges (1967, 1968), Taylor, Wheeler, and Altman (1968), Lamb (1969), McAdoo (1969), O'Neil (1969), and O'Neil, Spielberger, and Hansen (1969b).

The STAI A-Trait scale measures individual differences in anxiety proneness, i.e., the disposition to respond to psychological stress with different levels of A-State intensity. Low scores are obtained by persons who experience anxiety states relatively infrequently, whereas high scores are obtained by persons who frequently experience anxiety symptoms. The STAI A-Trait scale is highly correlated with other standard measures of trait anxiety, such as the J. A. Taylor (1953) Manifest Anxiety Scale (TMAS) and the IPAT Anxiety Scale (Cattell & Scheier, 1963). Since the intercorrelations among these anxiety scales for college students and neuropsychiatric patients approach the reliabilities of the individual scales (Spielberger *et al.,* 1970), the STAI A-Trait scale, the TMAS, and the IPAT Anxiety Scale may be considered as alternative measures of A-Trait.

III. Spence-Taylor Drive Theory

In order to study the effects of anxiety on learning, a theory of learning that specifies the complex relationships between anxiety and performance is needed. Over the past two decades, much of the research on the effects of individual differences in anxiety on the learning process has been guided by a theory of emotionally based drive formulated by K. W. Spence (1958) and J. A. Taylor (1956). A detailed statement of the current status and empirical evidence supporting Drive Theory was recently published by J. T. Spence and Spence (1966). The theory proceeds from Hull's (1943) basic assumption that excitatory potential, E, which determines the strength of a given response, R, is a multiplicative function of total effective drive state, D, and habit strength, H. Thus:

$$R = f(E) = f(D \times H)$$

Total effective drive state, D, results from the summation of all individual need states existent in a person at a given period of time, irrespective of their source. The number and strength of the specific habits that are elicited in any situation is determined by an individual's previous experience in the same, or in similar situations. All habit tendencies that are evoked in a person by a particular situation are multiplied by D.

Drive Theory proper begins with the assumptions that: (1) noxious or aversive stimuli arouse a hypothetical emotional response, r_e; and (2) that drive level, D, is a function of the strength of r_e. The TMAS was developed as an operational measure of individual differences in r_e. It was originally assumed that scores on this scale were positively related to characteristic differences among people in r_e and, therefore, reflected consistent individual differences in D. Evidence of the construct validity of the TMAS as an index of D has been consistently demonstrated in classical conditioning experiments in which the UCS is typically a noxious stimulus (K. W. Spence, 1964).

Verbal learning and concept attainment tasks do not generally involve noxious stimulation, and the evidence bearing on whether persons with high anxiety, as measured by the TMAS, have higher D than low-anxiety subjects when performing on such tasks is inconclusive. This led K. W. Spence (1958) to propose two alternative hypotheses concerning the relation between TMAS scores and D: (a) The "Chronic Hypothesis" posits that high TMAS subjects are more emotional than low TMAS subjects, and this causes them to manifest higher D in *all* situations, whether stressful or not; (b) The "Reactive Hypothesis" posits that high TMAS subjects are more emotionally reactive than low TMAS subjects, which disposes them to respond with higher D in situations involving some form of stress.

Investigations of learning under neutral and stressful experimental conditions provide strong empirical support for the Reactive Hypothesis (e.g., Nicholson, 1958; I. G. Sarason, 1960; J. T. Spence & Spence, 1966; Spielberger, 1966a). Differences in the performance of subjects who differed in anxiety as measured by scales such as the TMAS were obtained only when the experimental conditions involved some form of psychological stress. For example, Spielberger and Smith (1966) found a complex relationship between anxiety and performance on their serial verbal learning task when it was given with stressful instructions, but no relationship with neutral instructions. Apparently, the neutral instructions failed to elicit differential levels of A-State for subjects who differed in A-Trait. Most previous studies of anxiety and learning have used measures of anxiety such as the TMAS to select subjects on the assumption that those with high scores were higher in D than subjects with low scores. Since the TMAS appears to be a measure of trait anxiety (Spielberger, 1966b), this procedure is questionable in that the concept of D is logically more closely associated with A-State than with A-Trait. While Drive Theory does not differentiate between trait and state anxiety, most of the evidence supporting this theory is based on experimental applications of A-Trait measures. As previously noted, persons high in A-Trait tend to show performance changes attributed to higher D in situations characterized by failure or ego-involving instructions. It has also been shown that situations involving threats of physical danger or harm do not evoke differential levels of A-State for subjects who differ in A-Trait (Hodges, 1967; Hodges & Spielberger, 1966). Thus, in order for an experimental situation to have differential impact on A-State for subjects who differ in A-Trait, some type of interpersonal stress appears to be required.

Consistent with Hullian learning theory (Hull, 1943), Drive Theory posits that the effects on performance of individual differences in D will depend upon the relative strengths of the correct and competing response tendencies that are evoked in a learning task. On simple tasks, in which there is a single dominant response tendency, or in which correct response tendencies are stronger than competing responses, it would be expected that the high D associated with high levels of A-State intensity would facilitate performance. On complex or difficult tasks, in which competing error tendencies were numerous and/or stronger than correct response tendencies, the high D associated with high A-State would be expected to interfere with performance.

The findings in research on anxiety and learning are consistent with the hypothesis from Trait-State Anxiety Theory (Spielberger, 1972) that high A-Trait (HA-Trait) subjects respond with higher levels of A-State than low A-Trait (LA-Trait) subjects in situations that are made stressful by failure or ego-involving instructions. It follows from Drive Theory that high D associated with higher levels of A-State facilitates performance on simple tasks, in which correct responses are dominant, and leads to performance decrements on difficult tasks, in which there are strong error tendencies, through the activation of erroneous responses.

Drive Theory specifies the effects of individual differences in D on performance in learning experiments. It seems more logical, however, to infer differences in D from measures of A-State than by selecting subjects who differ in A-Trait, as has been the custom in research in the Drive Theory tradition. Trait-State Anxiety Theory augments predictions derived from Drive Theory by specifying the conditions in which subjects differing in A-Trait will be expected to show differences in A-State in learning experiments. The extent to which Drive Theory has been supported in the research literature is probably due to the fact that in many studies in which subjects were selected on the basis of an A-Trait measure, they were also exposed to ego-involving or failure instructions. Such instructions would induce differential levels of A-State in persons who differed in A-Trait.

In the next section, research on anxiety and programmed learning will be examined from the point of view of Drive Theory and Trait-State Anxiety Theory.

IV. The Effects of Anxiety in Programmed Instruction

Research dealing with anxiety and PI is reviewed in this paper for two reasons. First, the impetus for much of the progress in CAI grows out of earlier work on PI; secondly, in both PI and CAI, learning materials are presented in systematic order designed to lead to intended instructional outcomes. Thus, many of the results concerning anxiety and PI can be generalized to CAI.

A search of the psychological and educational literature revealed only a few investigations of the effects of anxiety on PI. Kight and Sassenrath (1966) report that college students with high anxiety scores on the Test Anxiety Questionnaire (Mandler & Sarason, 1952) worked faster and made fewer errors than low anxiety subjects, but they did not differ from the low anxiety subjects with regard to retention scores. Since Kight and Sassenrath's PI task was relatively easy, with a low error rate indicating few competing responses, their results were consistent with the prediction from Drive Theory that high anxiety would facilitate performance on such tasks.

The effects of test anxiety and feedback about performance on a programmed learning task were evaluated by Chapeau (1968) for fifth-grade school children whose anxiety was measured by the Test Anxiety Scale for Children (S. B. Sarason, Davidson, Lighthall, Waite, & Ruebush, 1960). There were no significant differences in the performance of high and low anxiety males in either immediate or delayed retention tests as a function of feedback. In contrast, while there were no differences for low anxiety females in the two feedback conditions, high anxiety females given feedback about the correctness of their responses performed better on both immediate and delayed retention tests than they did without such feedback. The results for females are seen as consistent with Drive Theory, if it is assumed that: (1) there were fewer competing responses in the feedback condition than in the no-feedback condition; and (2) high *D* adversely affected the performance of high anxiety females in the no-feedback condition.

O'Reilly and Ripple (1967) investigated the impact of anxiety and other individual difference variables for sixth-grade subjects who learned programmed materials. They found a correlation of −.53 between scores on the Test Anxiety Scale for Children (S. B. Sarason *et al.,* 1960) and a difficult posttest with a high error rate. These results are consistent with the Drive Theory interpretation that high anxiety subjects perform more poorly than low anxiety subjects on tasks with numerous competing error tendencies.

In contrast to the results of the anxiety-PI studies cited above, Tobias and Williamson (1968) found no significant differences in the performance of high and low TMAS subjects on a PI binary numbers program. In discussing their results, they noted that the anxiety reflected in their test scores was not manifested in the performance of their subjects and concluded that: "In order to provide a really adequate test of the effects of anxiety on programmed instruction, *S*s who are both high and low on anxiety as measured by a questionnaire could be given stress and nonstress instruction . . . and *S*s who are high on a measure (of anxiety) . . . ought to be more susceptible to such stress instructions [Tobias & Williamson, 1968, p. 7]." In effect, Tobias and Williamson acknowledge a fundamental assumption of Trait-State Anxiety Theory, namely, that persons who are high in A-Trait will be high in A-State only if appropriate stress-inducing experimental procedures are used. Their results also serve to highlight the need to specify the classes of stimuli that induce differential levels of A-State in subjects who differ in A-Trait.

In summary, the findings in the studies that have been reviewed in this section can be accounted for in terms of Trait-State Anxiety Theory which explains the arousal of A-State in persons who differ in A-Trait, and by Drive Theory which predicts the effects of differences in A-State on behavior. It should be noted, however, that none of these studies were specifically designed to test either of these theories. A series of studies of anxiety and computer-assisted learning carried out at Florida State University that were conceptualized and designed to test specific hypotheses derived from Trait-State Anxiety Theory and Drive Theory are reported in the next section.

V. The Effects of Anxiety on Computer-Assisted Learning

Most studies concerning the effects of anxiety on learning have originated either in artificial laboratory settings or in realistic but poorly controlled natural settings. CAI systems provide a convenient natural setting in which it is possible to evaluate the learning process under carefully controlled experimental conditions. Furthermore, learning materials may be selected that are more relevant to the needs and interests of the subject than is typically possible with traditional laboratory learning tasks. Before reporting the findings of our research on anxiety and computer-assisted learning, the general characteristics of CAI systems and procedures will be considered, and the particular systems that were used in our research will be described.

A. CAI Systems and Procedures

CAI can be defined as a form of man–machine interaction which is designed to make the learning of instructional materials more efficient. The experimental alternatives which are appropriate for a psychologist to investigate with CAI systems have been described by Groen and Atkinson (1966), Hansen (1966), and Suppes (1964). These alternatives may be summarized as follows: (1) selection of a media (visual, audio, tectile) and its associated terminal devices for the presentation of the stimuli; (2) programming the sequence and the rate of presentation of stimulus items; (3) concurrent recording of all relevant responses, including response latencies; and (4) the formulation of design rules which allow for contingent control of the rate and the sequence of stimuli.

CAI systems are organized so that the experimental treatment received by each subject may be achieved independently of other subjects who are interacting on the system. The subject's independence is referred to as *time sharing*. Before proceeding further, however, it may be useful to characterize more explicitly the experimental paradigm for CAI. One may begin with stimuli to be learned, which can be conceptualized as a set of presentation elements, S_i. These include both elements of new information and correctional messages. For each S_i element, there is one or more correct responses, R_i. These S-R pairs may be simple paired-associate items, such as "boy-girl." Or they may be complex questions with abstract conceptual answers. For example, given the S_i, "What is the distribution for a large number of mean values?," the R_i would be, "A normal distribution."

An experimental event paradigm for CAI is given in Fig. 2 in which each event represents a discrete computer operation. The learning session is started by assigning the subject to a particular experimental treatment, and the computer then determines which stimulus item to present. Immediately after the stimulus item is presented, a response is requested by the computer. The subject's response (along with the response latency) is evaluated by the computer via a prestored set of answers or by a symbolic

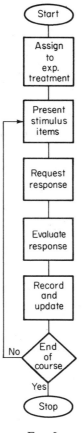

FIG. 2.

matching algorithm. After the response is evaluated, it is recorded, and the learning history of the subject is updated. The system then branches back to the decision rule which governs the stimulus to be presented next.

In a CAI system, the learning items and the correctional stimuli can be intermeshed according to the design characteristics prescribed by the psychologist. It is also possible to intersperse personality measures within the learning materials, such as brief anxiety scales, so that changes in personality states can be assessed as the subject progresses through the task. In essence, a CAI system allows the psychologist to program an array of differential treatments and to pursue the execution of an experiment according to specified contingent rules which determine each event or sequence of events for each subject.

In terms of the computer equipment (hardware) needed to implement various experimental design alternatives, CAI systems have an array of terminals that vary with respect to: (1) the type of terminal (typewriters, cathode-ray tubes, film projectors, audio tape players, and combinations of these); (2) the response devices (keyboards, light pens, and touch-sensitive surfaces); and (3) the number of terminals (typically 4–32). The experimental stimuli and response recordings are usually stored on random-access disks or magnetic tapes. The control of each subject's program is implemented in the CAI central processing unit, or "core." While other devices may also be found within CAI systems, the above units of equipment are essential.

B. The Florida State University CAI System

The studies that are described below were conducted at the Florida State University Computer-Assisted Instruction (CAI) Center. An IBM 1500 CAI system was used in each of the studies except for Study II. The 1500 system has a 32K central processor, 5,000,000 characters of disk storage, two 9-track magnetic tape drives, and the usual input/output devices such as a card reader and a printer. The stimulus materials for this system are presented on individually controlled cathode-ray tube (CRT) terminals with 7 in. by 9 in. screens. The stimulus presentation rate is extremely fast (400 characters per second). For each problem, the subject enters his response on an attached typewriter keyboard, or with a light-pen for CRT response probing.

An IBM 1440 CAI system was used in Study II. While generally similar to the 1500 system, the terminals of the 1440 system consist of automated typewriters, whereas the CRT serves a similar function for the 1500 system. An important difference between the typewriter terminal and the CRT is the relatively slow rate of presentation of the typewriter (13 characters per second as compared with 400 for the CRT). Another important difference between these systems is that the stimulus array on the CRT is typically programmed to disappear immediately after the subject responds, whereas the materials presented by the automated typewriter are continuously available for visual inspection by the subject.

C. Studies of Anxiety and Computer-Assisted Learning

The effects of anxiety on computer-assisted learning were investigated in a series of studies in which the STAI was used to obtain measures of A-State and A-Trait for subjects who performed on various CAI learning tasks. Four studies will be reported in detail, and the results of several others will be briefly described.

1. Study I: Anxiety and Performance in CAI and
Laboratory Settings

The subjects in this study were 16 seventh-grade students (eight males and eight females) from the Florida State University Laboratory School who were participating in the first year of a 3-year Intermediate Science Curriculum Study (ISCS). The ISCS project was based on science learning materials developed by Burkman (1970). These materials consisted of conceptual and laboratory components which were self-pacing. The special adaptation of the ISCS materials for the Florida State University study consisted of: (1) the presentation of selected science concepts using the CAI media; and (2) the subsequent demonstration and testing of these concepts in a laboratory setting.

The subjects who participated in this study were selected at the beginning of the fall term from a pool of approximately 80 subjects. At the time of the data collection, the subjects' mean age was 12.9 years. The sample was representative of the total population of seventh graders at the Laboratory School with regard to IQ and performance in previous science courses. The mean IQ for the group was 101.2 as measured by the California Test of Mental Maturity.

The ISCS curriculum was presented in a CAI setting and a small science laboratory (LAB). The CAI learning took place in a 12 ft by 20 ft room containing the CRT terminals. Each terminal was located on a table within a small booth formed by wooden partitions. There was sufficient space beside the terminal for work sheets and graphic materials. The science laboratory exercises were conducted in an adjacent 8 ft by 16 ft room which contained the work tables and the laboratory apparatus.

The initial presentation of information relating to the conceptual aspects of the science materials, for example, the relationship between force, mass, and momentum, was given in the CAI setting. The students then took part in an individualized laboratory exercise. With regard to the example noted, each student performed an experiment that involved rolling an object down an inclined plane to demonstrate the relationships among the science concepts.

Study I was initiated in the late spring. Prior to the beginning of this experiment, the students had been working on the ISCS materials via CAI for approximately 8 months. On the average, they spent about an hour each day on the experimental science curriculum, of which 30–40 minutes was typically devoted to laboratory exercises. The observations on each subject were taken on a single day during the period that the subject was at the CAI Center.

In both CAI and laboratory settings, each student progressed at his own individual rate. During each session, the subjects were assisted by three proctors. The proctors were graduate students in science education who answered any questions that arose regarding the procedures or the curriculum. Since the CAI presentations were almost completely self-contained, the proctors spent most of their time in the laboratory setting where they functioned primarily as observers, evaluators of performance, and procedural problem-solvers with regard to the day-to-day instructional process.

Two independent observers (not proctors) took 10-minute time samples on each child in the CAI and LAB situations. They simultaneously observed the same child and rated his avoidance responses. The types of avoidance responses that were rated included nontask-oriented behaviors, such as social talking, staring into space, wandering around the room, yawning, rubbing the eyes, and nontask-related work. Prior to the study, the observers were given several practice sessions in rating specific avoidance behaviors. In the final practice session, the interrater reliability for these ratings was .93. During the experiment, the interrater reliability was .87.

The experimental procedures for each subject can be divided into five stages as follows: (1) the administration of the STAI A-Trait scale; (2) the presentation of the science concepts in the CAI setting; (3) the administration of the STAI A-State scale immediately after the CAI presentation, with instructions to indicate how the subjects felt while responding to the CAI materials; (4) performance in the science LAB; and (5) the second administration of the STAI A-State scale, with instructions to report how the subjects felt while they were working in the laboratory. With the exception of the administration of the anxiety scales, the procedures for the students were essentially the same as they had been each day during the preceding 8 months.

Results and Discussion. The mean STAI A-State scores obtained by the 16 subjects in the CAI and LAB settings were 34.84 and 40.66, respectively, and the *t*-test for the difference between these means was statistically significant. Since the LAB setting induced higher levels of A-State in the subjects, it may be concluded that it was more threatening than the CAI setting.

The effects of the CAI and LAB situations on A-State for subjects who differed in A-Trait were evaluated next. The eight subjects with scores above the A-Trait median were designated the high A-Trait (HA-Trait) group, while those with scores below the median were designated the low A-Trait (LA-Trait) group. The median score on the STAI A-Trait scale given at the beginning of the experiment was determined to be 36.

The mean STAI A-State scores obtained by the HA- and LA-Trait

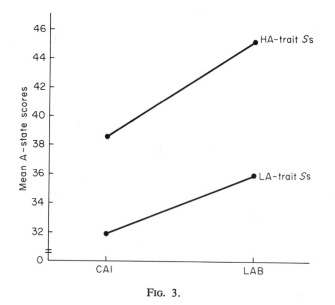

Fɪɢ. 3.

subjects in the CAI and LAB settings are shown in Fig. 3. These data were evaluated by a two-factor, mixed-design analysis of variance (ANOVA) in which A-Trait and experimental settings (CAI vs. LAB) were the independent variables, with repeated measures on the second factor. The significant A-Trait by settings interaction, when considered along with the data presented in Fig. 3, indicated that the impact of the LAB setting on A-State was relatively greater for the HA-Trait subjects than for the LA-Trait subjects. The main effects of A-Trait and experimental settings were also statistically significant. Individual t-tests revealed that level of A-State was significantly higher in the LAB setting than in the CAI setting for both the HA- and LA-Trait subjects.

The mean number of avoidance responses for HA- and LA-Trait subjects in the CAI and LAB settings are presented in Table I. These

TABLE I

Mᴇᴀɴ Nᴜᴍʙᴇʀ ᴏꜰ Aᴠᴏɪᴅᴀɴᴄᴇ Rᴇsᴘᴏɴsᴇs ᴀɴᴅ Mᴇᴀɴ Pʀᴏᴘᴏʀᴛɪᴏɴ ᴏꜰ Eʀʀᴏʀs ꜰᴏʀ HA-Tʀᴀɪᴛ ᴀɴᴅ LA-Tʀᴀɪᴛ Sᴜʙᴊᴇᴄᴛs ɪɴ ᴛʜᴇ CAI ᴀɴᴅ LAB Sᴇᴛᴛɪɴɢs

Groups	Mean avoidance response		Mean proportion of errors	
	CAI	LAB	CAI	LAB
HA-Trait	45.84	62.76	.289	.437
LA-Trait	37.92	49.56	.245	.379

data were evaluated by the same type of two-factor, mixed-design ANOVA that was used to evaluate the A-State scores. In this analysis, only the main effect of settings was significant, which indicated that the students exhibited fewer avoidance responses in the CAI setting than in the LAB setting.

Since the number of learning trials differed in the CAI and LAB settings, in order to compare the performance of subjects in these settings, the mean proportion of errors was determined for the HA- and LA-Trait groups. These data are presented in Table I. The results of a two-factor mixed-design ANOVA, similar to the one used in the preceding analyses of A-State scores and avoidance responses, yielded only a significant main effect of settings. This finding indicated that the mean proportion of errors was higher in the LAB setting than in the CAI setting, as may be noted in Table I.

In the preceding analyses, no relationship was found between level of A-Trait and avoidance responses nor between A-Trait and errors. For both HA- and LA-Trait subjects, however, level of A-State was significantly higher in the LAB setting than in the CAI setting, and the LAB setting was particularly threatening for the HA-Trait group. Therefore, in the next analysis, avoidance responses and errors in the two experimental settings were examined as a function of level of A-State. Subjects with A-State scores above the median in each setting were designated as the high A-State (HA-State) group, and those with scores below the median were designated the low A-State (LA-State) group. The median A-State scores in the CAI and LAB settings were determined to be 35 and 39, respectively.

The mean number of avoidance responses and the mean proportion of errors for the HA- and LA-State subjects in the CAI and LAB settings are reported in Table II. Although the HA-State subjects showed more avoidance responses than the LA-State subjects in both settings, the

TABLE II
MEAN ERROR PROPORTIONS AND AVOIDANCE RESPONSES

Measures	CAI				LAB			
	LA	HA	t	p	LA	HA	t	p
Avoidance responses								
Mean	28.44	40.56	1.37	NS	14.16	85.56	4.01	$<.01$
SD	9.72	12.27			8.17	12.74		
Error proportion								
Mean	.143	.376	2.68	$<.05$	.263	.519	3.17	$<.01$
SD	.047	.053			.062	.084		

differences between these groups was statistically significant only in the LAB setting. A similar analysis for the error data indicated that the HA-State subjects had a significantly higher mean proportion of errors in both settings than did the LA-State subjects.

In summary, even though the science concepts were initially presented in the CAI setting and subsequently demonstrated in the LAB, the results of Study I indicated that: (1) level of A-State was higher in the LAB setting than in the CAI setting for both HA- and LA-Trait subjects; (2) the mean number of avoidance responses and the mean proportion of errors were greater in the LAB setting than in the CAI setting; (3) the LAB setting was particularly threatening for the HA-Trait subjects; (4) level of A-Trait was not related to either avoidance responses or errors in either setting; and (5) the HA-State subjects made significantly more errors in both settings, and significantly more avoidance responses in the LAB setting.

It would appear that the LAB setting was more threatening than the CAI setting as indicated by higher A-State scores, more avoidance responses, and a higher proportion of errors. Furthermore, consistent with Trait-State Anxiety Theory (Spielberger, 1972), these results may be attributed to the fact that the subjects' performance was more closely observed and evaluated by the proctors in the LAB setting than in the CAI setting, and this made the LAB setting more threatening, especially for the HA-Trait subjects.

2. Study II: The Effects of A-State and Task Difficulty on Computer-Assisted Learning

This study investigated the relationship between A-State and performance for college students who learned difficult and easy mathematics concepts by CAI (O'Neil et al., 1969b). According to Spence-Taylor Drive Theory, assuming that drive level is associated with A-State, it would be expected that the performance of high A-State subjects would be inferior to that of low A-State subjects on tasks in which competing error tendencies were stronger than correct responses, and superior on tasks in which correct responses were dominant relative to incorrect response tendencies. In the present study, it was hypothesized that subjects who were high in A-State would make more errors than low A-State subjects on the difficult CAI task, and that this relationship would be reversed on the easy task. A unique feature of this study was that A-State measures were obtained while the subjects actually performed on the CAI learning tasks.

The subjects were undergraduate students enrolled in the introductory psychology course at Florida State University. The A-State scale of the

STAI provided a self-report measure of the phenomenological aspects of state anxiety. Measures of systolic blood pressure (SBP) were obtained as indicants of the physiological component of A-State. SBP was measured by means of a desk model Baumanometer. A CAI typewriter terminal controlled by an IBM 1440 System presented the learning materials and recorded the subjects' responses.

The CAI program was written in a linear format using COURSE-WRITER I, an author programmer language. This program was comprised of two main parts: a difficult section, which involved proofs relating to the field properties of complex numbers; and an easy section, which consisted of problems about compound fractions. The programming logic required the subject to solve each succeeding problem correctly before he could attempt the next one. The learning materials are described in detail by O'Neil et al. (1969b).

Two experimenters supervised as many as eight subjects at the same time. The subjects were seated at CAI terminals located in a sound-deadened, air-conditioned room which the experimenters entered only to read instructions, administer the anxiety scales, and take blood pressure. The experimental procedures, which were the same for all subjects, were divided into four periods: pretask, difficult and easy performance periods, and posttask. During the performance periods, each subject first progressed through the difficult learning materials and then the easy materials. A brief four-item A-State scale was also presented during the task by the computer, and the subjects were instructed to respond to it according to how they felt while working on the task. At the end of each period, SBP was taken, and the 20-item STAI A-State scale was administered. The possibility of systematic experimenter bias was minimized by insuring that neither experimenter took a complete series of SBP measures for any single subject.

Results and Discussion. The mean STAI A-State scores for the pre-task period, the difficult and easy performance periods, and the posttask period were 36.4, 43.0, 32.3, and 33.4, respectively. Thus A-State scores increased from the pretask period to the difficult task, decreased on the easy task, and showed essentially no change from the easy task to the post-task period. In a two-factor ANOVA, in which sex and periods were the independent variables, only the periods main effect was statistically significant. Individual *t*-tests revealed that A-State scores were significantly higher in the difficult task period than in any of the other periods. There were no significant differences in the A-State scores of men and women.

The mean SBP values, corresponding to the periods for which STAI A-State measures were available, are presented in Fig. 4. It may be noted that SBP increased during the difficult task period, decreased during the easy task period, and showed little change from the easy task period to

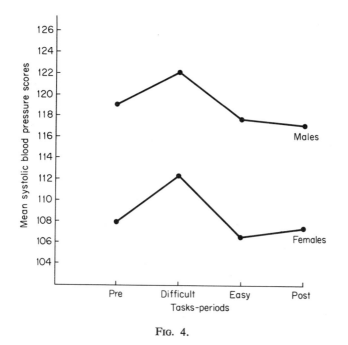

Fɪɢ. 4.

the posttask period. In the analysis of variance for these data, the main effects for sex and periods were statistically significant, indicating that: (a) SBP for males was considerably higher than for females; and (b) SBP showed changes over task periods similar to those obtained for the STAI A-State scores. For both men and women, SBP measures taken immediately after subjects performed on the difficult task were significantly higher than in any other period.

In the analysis of the error data for the difficult and the easy CAI tasks, each task was divided into two sections. For the difficult task, the first section consisted of five proof statements, Diff/(1–5), and the second section consisted of the remaining 12 proof statements, Diff/(6–17). Similarly, for the easy task, the two sections corresponded to the first five items, Easy/(1–5), and the remaining 11 items, Easy/(6–16). Brief A-State scales had been given by the computer between the two sections of each task.

The mean number of errors per problem for the first and second sections of the difficult task were 2.8 and 1.6. For the two sections of the easy task, the mean number of errors were .1 and .02. These data were evaluated in an ANOVA in which the significant F ratio for Tasks indicated that errors declined across the four periods, falling almost to zero in both sections of the easy task. Since there were so few errors on the easy task, the data for this task were not considered in the analysis of the relationship between A-State and errors.

As previously noted, there were no differences between men and women in either STAI A-State scores or in mean number of errors. Therefore, in evaluating the relationship between A-State and errors, the data for men and women were combined. For this analysis, the subjects were divided at the median STAI A-State score obtained following the difficult task. Subjects whose scores were above the median were designated the HA-State group; those with scores below the median were designated the LA-State group.

The mean number of errors made by the HA- and LA-State groups on the two sections of the difficult task are reported in Fig. 5. The ANOVA for these data yielded a significant A-State by tasks interaction and a main effect of tasks. These statistical findings reflected the fact that the HA-State subjects made nearly twice as many errors as the LA-State subjects on the Diff/(1–5) section, and fewer errors than the LA-State subjects on the Diff/(6–17) section, as may be noted in Fig. 5.

To summarize the results for Study II, it was found that state anxiety increased when subjects worked on difficult CAI materials and decreased

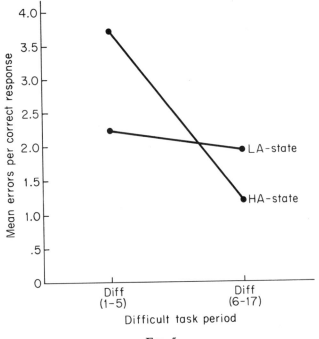

FIG. 5.

when they performed on easy materials. This pattern of change in A-State was observed for the 20-item STAI A-State scales, the brief A-State scales embedded in the learning materials, and the SBP measures. There were no differences in the STAI A-State scores for men and women, but the SBP scores for males were significantly higher than for females. This latter finding apparently reflected the fact that SBP is dependent upon physical characteristics such as height, weight, and body build (Gregg, 1961). Since the males, on the average, were taller, heavier, and more muscular than the females, higher levels of SBP would be expected for them on the basis of these physical differences.

It may be noted in Fig. 5 that the HA-State subjects made more errors than LA-State subjects on Diff/(1–5), whereas the LA-State subjects made more errors than the HA-State subjects on Diff/(6–17). The finding that performance on the CAI task was an interactive function of level of A-State and Task Difficulty was consistent with: (1) the assumption that A-State reflected D; and (2) the prediction from Drive Theory that the effects of anxiety on learning would depend upon the relative strengths of correct responses and competing error tendencies (J. T. Spence & Spence, 1966). In the present study, A-State apparently influenced performance by: (a) activating error tendencies on the initial section of the difficult CAI task, for which error rate was relatively high; and (b) enhancing the production of correct responses on the second section of the difficult task, for which error rate was relatively low.

3. Study III: The Effects of A-Trait and A-State on Computer-Assisted Learning

In this study (O'Neil et al., 1969a), the subjects were selected on the basis of extreme scores on the STAI A-Trait scale. The same learning materials that were used in Study II were presented on an IBM 1500 system, and order of presentation of the difficult and easy tasks was counterbalanced.

On the basis of the findings in Study I, it was hypothesized that HA-Trait subjects would respond to the CAI tasks with higher levels of A-State than would LA-Trait subjects. On the basis of the results obtained in Study II, it was expected that level of A-State would be higher on the more difficult CAI task than on the easy task. In both previous studies, the results suggested that the relationship between A-State and errors would be an interactive one in which the HA-State subjects would make relatively more errors than LA-State subjects on difficult CAI materials but not on easy materials.

The A-State and A-Trait scales of the STAI were administered to approximately 1100 introductory psychology students at Florida State University. From this population, males with extreme scores on the STAI

A-Trait scale (upper and lower 20%) were invited to participate in an experiment on computer-assisted learning. Of the 44 subjects who were selected for the study, 22 had high A-Trait scores and 22 had low A-Trait scores.

The CAI mathematics program used in the previous study (O'Neil *et al.,* 1969b) was adapted for the present experiment by recoding the learning materials in COURSEWRITER II. The learning materials were presented on the CRT of an IBM 1500 CAI system (IBM, 1967). For each problem, the subject selected a response from 24 alternative choices that were printed in an auxiliary booklet, and entered his choice by typing it on the attached typewriter keyboard. If the response was correct, the next problem was presented; for incorrect responses, a corrective message was given and the same problem was presented again.

The CAI system also administered the STAI A-State scales during the learning tasks and recorded the subjects' responses. Seven measures of A-State were obtained. Except for the pretask A-State scale, which was given with standard instructions ("indicate how you feel right now"), the subjects were asked to respond to each scale by indicating how they felt while performing on the preceding section of the learning task. The several administrations of the A-State scales were programmed so that the order of item presentation on different occasions was random.

The experimental procedures were divided into three periods: (a) the pretask period, in which the subjects learned how to operate the CAI terminal; (b) the performance period, in which the computer presented the learning materials; and (c) the posttask period in which subjects were interviewed and debriefed. These procedures were essentially the same as in Study II, except that blood pressure was not taken, and the easy and difficult CAI tasks were presented in counterbalanced order. Each subject was assigned either to the D/E order, in which he progressed through the difficult task first and then the easy task, or the E/D order, in which the easy task was followed by the difficult task.

Results and Discussion. The mean STAI A-State scores for the HA- and LA-Trait subjects in each of the three sections of the difficult and easy tasks are shown in Fig. 6. The data as presented have been collapsed over task order, since level of A-State was approximately the same during the difficult task, irrespective of whether it was given first or preceded by the easy task. Similarly, A-State during the easy task was approximately the same whether or not it was given first or second. It may be noted in Fig. 6 that: (a) the HA-Trait subjects responded with higher levels of A-State throughout the experiment than the LA-Trait subjects; and (b) level of A-State increased from the pretask measure to Diff/A, decreased somewhat during Diff/B and Diff/C, and was relatively low in all three sections of the easy task.

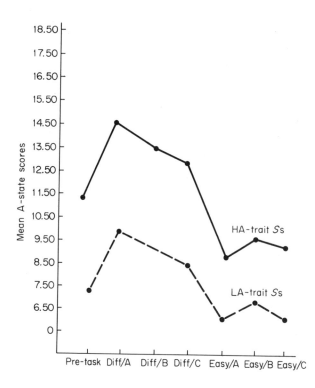

FIG. 6.

In the ANOVA for the data presented in Fig. 6, the main effects of A-Trait and Periods were significant. Further analyses of the A-Trait and Periods effects indicated that A-State was significantly higher for the subjects while they performed on the difficult CAI task than on the easy task, and that the HA-Trait subjects had higher levels of A-State on both tasks than did the LA-Trait subjects. Thus, A-State scores varied as a function of both A-Trait and task difficulty, but not as a function of task order, and higher levels of A-State were associated with the more difficult task.

Since there were so few errors on the easy CAI task, the relationship between A-Trait, A-State, and errors was evaluated only for the difficult task. In the analysis of the relationship between A-Trait and errors on the difficult task, the only significant finding was the main effect of tasks which reflected the decline in the mean number of errors as the subjects progressed through the three sections of the difficult task. The mean number of errors on Diff/A, Diff/B, and Diff/C were 4.8, 3.3, and 2.9, respectively. The failure to find any relationship between A-Trait and errors in the present study was consistent with the results in Study II, in which A-Trait and errors were also unrelated.

In both Study I and Study II, there was a significant relationship between A-State and errors. Consequently, in the present study, the relationship between A-State and errors was evaluated for the three sections of the difficult task. For this analysis, the subjects were divided at the median STAI A-State score obtained during Diff/A, which was 13. The mean number of errors made by the HA- and LA-State subjects in the difficult task are presented in Fig. 7. It may be noted that HA-State subjects made more than twice as many errors on Diff/A than did the LA-State subjects, whereas there was relatively little difference in the error rate for the HA- and LA-State subjects on Diff/B and Diff/C. The analysis of variance for these data yielded a significant A-State by Periods interaction similar to the one obtained for these same variables in Study II (compare Figs. 5 and 7). In both Study II and Study III, the HA-State subjects made many more errors on the CAI materials presented early in the task (Diff/A) than on the materials presented later in the task (Diff/B and Diff/C). In contrast, there was relatively little difference in the error rate for LA-

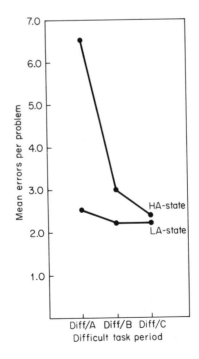

FIG. 7.

State subjects on materials presented earlier and later in the learning task.

A comparison of the results presented in Figs. 5 and 7 reveals that the same learning materials produced more errors when presented with the CRT in Study III than with the automated typewriter which presented the learning materials in Study II. The higher error rate in Study III may be due to the fact that the subject's responses were only briefly displayed on the CRT and removed immediately after feedback was given. With the automated typewriter, the subject's responses and the computer feedback for each item were printed out, and were thus continuously available for visual inspection. Apparently, the greater memory load associated with the CRT terminal in Study III produced a higher error rate because information with regard to previous responses was not available to the subjects.

The results of Study III may be summarized as follows: (a) level of state anxiety was higher on the difficult CAI task than on the easy task; (b) on both the difficult and easy CAI tasks, the HA-Trait subjects responded with higher levels of A-State than did LA-Trait subjects; (c) there was no relationship between A-Trait and errors on the CAI tasks; (d) the HA-State subjects made more errors than the LA-State subjects on the difficult task, and especially on the materials presented at the beginning of this task; and (e) the HA-State subjects made more errors on the materials presented at the beginning of the difficult task than they did on the materials presented later in this task, whereas there was little change in the error rate for LA-State subjects as they progressed through the learning task.

Thus, in Study III, higher levels of A-State were observed for students who worked on difficult mathematics materials than for these same students as they worked on easy materials. On the more difficult materials where overall error rate was high, subjects with high A-State scores showed impaired performance relative to subjects who were low in A-State. In contrast, there was relatively little difference in error rate between HA- and LA-State subjects on CAI materials for which the overall error rate was relatively low. It may be concluded that task difficulty influences level of A-State, and that whether or not individual differences in A-State impair or facilitate performance will depend upon the overall error rate. In general, these findings are consistent with Spence-Taylor Drive Theory and Trait-State Anxiety Theory (Spielberger, 1972).

4. Study IV: The Effects of Stress on A-State and Performance in Computer-Assisted Learning

This study investigated the effects of stress on state anxiety and learning in a CAI task in which subjects were given either neutral or negative feedback regarding their performance (O'Neil, 1969). In order to facilitate comparison with the research previously described, the task selected for this study was the difficult CAI mathematics program that was used in Studies II and III. As in Study III, the task was divided into three sections and presented on the CRT of an IBM 1500 CAI system.

The STAI A-State and A-Trait scales were administered to 583 students enrolled in the introductory psychology course at Florida State University. From this population, females with extreme STAI A-Trait scores (upper and lower 20%) were invited to participate in an experiment on computer-assisted learning. The HA- and LA-Trait subjects who volunteered for the experiment were randomly assigned to either stress or nonstress experimental conditions. The resulting HA- and LA-Trait groups were well-matched with respect to both A-Trait and A-State scores.

The subjects in the stress condition were told, "The computer has been programmed to evaluate your performance as you progress through the learning materials," and they were given negative feedback about their performance during the learning task by the computer. Different negative feedback statements were given during each section of the task. The subjects in the nonstress condition were given brief rest periods in place of the negative feedback statements.

As in Study III, the experimental procedures were divided into three periods: (1) a pretask period in which the subjects were instructed in the operation of the CAI terminal; (2) a task period in which the subjects learned the field properties of complex numbers and received differential feedback regarding their performance; and (3) a posttask period in which the subjects were interviewed and debriefed. With the exception of the introduction of the feedback conditions and the elimination of the easy task, the procedures for Study IV were essentially the same as those used in Study III.

Results and Discussion. The mean STAI A-State scores for the HA- and LA-Trait subjects in the stress and nonstress conditions are shown in Fig. 8A and B. The most important finding in the ANOVA for these data was the significant A-Trait by Conditions by Periods interaction. This triple interaction indicated that the A-State scores of the HA- and LA-Trait subjects in the stress and nonstress conditions showed a differential pattern of change during the experiment. To clarify the interaction, two subsidiary analyses were run: The first evaluated the subjects' *initial* reactions to the CAI learning task; the second examined changes in A-State *during* the task.

In the analysis of the initial reactions to the learning task, changes in A-State from the pretask period to Diff/A were examined as a function of A-Trait and experimental conditions. As in the overall analysis of

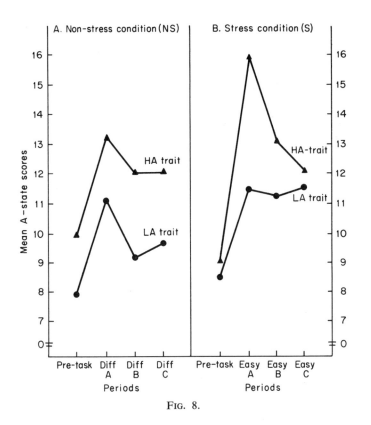

FIG. 8.

variance, a significant triple interaction involving A-Trait, Conditions, and Periods was obtained. When considered with the means presented in Fig. 8A, this finding indicated that the HA-Trait subjects in the stress condition showed a greater initial increase in A-State than did any other group. Further analyses of these data indicated that the HA-Trait subjects showed a greater increase in A-State in the stress condition than in the nonstress condition, and that LA-Trait subjects reacted in a similar manner in both experimental conditions.

Changes in A-State during learning were evaluated by comparing the A-State scores obtained in the three sections of the CAI task. The overall three-factor ANOVA for these data yielded a significant triple interaction which involved A-Trait, Conditions, and Periods. When considered with the means presented in Fig. 8B, this finding indicated that: (a) the HA-Trait subjects in the stress condition showed a marked decline in A-State during the task, whereas level of A-State remained relatively constant for the LA-Trait subjects in the stress condition; and (b) changes in A-

State for the HA- and LA-Trait subjects in the nonstress condition were quite similar, with both groups showing a parallel decline in A-State levels during the learning task.

Further analyses of the changes in A-State scores during the task suggested that the statistically significant interaction could be attributed to three factors. First, level of A-State was higher in Diff/A for the HA-Trait subjects in the stress condition than for the HA-Trait subjects in the nonstress condition, apparently due to the initial impact of negative feedback on level of A-State (see Fig. 8A). Second, the HA-Trait subjects in the stress condition showed a greater decline in A-State during the learning task than did the HA-Trait subjects in the nonstress condition so that, by Diff/C, the level of A-State for both groups was about the same. And, finally, level of A-State for the LA-Trait subjects in the stress condition remained relatively asymptotic throughout the learning task, whereas the A-State scores for LA-Trait subjects in the nonstress condition declined, as may be noted in Fig. 8B.

In the analysis of the effects of stress and A-Trait on errors, a three-factor ANOVA was used. The only significant finding in this analysis was the main effect for Periods which indicated that the number of errors declined from Diff/A to Diff/C, as was previously noted. The absence of any statistically significant effects involving either A-Trait or experimental conditions indicated that, although these variables influenced A-State, they had no direct influence on errors. It may be recalled that no relationship was found between A-Trait and errors in either Study I or Study III.

In the present study, level of A-State declined during the learning task for three of the four experimental groups (see Fig. 8B). Therefore, in examining the relation between A-State and errors, performance on each section of the learning task was separately evaluated as a function of the A-State scores actually obtained during the three sections of the task. The median A-State scores on Diff/A, Diff/B, and Diff/C were 13, 13, and 12, respectively. Subjects with A-State scores above and below the median on Diff/A were designated, for this section of the learning task, the HA-State and LA-State groups. A similar procedure was used to define the HA- and LA-State groups for Diff/B and Diff/C.

The mean number of errors made by the HA- and LA-State groups on the three sections of the learning task are reported in Table III in which it may be noted that the HA-State groups made more errors on each section of the task than did the LA-State groups. However, when these data were evaluated by separate one-way ANOVA's, it was found that the HA-State groups made significantly more errors on Diff/B and Diff/C, but not on Diff/A.

TABLE III
MEAN ERRORS FOR HA-STATE AND LA-STATE SUBJECTS IN THE THREE SECTIONS OF
THE CAI MATHEMATICS LEARNING TASK

Groups	Diff/A	Diff/B	Diff/C
HA-State			
Mean	3.5	2.3	2.2
SD	2.1	2.8	2.0
LA-State			
Mean	2.9	1.1	0.8
SD	2.1	2.1	1.3

The results for Study IV may be summarized as follows: (1) Negative feedback about performance led to greater initial increments in A-State for HA-Trait subjects than for LA-Trait subjects in the stress condition. (2) The HA- and LA-Trait subjects given nonevaluative feedback about their performance (nonstress condition) showed parallel initial increases in A-State. (3) Level of A-State for the HA-Trait subjects in the stress condition decreased during the learning task, despite repeated negative feedback, whereas level of A-State for the LA-Trait subjects in this condition was sustained at initial high levels. (4) During the task, the HA- and LA-Trait subjects in the nonstress condition showed parallel decreases in A-State. (5) No relationship was found between A-Trait and errors. (6) The HA-State subjects made more errors than the LA-State subjects on all three sections of the learning task, and the differences between these groups were statistically significant for Diff/B and Diff/C.

On the assumption that the negative feedback in the stress condition was interpreted as more threatening by the HA-Trait subjects than by the LA-Trait subjects, the results are consistent with Trait-State Anxiety Theory (Spielberger, 1972) which predicts that HA-Trait subjects will respond with greater increments in A-State than LA-Trait subjects in situations that pose a threat to self-esteem. The finding in the stress condition that the HA-Trait subjects adapted better than the LA-Trait subjects was unexpected and somewhat surprising. We may speculate that HA-Trait college students, who presumably experience anxiety states more frequently than LA-Trait students, develop more effective mechanisms for coping with such states when they arise.

The findings in Study IV with regard to changes in A-State in the nonstress condition were essentially the same as in Study II and III. However, with regard to the relationship between A-State and errors, somewhat different results were obtained. In Study II and III, the HA-State subjects made significantly more errors on Diff/A than the LA-State subjects but not on Diff/B and Diff/C. In contrast, in the present study, HA-State subjects made significantly more errors on Diff/B and Diff/C than LA-State subjects, but not on Diff/A. The differences in the relation between A-State and errors in Study IV, as compared to Study II and III, will be further considered in the next section.

D. RECAPITULATION OF THE FINDINGS

The most important results of the four studies described in the previous section will be briefly summarized, and the implications of these findings will then be evaluated from the standpoint of Trait-State Anxiety Theory and Drive Theory. In Study I, level of A-State was higher for junior high school students in the laboratory setting than in the CAI setting, and the mean number of avoidance responses and the mean proportion of errors was also greater in the LAB. Subjects with high A-State scores made significantly more errors in both the LAB and the CAI settings, and they exhibited more avoidance responses in the LAB than did subjects who were low in A-State.

In Study II, higher levels of A-State were evoked by the more difficult CAI materials than by the easy CAI materials, as reflected in greater increases in SBP and higher scores on the STAI A-State scale. Performance on the CAI learning task was found to be an interactive function of level of A-State and task difficulty. The HA-State subjects performed more poorly on the more difficult CAI materials than LA-State subjects, and did somewhat better than LA-State subjects on the easier CAI materials.

Level of A-State was also higher on the more difficult CAI materials in Study III. The HA-Trait subjects responded with higher levels of A-State than LA-Trait subjects throughout the learning task, but no relationship was found between A-Trait and errors. However, an interactive relationship between A-State and errors was found. This interaction reflected the fact that HA-State subjects did more poorly on the more difficult CAI materials than LA-State subjects, and there was relatively little difference in error rate between these groups on the easier CAI materials.

Negative feedback about performance in Study IV evoked greater initial increments in A-State for HA-Trait subjects than for LA-Trait subjects, and also produced a different pattern of change in A-State for these groups during the learning task. In contrast, the HA- and LA-Trait subjects who were given nonevaluative feedback showed comparable initial increments in A-State, and parallel changes in A-State during the learning task. While no relationship between A-Trait and errors was found, the relationship between A-State and errors was somewhat different than in the previous study. The HA-State subjects made more errors than LA-State subjects on all three sections of the CAI learning task, and the difference between these groups was greatest on the easy materials.

The findings in these studies that HA-Trait subjects showed greater elevations in A-State than LA-Trait subjects under circumstances that posed a threat to self-esteem was consistent with Trait-State Anxiety Theory. In Study I, level of A-Trait interacted with the learning situation to influence A-State scores. While HA-Trait subjects had higher levels of A-State in both the LAB and CAI settings, and the LAB setting evoked higher levels of A-State than the CAI setting, the relative difference between A-State scores of the HA- and LA-Trait subjects was greater in the LAB setting. These findings suggest that the LAB was more threatening for both groups than the CAI setting, and that it was especially threatening for the HA-Trait subjects. Apparently this was due to the fact that performance in the LAB was more closely supervised and evaluated by the proctors than in the CAI setting, and there was more overt competition in the LAB among subjects.

The finding in Study IV that negative feedback about performance led to greater initial increases in A-State for HA-Trait subjects than for LA-Trait subjects was also consistent with Trait-State Anxiety Theory. This finding suggests that the negative feedback was perceived as a threat to self-esteem to which the HA-Trait subjects responded with greater elevations in A-State. In contrast, there were no differences in the A-State reactions of the HA- and LA-Trait subjects in Study III, nor in the non-stress condition of Study IV. Thus, HA-Trait subjects who were given factual, nonevaluative feedback about their performance by the computer showed about the same change in A-State as LA-Trait subjects. Apparently, CAI is no more threatening to HA-Trait subjects than it is to LA-Trait subjects when feedback about performance is concerned only with the correctness of the subjects' responses.

It should be noted that the more difficult CAI materials evoked higher levels of A-State in Study II and III than did the easier CAI materials. The fact that level of A-State was higher for the subjects as they worked on the more difficult materials suggests that they appraised these materials as more threatening than the easy materials. However, only in situations in which performance was evaluated by proctors (Study I), or where explicit negative evaluation about performance was given by the computer (Study IV), did the HA-Trait subjects show a greater increase in A-State than LA-Trait subjects. In other words, there were no interactive effects of A-Trait and task difficulty on level of A-State, except under experimental conditions in which the subjects' personal adequacy was evaluated or explicitly challenged.

The findings in these studies emphasize the importance of the conceptual distinction between A-Trait and A-State, and point up the need to provide operational measures of both of these constructs. The results also suggest that it is more appropriate to infer differences in D from measures of A-State, which are obtained in the experimental situation, than from measures of A-Trait. In the three studies in which A-Trait measures were available, no relation was found between A-Trait and performance, whereas systematic relationships were found between A-State and performance.

While the data from Study I are difficult to evaluate from the standpoint of Drive Theory, the findings in Study II and III clearly support this theory. In both studies, performance was an interactive function of level of A-State and task difficulty. These results would seem to indicate that higher levels of D, as inferred from higher A-State scores, activated error tendencies on the more difficult sections of the CAI task (for which error rate was relatively high) and enhanced the production of correct responses on the easy sections of the CAI task (for which error rate was relatively low).

In Study IV, the relationship between A-State and errors clearly failed to support Drive Theory, and the findings in this study were inconsistent with the results obtained in Study II and III. While it is difficult to compare Study II with Study IV, because different procedures were used, the same task and procedures were used in Study III and IV. The only difference between these studies was in the sex of the subjects; females were used in Study IV, whereas the subjects in Study III were males.

Katahn and Lyda (1966) have reported sex differences in several studies of anxiety and learning, and they suggest that situational variables may have different significance for men and women. We are at a loss to explain why the HA- and LA-State males and females performed differently in Study III and IV. However, future research will be designed to evaluate sex differences in anxiety and learning, and to clarify possible interactions between the sex of the subjects and the experimenters.

E. NEW DIRECTIONS IN RESEARCH ON ANXIETY AND COMPUTER-ASSISTED LEARNING

In the studies previously reported in this chapter, CAI was used to evaluate the effects of anxiety on the learning process under carefully controlled experimental conditions. The science and mathematics learning materials used in these studies were more meaningful to the subjects than is typically the case in traditional laboratory learning experiments, but the research was limited to observations of performance in a single experimental session. The preliminary findings in two studies of anxiety and learning that are reported in this section investigated these effects over a longer period of time. The first study evaluates the effects of anxiety on performance in a CAI undergraduate physics course. The second investigates the effects of anxiety on computer-managed instruction in a graduate course in educational research.

1. Anxiety and Performance in a CAI Physics Course

Hansen, Dick, and Lippert (1968) investigated the effects of anxiety on performance in a general education physics course which was presented by CAI. The course was given for credit to 37 undergraduate, nonscience majors at Florida State University. An IBM 1500 CAI system guided the students through a self-paced program of textbook reading assignments, CAI homework problems, audio-taped lectures, movies, and film strips of demonstration experiments. The computer provided information about each course assignment and then administered quizzes that covered the textbook reading, the taped lectures, and the movies. The students were required to pass these quizzes before being allowed to proceed to the next assignment. It should be noted, however, that course grades were not dependent upon performance on the CAI quizzes, but were determined by grades on the midterm and final exams which were given in a conventional manner. Thus, students were not penalized for doing poorly on the CAI quizzes.

As an integral part of the CAI physics course, measures of A-State were obtained following each of the 29 quizzes. The computer administered the same five-item STAI A-State scale that was used in Study II, III, and IV, and instructed the subjects to respond according to how they felt while working on the physics assignment they had just completed. To evaluate changes in A-State during the course, the curriculum was divided into five sequentially-presented content areas: (1) introduction; (2) light; (3) mechanics; (4) electricity and magnetism; and (5) modern physics. Mean A-State scores were determined for each student for each of these areas. It was found that A-State scores were significantly higher in the first section of the course than in any of the subsequent sections. There were no differences in mean A-State scores in sections 2–5 of the course.

Only those CAI quizzes which covered the taped lectures were significantly correlated with final course grades. For 24 of the taped lecture quizzes, A-State scores were negatively correlated with quiz grades, and the strongest correlations were found for the introductory section of the course during which level of A-State was highest. No consistent relationships were obtained between A-State scores and performance on the quizzes which covered the textbook reading assignments and the movies.

There were many uncontrolled variables with regard to the rate and manner in which the curriculum materials were presented in this self-pacing physics course. To cite an extreme example, one student completed all 29 assignments in only four sessions at the CAI Center, and covered 11 assignments in a single session. Most students completed two or more assignments during each session, and the subjects' learning strategies were highly idiosyncratic. Some studied intensively before working on the computer and made very few errors, while others did very little preparation and made many errors. Apparently, the latter group adopted the strategy of having the computer present questions to which they guessed at the answers, and then memorized the correct answers when these were given by the computer.

At the conclusion of the course, each student was interviewed to determine his attitudes toward CAI and how he felt about the anxiety scales. Most students (70%) reported that they liked CAI, and would take another course on CAI (73%) if it was offered. Almost all of the students liked the self-pacing aspect of the CAI course (95%), and most felt that the knowledge that they gained was useful (90%). With regard to the anxiety scales, the majority of the students indicated that they responded "sincerely" each time the scale was given (73%), and that they did not spend a great deal of time in determining their answers (62%).

In the interview, the students were also asked to indicate in which part of the course they had felt most anxious or upset. In response to this question, 15% indicated that it was at the beginning of the course, 16% reported that it was after poor performance on one of the assignments, 10% stated that they felt more anxious when the materials were difficult, and 11% said they experienced no anxiety. These comments are consistent with the finding that mean A-State scores were highest at the beginning of the course. Apparently there were no differences in A-State in any of the other sections of the course, because the difficulty level for the several content areas differed for various members of the class.

2. Anxiety and Computer-Managed Instruction

Gallagher (1970) investigated the effects of trait and state anxiety on performance in a course on "Techniques of Programmed Instruction" which was given for credit to 59 graduate students in education at Florida State University. During the first half of the course, the students completed a series of 13 assignments designed to teach them how to develop a programmed text. During the second part of the course, the subjects were required to develop a programmed text using the principles they learned in the first part of the course.

Each of the assignments in the first part of the course pertained to different aspects of programmed instruction. After studying an assignment on his own, the subject reported to the CAI Center where he took a quiz presented by the computer which evaluated his understanding of a particular task. The computer also presented five-item STAI A-State scales immediately before and immediately after the quiz. The A-State measure which preceded the quiz required the subject to indicate how he felt, "Right now, at this moment"; the measure taken after the quiz asked the subject to report how he felt while he was taking the quiz. There were 13 quizzes, one covering each assignment.

Pearson product–moment correlations were computed between the subjects' quiz grade and the two A-State measures. There was little evidence of any systematic relationship between prequiz A-State scores and quiz grades in that only two of the 13 correlations were statistically significant. In contrast, 9 of the 13 correlations between the postquiz A-State measure and quiz grades were statistically significant, and all 13 correlations were negative. Thus, while there was no relationship between quiz grades and A-State level immediately prior to the quiz (anticipation), subjects who reported higher levels of A-State while they worked on the quiz did more poorly than those with low A-State scores. There are at least two possible interpretations of these findings. First, the poorer performance of the HA-State subjects could be attributed to their higher levels of A-State. An alternative explanation is that higher levels of A-State resulted from the subjects' reactions to their poor performance.

During the second part of the course, the programmed text that each student was required to develop was evaluated by either an instructor or by the computer. The subjects in the instructor-evaluated group presented their products (e.g., lists of behavioral objectives, test items, etc.) to the course instructor (or one of his assistants) who rated each product according to a checklist of course objectives. The quality of the products developed by the subjects in the computer-evaluated group was determined through an interactive dialogue with the computer. On the basis of computer feedback, each subject passed or failed himself according to the same checklist used by the instructor.

At the conclusion of the course, when the programmed text and documentation were completed, all subjects submitted their final products to the course instructor. The final grade for the course was based primarily on the instructor's evaluation of the merits of the programmed text and documentation which each student submitted at the end of the term.

No differences were found in the final grades obtained by the subjects in the instructor-evaluated and computer-evaluated groups. However, the correlation between scores on the STAI A-Trait scale given at the beginning of the term and the students' final grade for the course was −.51 for the instructor-evaluated group, and only −.03 for the computer-evaluated group. Thus, the HA-Trait subjects in the instructor-evaluated group did more poorly than the LA-Trait subjects in this group, whereas there were no differences in the performance of the HA- and LA-Trait subjects in the computer-evaluated group.

The finding that HA-Trait subjects did more poorly when evaluated by the instructor than LA-Trait subjects is of considerable theoretical and practical interest. According to Trait-State Anxiety Theory, being evaluated by an instructor should pose a greater threat to self-esteem than computer feedback about performance, and should evoke higher levels of A-State in HA-Trait subjects than in LA-Trait subjects. Drive Theory would then lead us to predict decrements in the performance of the HA-Trait subjects if higher levels of D associated with elevations in A-State activate error tendencies on a relatively difficult task. Thus, the results suggest that the performance of HA-Trait subjects will be facilitated if the threats that are inherent in learning situations are minimized. It is also possible that LA-Trait subjects may do better under conditions where their performance is more closely evaluated.

The results of these studies, in which the effects of anxiety on learning were investigated over several months, reflect both the complexity and the potential significance of this type of research. The learning situations were so unstructured in both the physics and education courses that individual subjects proceeded in a highly idiosyncratic manner. This led to many different learning strategies and a host of uncontrolled variables which may have obscured detection of the possible influence of anxiety on performance. In the graduate education course, however, the content was more limited than in the physics course, and the subjects were more homogeneous in ability and motivation. These factors may account for the finding that individual differences in A-State and A-Trait were more directly related to performance in the education course than in the physics course.

While the findings in these studies are tentative and require further analysis and replication, they provide some evidence that anxiety may influence performance in real-life learning situations in much the same manner that it does in laboratory contexts which are more structured and restricted in time. Given the complexity of the learning process that takes place in college courses, it will be interesting in future research to evaluate the learning strategies that are employed by HA- and LA-Trait subjects, as well as the relationships between stress, A-Trait, A-State, and performance.

VI. Summary

In this chapter, Spence-Taylor Drive Theory and Spielberger's Trait-State Conception of Anxiety were reviewed, along with methods for measuring A-State and A-Trait. The research literature on anxiety and programmed instruction was then evaluated, and hypotheses about the effects of anxiety on performance in computer-assisted learning were formulated in the context of Drive Theory and Trait-State Anxiety Theory. These hypotheses were tested in a series of studies on anxiety and CAI.

The results of four laboratory studies carried out at the Florida State University CAI Center were described in detail. In addition, the preliminary results of two studies were presented in which the effects of anxiety on performance were evaluated for students taking a CAI course in physics and a computer-managed course in educational research.

The findings that emerged in the four studies of anxiety and computer-assisted learning may be summarized as follows:

1. Level of A-State was higher when learning materials were presented in a laboratory setting than it was for related materials presented in a CAI setting.

2. Higher levels of A-State were evoked by more difficult CAI materials than by easy CAI materials.

3. Subjects who were high in A-Trait responded to the learning tasks with higher levels of A-State than LA-Trait subjects.

4. HA-Trait subjects showed greater elevations in A-State than LA-Trait subjects under circumstances in which performance was closely evaluated by proctors, or in which subjects were given negative feedback about performance.

5. Students with high A-State scores made more errors and more avoidance responses in a laboratory setting than they did in a CAI setting.

6. Performance on CAI learning tasks was found to be an interactive function of level of A-State and task difficulty. HA-State subjects consistently performed more poorly on difficult CAI materials than LA-State subjects. No consistent relationship was found between A-State and performance on easier CAI materials.

7. Although performance was related to A-State, and A-State was moderately correlated with A-Trait, no systematic relationships between A-Trait and performance on the CAI learning tasks were found.

8. CAI appears to be no more threatening to HA-Trait subjects than it is to LA-Trait subjects when they are given factual, nonevaluative feedback about the correctness of their responses.

These results were discussed in terms of their implications for Trait-State Anxiety Theory and Drive Theory. It was concluded that the findings supported Trait-State Anxiety Theory in affirming the importance of the conceptual distinction between A-Trait and A-State, and in the prediction that HA-Trait subjects will show greater elevations in A-State than LA-Trait subjects in learning situations in which the subject's personal adequacy is evaluated, or which pose a threat to self-esteem. The findings were also interpreted as generally consistent with Drive Theory, although certain results suggested that the effects of anxiety on learning may not be the same for men and women. It was concluded that investigators should evaluate sex differences in research on anxiety and learning, as well as the possibility of interactions between the sex of subjects and experimenters.

The tentative findings in the two studies of the effects of anxiety on the complex learning that occurs in college courses revealed both the problems and the promise that are inherent in this type of research. The relatively unstructured nature of the learning situations, and the fact that the studies were carried out over a period of several months, made it difficult to evaluate the influence of anxiety on performance. However, the potential significance of this research was suggested by the tentative evidence that the effects of anxiety on performance in real-life learning situations may be similar to what has been found in the laboratory.

References

Atkinson, J. W. *An introduction to motivation.* Princeton, N. J.: Von Nostrand, 1964.

Burkman, E. Development and education of a coordinated science curriculum for grade seven through nine. Technical Progress Report, 1970, Contract No. OEC-2-6-061762-1745, Office of Education. (Period covered by report, March 1, 1970 through May 31, 1970.)

Cattell, R. B., & Scheier, I. H. *Handbook for the IPAT anxiety scale.* (2nd ed.) Champaign, Ill.: Institute for Personality and Ability Testing, 1963.

Chapeau, P. L. Test anxiety and feedback in programmed instruction. *Journal of Educational Psychology,* 1968, **59**, 159–163.

Gallagher, P. D. An investigation of instructional treatments and learner characteristics in a computer-managed course. Technical Report No. 12, 1970, Computer-Assisted Instruction Center, Florida State University.

Gregg, D. E. The regulation of pressure and flow in systemic and pulmonary circulation. In C. H. Best & N. B. Taylor (Eds.), *The physiological basis of medical practice.* Baltimore: Williams & Williams, 1961.

Groen, G., & Atkinson, R. C. Models for optimizing the learning process. *Psychological Bulletin,* 1966, **66**, 309–320.

Hansen, D. N., Dick, W., & Lippert, H. T. Research and implementation of collegiate instruction of physics via computer-assisted instruction. Technical Report No. 3, 1968, Computer-Assisted Instruction Center, Florida State University.

Hodges, W. F. The effects of success, failure and threat of shock on physiological and phenomenological indices of state anxiety. Unpublished doctoral dissertation, Vanderbilt University, 1967.

Hodges, W. F. Effects of ego threat and threat of pain on state anxiety. *Journal of Personality and Social Psychology,* 1968, **8**, 364–372.

Hodges, W. F., & Spielberger, C. D. The effects of threat of shock on heart rate for subjects who differ in manifest anxiety and fear of shock. *Psychophysiology,* 1966, **2**, 287–294.

Hull, C. L. *Principles of behavior.* New York: Appleton, 1943.

Katahn, M., & Lyda, L. L. Anxiety in the learning of response varying in initial rank in the response hierarchy. *Journal of Personality,* 1966, **34**, 287–299.

Kight, H. R., & Sassenrath, J. M. Relationship of achievement motivation and test anxiety to performance in programmed instruction. *Journal of Educational Psychology,* 1966, **14**, 185–191.

Lamb, D. H. The effects of public speaking on self-report, physiological, and behavioral measures of anxiety. Unpublished doctoral dissertation, Florida State University, 1969.

Mandler, G., & Sarason, S. B. A study of anxiety and learning. *Journal of Abnormal and Social Psychology,* 1952, **47**, 166–173.

McAdoo, W. G. The effects of success, mild failure feedback on A-State for subjects who differ in A-Trait. Unpublished doctoral dissertation, Florida State University, 1969.

Nicholson, W. M. The influence of anxiety upon learning: Interference or drive increment? *Journal of Personality,* 1958, **26**, 303–319.

O'Neil, H. F. Effects of stress on state anxiety and performance in computer-assisted learning. Unpublished doctoral dissertation, Florida State University, 1969.

O'Neil, H. F., Hansen, D. N., & Spielberger, C. D. The effects of state and trait anxiety on computer-assisted learning. Paper presented at the meeting of the American Educational Research Association, Los Angeles, 1969. (a)

O'Neil, H. F., Spielberger, C. D., & Hansen, D. N. The effects of state-anxiety and task difficulty on computer-assisted learning. *Journal of Educational Psychology,* 1969, **60**, 343–350. (b)

O'Reilly, R. P., & Ripple, R. E. The contribution of anxiety, creativity and intelligence to achievement with programmed instruction. Paper presented at the meeting of the American Education Research Association, New York, 1967.

Sarason, I. G. Empirical findings and theoretical problems in the use of anxiety scales. *Psychological Bulletin,* 1960, **57**, 403–415.

Sarason, S. B., Davidson, K. S., Lighthall, F. F., Waite, R. R., & Ruebush, B. K. *Anxiety in elementary school children.* New York: Wiley, 1960.

Spence, J. T., & Spence, K. W. The motivational components of manifest anxiety: Drive and drive stimuli. In C. D. Spielberger (Ed.), *Anxiety and behavior.* New York: Academic Press, 1966. Pp. 291–326.

Spence, K. W. A theory of emotionally based drive (D) and its relation to performance in simple learning situations. *American Psychologist,* 1958, **13**, 131–141.

Spence, K. W. Anxiety (drive) level and performance in eyelid conditioning. *Psychological Bulletin,* 1964, **61**, 129–139.

Spielberger, C. D. The effects of anxiety on complex learning and academic achievement. In C. D. Spielberger (Ed.), *Anxiety and behavior.* New York: Academic Press, 1966. Pp. 361–398. (a)

Spielberger, C. D. Theory and research on anxiety. In C. D. Spielberger (Ed.), *Anxiety and behavior.* New York: Academic Press, 1966. Pp. 3–20. (b)

148   C. D. SPIELBERGER, H. F. O'NEIL, JR., AND D. N. HANSEN

Spielberger, C. D., & Gorsuch, R. L. The development of the state-trait anxiety inventory. In C. D. Spielberger & R. L. Gorsuch, Mediating processes in verbal conditioning. Final Report, 1966, Grants MH 7229, MH 7446, & HD 947, National Institutes of Health, U. S. Public Health Service.

Spielberger, C. D., Gorsuch, R. L., & Lushene, R. E. *The state-trait anxiety inventory (test manual)*. Palo Alto, Calif.: Consulting Psychologists Press, 1970.

Spielberger, C. D. Anxiety as an emotional state. In C. D. Spielberger (Ed.), *Anxiety: Current Trends in Theory and Research*. New York: Academic Press, 1972.

Spielberger, C. D., & Smith, L. H. Anxiety (drive), stress, and serial-position effects in serial-verbal learning. *Journal of Experimental Psychology*, 1966, **72**, 589–595.

Suppes, P. Problems of optimization in the learning of a simple list of items. In M. Shelly & G. Bryan (Eds.), *Human judgements and optimality*. New York: Wiley, 1964.

Taylor, D. A., Wheeler, L., & Altman, I. Stress reactions in socially isolated groups. *Journal of Personality and Social Psychology*, 1968, 9, 369–376.

Taylor, J. A. A personality scale of manifest anxiety. *Journal of Abnormal and Social Psychology*, 1953, 48, 285–290.

Taylor, J. A. Drive theory and manifest anxiety. *Psychological Bulletin*, 1956, **53**, 303–320.

Tobias, S., & Williamson, J. Anxiety and response to programmed instruction. Paper presented at the meeting of the American Education Research Association, CElcago, Feb., 1968.

THE EFFECTS OF REINFORCEMENT PROCEDURES UPON SCHIZOPHRENIC PATIENTS: A SURVEY OF THE DATA[1]

Donald R. Stieper, Edward M. Ells, Erwin Farkas,[2] and Arline Caplan

VETERANS ADMINISTRATION, ST. PAUL, MINNESOTA

[1] The authors wish gratefully to acknowledge the contributions of the following people: Dr. David H. Kaplan, Chief, Outpatient Service, for his help in procuring Veterans Administration research funds for the conducting of the study; Dr. Daniel W. Ferguson, Chief, Mental Hygiene Clinic, for his help and encouragement in the initial stages of the study and for his continuing interest throughout the progress of it; Dr. Norman Garmezy, University of Minnesota, for his counsel and guidance; Dr. Naomi Quevillon, Mr. William Percy, Mrs. Sara Page, Dr. John Steinhelber, Miss Florence Christopher, and Miss Elvira Butler for their ideas and help at various stages of the project; and Mrs. Sharon Gorton and Miss Patricia Schaff for their help in typing and reproducing the manuscript.

The opinions and conclusions are those of the authors and not necessarily those of the Veterans Administration.

[2] Present address: Rochester State Hospital, Rochester, Minnesota.

149

150 DONALD R. STIEPER ET AL.

I. Introduction

A. RATIONALE

Learning is a psychological process in terms of which many of the clinical symptoms of schizophrenia might, perhaps, be understood. If the schizophrenic learns differently from the nonschizophrenic (or if the parameters of his basic biological learning capacities differ) this might explain the origins of some of his strange associations, his unusual discriminations, his failures to respond to relevant stimuli, his strange value systems, and his bizarre ideas.

Specifically, we wanted to know what kinds of variables enhance learning and performance in schizophrenic subjects, and what kinds of manipulations or devices have proven useful in such enhancement. The literature, however, is a source of discouragement. The findings have been a baffling jumble of contradictory outcomes, dead-end hypotheses, with many different learning tasks assessed under an infinite variety of conditions. Rather than providing a research foundation on which to build subsequent work, the literature on schizophrenic learning generally leads the reader to frustration and bewilderment. Even the literature reviews have provided little other than summaries of summaries; they have offered few directions in which the new researcher could expand the work with any degree of confidence that he was laboring on a meaningful variable.

At this point, the writers decided to attempt an analytic as well as a systematic literature review of the research on schizophrenic learning. But rather than simply collate findings from studies investigating a common area, we wished to construct an analysis that could conceivably compare studies, step by step and variable by variable, to see why they led so frequently to disparate and confusing findings.

B. SCOPE OF THE PROBLEM

Because of the vastness of the literature dealing with schizophrenic learning variables and the number of journals reporting studies in that area, the field of investigation was limited to that of reinforcement procedures with schizophrenic patients—the largest single segment of the literature. It was found that from the years 1949 to 1966, in excess of 150 experimental studies had been completed, many of them doctoral dissertations. Seventy-nine percent of this group was from the 1960 to 1966 period—the heyday of research on reinforcement procedures with schizophrenics.

These were studies of major proportions, some of them using hundreds of subjects. In addition, there were numerous smaller studies with tiny Ns and modest goals which appeared in textbook footnotes and in "brief reports" sections of journals.

In reviewing these studies, a striking lack of uniformity in both actual procedures and in the reporting of procedures becomes immediately apparent. There is also a disturbing inconsistency in the substantive findings. The differing procedures might constitute a source of crucial variables that are usually uncontrolled and unrecognized. As illustrations of how these sources of uncontrolled variability operate, consider two studies concerned with the same problem—the effects of social reinforcement on schizophrenic behavior. The variable expressly manipulated is identical for both studies, and the samples are comparable on the obvious demographic variables: age, intellectual range, educational level, etc. Yet they might differ in the following ways: (1) In one study, the majority of subjects are receiving tranquilizing medication, in the other they are not; (2) one study uses a motor task, the other a verbal task; (3) in one study, the subject is sent to the experimental room by an aide, in the other the experimenter goes to get subject and chats with him on the way.

Our basic premise was that this lack of uniformity in procedures was directly related to the discrepancies in results of studies dealing with similar problems.

C. Procedure

The present study consists of a systematic comparative analysis of 84 studies, 55 of which were microfilmed doctoral dissertations. Eighty-four studies constitute a 56% sample of pertinent *experimental* research from 1949 to 1966. The selection of the 84 sample studies was not random. All the available doctoral dissertations were used plus those studies that appeared in journals that were possible for us to locate. In all, the 84 studies contained 90 separate experiments.

Each study was compared on 448 variables, divided into 72 major categories of information. The 448 items were described as clearly as possible in a manual, to which each of our research analysts had access. (See copy of the manual in the Appendix.) The 72 major categories were in turn grouped into eight large sections, each constituting a segment of data about the study:

I. *Characteristics of the schizophrenic sample group,* kinds of information reported in restricting sample, symptoms, premorbidity, chronicity, stage of remission, source of diagnosis, drug status.

II. *Characteristics of the experimenter(s),* such as sex, status, familiarity with the hypotheses, the experimenter's personality, etc.

III. *Characteristics of the nonschizophrenic comparison group(s),* similar to I above.

IV. *Situational variables,* covering such items as rewards for the subject's participation in study, antecedent contact with the subject, purpose of contact with the subject, social setting of the experiment, etc.

V. *Experimental task stimuli,* focusing on methods of presentation, control of rate of presentation, sense modality stimulated, nature of stimulus materials, "humanness" of materials, meaningfulness, affective tone, etc.

VI. *Task instructions,* referring to motivational instructions, instructions concerning correct response, nature of task assignment, mode of response, etc.

VII. *Acquisition and related areas,* identifying such features as classical conditioning, instrumental conditioning with explicit or implicit reinforcement, method of presentation of reinforcement or punishment, type of behavioral manipulation, reinforcement or punishment schedules, extinction schedules, affective tone of reinforced responses, etc.

VIII. *Dependent variables,* or response measures, generalization measures, such as "number of trials to criterion," "number of errors," etc.

Each experiment was coded in all eight sections, on all 448 items by two research analysts. Where the two analysts disagreed on coding, a third analyst was brought in to settle the dispute. The data on each study were then keypunched on data cards.

The Royal-McBee KeyDex system was used as the rapid-data-retrieval method for handling these data. The Royal-McBee system consists of a card-file system, a key punch, and a viewer.

Each of the 448 items was allotted a separate card; e.g., Card 001 Male, Card 002 Female. Each card had space for punching in as many as 10,000 entries. The entries were studies in this project. Each study was assigned a coordinate number that determined its location on all 448 cards. It was possible to identify quicky, by stacking cards on the viewer, all the studies which used a particular combination of variables.

Another set of KeyDex cards was used to code the outcomes of the studies in the manner described in Section II,A below.

Essentially two kinds of data were separated out of this body of information: first, frequency data, which is presented in terms of percentages of experiments reporting use of each variable included in our coding manual. The second kind of data results from sifting out those items that appeared to enhance learning and/or performance.

The following sections follow the general outline of the coding manual, and in each section the data will be broken down into the following subsections: Introduction, Frequency Data, Major Findings, Minor Trends, and Discussion. The Appendix will present some general comments on literature reviews and a how-to-do-it "manual," dedicated principally to the neophyte researcher who has the courage to attempt an experiment in this area.

II. Overall Outcomes

A. Introduction

Since the entire sample of 84 studies was involved with reinforcement practices with schizophrenic patients, essentially four different kinds of treatment modalities (cf. Skinner, 1959) were used:

Positive Reinforcement or reward refers to stimuli which increase the strength of the preceding response.

Punishment refers to the presentation of aversive stimuli or the removal of positive reinforcers following a definable response or series of responses.

Negative Reinforcement refers to stimuli which, when removed, increase the strength of the preceding response.

The fourth treatment modality, *Mixed Type,* represents any combination of the above three in a *unitary treatment condition,* but is most commonly a combination of reward and punishment following correct and incorrect responses, respectively.

These four types of manipulations will be referred to henceforth as "treatments." The remainder of this section will describe the system for the coding of treatment effects, a comparison of the overall treatment effects, and a summary of the ways in which coding manual items were related to treatment effects.

B. The Relationship between Outcomes and Treatments

Treatment effects will hereafter be referred to simply as "outcomes." The coding of the outcomes was done in the following manner:

An outcome was coded as *plus* if the treatment had an enhancing effect on learning and/or performance. It was coded *zero* if the treatment had no effect on learning and/or performance. An outcome was coded *minus* if the treatment had an impairing effect on learning and/or performance. And it was coded *cannot say* if the treatment had an indeterminable effect on learning and/or performance. In order to be coded *plus* or *minus,* the outcome had to be significant at the conventionally accepted 5% level of confidence (or better) as reported by the author(s). *Zero* coding reflects the outcome's failure to reach the 5% level of significance.

The *cannot say* coding was resorted to under two conditions: (1) when there was neither a baseline nor an independent control group with which to compare the effects of the treatment; and (2) where no statistical analysis was done, or where the analysis performed was too confusing to interpret.

Outcomes were coded for each experimental subgroup rather than for each study. This procedure yielded somewhat more than twice as many outcomes (207) as there were studies (84). Outcomes of studies cannot be coded because studies often have multiple and differing outcomes. Outcomes were also coded separately for interactions between independent variables and for "multiple outcomes" (where several dependent variables yielded differing outcomes).

Following this procedure, the analysis yielded 108 outcomes for positive reinforcement, 75 for punishment, 11 for negative reinforcement, and 13 for "mixed type" treatments. Table I summarizes the four treatments broken down by the four possible outcomes for schizophrenics. The numbers in parentheses are percentages within treatments.

It may be seen from Table I that, for positive reinforcement and punishment, the outcomes are rather evenly divided between enhancing and nonenhancing effects of treatment. Or, using somewhat different terminology, it appears that the number of positive and negative findings are about equal with these two treatments in this sample of studies; in any case, the differences are *not* statistically significant.

Using negative reinforcement as the treatment, enhancement appears more likely than no-enhancement, although the number of outcomes is rather small here. With "mixed type" treatment, the *cannot say* outcomes predominate.

Outcomes were also coded for "normal" samples in those studies which used a "normal comparison group." Table II provides a summary of "outcomes by treatments" for the normal samples. The total number of studies involved here is 42.

A comparison of Tables I and II indicates that the distribution of overall outcomes for schizophrenics and normals is not too dissimilar. One difference that may be noted is the reversal of the proportions of *plus* and *zero* outcomes for the first three treatments (excepting mixed type). For *positive* reinforcement there is a weak trend ($\chi^2 = 2.37$,   df = 1, $p < .20$) for schizophrenics and normals to differ, with schizophrenics showing more *zero* outcomes and normals showing more *plus* outcomes. However, the effect of *punishment* on learning and/or performance is not signifi-

TABLE I

SUMMARY OF OUTCOMES ACROSS TREATMENTS, BROKEN DOWN BY FREQUENCIES AND PERCENTAGES, FOR SCHIZOPHRENIC SUBJECTS

Treatments	Outcomes				
	Plus (+)	Zero (0)	Minus (−)	Cannot say	Totals
Positive	40 (37%)	47 (44%)	3 (3%)	18 (16%)	108 (100%)
Punishment	31 (41%)	26 (35%)	7 (9%)	11 (15%)	75 (100%)
Negative	9 (82%)	2 (18%)	0 (0%)	0 (0%)	11 (100%)
Mixed type	3 (23%)	0 (0%)	1 (8%)	9 (69%)	13 (100%)

TABLE II
SUMMARY OF OUTCOMES ACROSS TREATMENTS, BROKEN DOWN BY FREQUENCIES
AND PERCENTAGES, ON COMPARISON GROUPS EMPLOYING "NORMAL"
SUBJECTS

	Outcomes				
Treatments	Plus (+)	Zero (0)	Minus (−)	Cannot say	Total
Positive	16 (44%)	10 (28%)	0 (0%)	10 (28%)	36 (100%)
Punishment	9 (32%)	10 (36%)	1 (4%)	8 (28%)	28 (100%)
Negative	1 (14%)	5 (72%)	1 (14%)	0 (0%)	7 (100%)
Mixed type	3 (30%)	0 (0%)	0 (0%)	7 (70%)	10 (100%)

cantly different ($\chi^2 = .07$, $p > .70$) for normals and schizophrenics in this sample of outcomes.

With *negative reinforcement* as the treatment modality, it can be seen that schizophrenics obtain more *plus* outcomes and normals more *zero* outcomes (Fisher's exact probability test, $p < .05$). It may be instructive to point out certain facts regarding the generality of this finding. First, six of the eight studies employing negative reinforcement used "white noise" as the aversive stimulus. Secondly, what generally tends to happen in these studies is that the response-contingent termination of the aversive stimulation *improves* the schizophrenics' performance, but not the normals', in a situation where the normals are outperforming the schizophrenics *without* the aversive stimulation. The usual explanation for this phenomenon is that normal subjects perform at an optimum level without any special stimulation, while schizophrenic subjects—presumed by many to have a general motivational defect—require special stimulation to bring their performances up to a more adequate level.

C. THE RELATIONSHIP BETWEEN INDIVIDUAL ITEMS
AND OUTCOMES

As an additional step in handling the data of this survey, each of the 448 coding manual items was observed in relation to the outcomes of learning and/or performance under positive reinforcement and punishment treatments. The number of experiments employing negative reinforcement (eight) was far too small for this kind of analysis, and the number of indeterminate outcomes (69%) in studies using "mixed type" treatments made it impractical to compare items with outcomes. The little data available for discussing an items-outcomes analysis with these two treatment modalities will be reserved for the section on Acquisition and Related Areas (Section IX).

In considering the outcome data for positive reinforcement and punishment, the *zero* and *minus* outcomes were combined and treated as a unitary outcome category in order to increase the number of cases per cell. The justification for such combining is the assumption of a continuum of treatment effect from "enhancing" to "impairing." *Cannot say* outcomes were ignored for the purpose of this analysis.

Table III is an abstraction from Table I, showing the collapsed categories on just the two treatment modalities—positive reinforcement and punishment.

The data retrieval system described above permitted obtaining counts of outcomes for each individual item or for any combination of items simply and expeditiously. Thus, the outcome split for the group of studies using a particular item (or combination of items) could be easily obtained. A simple check could then be made to see if the item split differed significantly from the "overall split" shown in Table III. The direction of the difference would indicate whether the item was contributing more to *plus* or more to *zero* outcomes.

As might be expected, some items were used by all studies in the sample, and some were used by none. If an item was used in 100% of the studies (or close to it), the outcome split on that item would be identical (or nearly so) to the overall split, and a deviation from the overall split would therefore not be possible. On the other hand, items which were never or rarely used could not be tested for deviation from the overall split. A minimum of five outcomes was used as the cutoff point for doing a statistical test on any particular item.

The null hypothesis tested was that the proportion of *plus* (or *zero*) outcomes for any subgroup of studies (those employing a particular item or combination of items) did not differ from the "population" of *plus* (or *zero*) outcomes in Table III.

With respect to the statistical procedure, it may also be pointed out that

TABLE III

SUMMARY OF POSITIVE REINFORCEMENT AND PUNISHMENT ACROSS OUTCOMES, BROKEN DOWN BY FREQUENCIES AND PERCENTAGES, FOR SCHIZOPHRENIC SUBJECTS

(Abstract of Table I)

	Outcomes		
Treatments	Plus (+)	Zero (0) (combined − & 0 outcomes)	Total
Positive	40 (44%)	50 (56%)	90 (100%)
Punishment	31 (48%)	33 (52%)	64 (100%)

the tests used were two-tailed, and that for items with a total number of outcomes less than ten (less than ten but greater than or equal to five), the *maximum* significance level used was .10 (even though the actual test may have resulted in greater significance).

A tabular summary of the items-outcome analysis is contained in the Appendix.

III. Characteristics of the Schizophrenic Sample Group

A. INTRODUCTION

Drawing an adequate (representative) sample is very important in production of useful research. The most ingenious and elegantly tight design can be rendered meaningless when the sample is badly drawn or poorly described. Bias in the sample then is unmeasured, unaccounted for, and—in many cases—undetected.

Famous in the history of "biased samples" is the case of the *Literary Digest* (LD) (Schor, 1968), a flourishing American periodical which placed its reputations (both soothsaying and financial) on the line in predicting the outcome of the 1936 presidential election. Their sample was drawn from people who owned telephones and/or cars, and in those days of the Depression and economic calamity, only the upper socioeconomic groups could afford telephones and cars. Consequently, the major findings (the basis of LD's predictions) were founded on a biased group—not a true representation of the voting population. And the magazine's predictions ended in disaster for the publication.

Not all biased samples lead to such dramatic consequences. Most biased samples come to the attention of only a few specialists who find them mouldering away in old periodicals. But the issue is the same—the research can be rendered meaningless by the drawing of a bad (nonrepresentative) sample.

This is generally true in the area of research on human behavior. It is particularly true in the research on schizophrenia, where the defining characteristics of "schizophrenia" itself are neither clear-cut nor well agreed upon. There is a wide range of disorders—with all kinds of genetic, social-learning and socioeconomic etiologic threads—that have been called forms of schizophrenia. Most researchers take the easy way out and define a patient as schizophrenic if the diagnosing psychiatrist(s) has diagnosed the patient "schizophrenic." Thus, for the time being, the problem is solved—or compounded.

But even if we can assume or pretend to assume—in a flight of fancy—that the parameters of schizophrenia are well defined and the diagnosis of the disorder is reasonably reliable, is the problem solved? Apparently, it is not. Most research projects require the cooperation of its subjects; are cooperating schizophrenics different from noncooperating schizophrenics? Most researchers confine themselves to one hospital or facility; is the schizophrenic population of one hospital representative of the schizophrenic population at large? The Veterans Administration, in their classic cooperative studies on psychotropic drugs (Veterans Administration, 1970), has partially handled this problem by drawing samples from many (up to 37) different hospitals in many localities. But are schizophrenic patients who are veterans different from nonveteran schizophrenics?

And even if we procured a representative sample of American schizophrenics, can we then say that all schizophrenics—anywhere in the world—are represented in the research? Lorr and Klett's (1969) work on psychotic prototypes suggests that there are national differences—even among nations that are highly "Westernized."

Following are some paragraphs which attempt to describe what researchers have actually done in the drawing and description of schizophrenic samples—where the purpose of the research was to ascertain something definitive about the effects of reinforcement practices upon schizophrenics' learning.

B. FREQUENCY DATA

Of foremost importance is the source of the diagnosis, "schizophrenia." As mentioned above, most investigators (57% of our sample) took at face value the hospital chart diagnosis which is presumably made or confirmed by the patient's current psychiatrist, probably in collaboration with his staff. None of the sample relied solely upon psychometric instruments; 1% used judges' opinions; and only 1% used a combination of two or more of the above three ways of arriving at a diagnosis. A deplorably high 41% of the experimental reports gave no information on the source of the diagnosis.

It might be of some value to list those demographic variables most frequently considered by researchers to be of importance in sample description. These are: age range of sample (98%), length of hospitalization (79%), absence of neurological disorder (68%), and educational level (66%). Probably the most easily determined of the demographic variables is "sex of subject." Yet 8% failed to describe the sex of their samples. Male subjects were much more frequent (79%) than females (6%). Males and females in the same group comprised 4%, and "sex of subjects" was used as an independent variable in 3% of the experiments.

In a collection of learning experiments, one would assume that the intellectual level of the subjects would be of some important descriptive value. Yet, only 29% provided information on the variable of "intelligence" as measured by some psychometric instrument.

Concerning other demographic variables, absence of recent shock treatment (ECT) was reported in 30%. (Unfortunately, this does not mean that the subjects in the remaining 70% were undergoing or had undergone ECT.) Eighty-four percent listed "other restricting characteristics" of their samples—which varied from study to study: items such as marital status, mental deficiency, alcoholism, absence of psychotherapy, etc.

Although psychotropic drugs (principally chlorpromazine and its simulators) have been widely used in the treatment of schizophrenia since 1954, 66% of the experiments provided no information on their subjects' current drug status. This may be an important variable, for Vestre (1965) found that phenothiazines reduced the effectiveness of verbal reward with his sample of chronic schizophrenics. When it is recalled that the vast majority of studies were conducted following 1960 (6 years after the introduction of the antipsychotic medications), the omission of information on drug status becomes even more glaring. In 15% of the experiments, subjects "on and off" drugs were lumped together indiscriminately, further clouding the issue in this group of experiments.

Despite increasing evidence of the diversity of disorders lumped under the "schizophrenic" rubric, researchers often appear oblivious to this possible source of variation. Bleuler (1911, 1950) listed four classical "subtypes," distinguishable descriptively, which are still a part of the psychiatric nomenclature. In addition to his four (simple, paranoid, catatonic, hebephrenic), six other subtypes have been added in the Second Edition of the American Psychiatric Association's (1968) Diagnostic Manual. Controversy has, of course, raged over whether or not these distinctions are more apparent than real, but their retention in diagnostic procedure and literature means that they still have some value to the psychiatric community.

Researchers give short shrift to this clinical hairsplitting—if that is what it is. Sixty percent of our sample of experiments had subject groups made up of mixed types of schizophrenia, without any information about the frequency of subtypes within their groups. Another 30% also used subject groups of mixed schizophrenics, but did give information about the frequency of subtypes in their samples. The remaining 10% made some attempt either to confine their samples to one or two subtypes of schizophrenia or used subtypes as one of their independent variables.

More recent in the discussions of subtyping in schizophrenia has been the introduction of several empirically derived "dichotomies." In addition to the more ancient concept of acute–chronic, more recent entries have been: good premorbid–poor premorbid; reactive–process; and paranoid–nonparanoid.

With regard to the first of these variables, acute–chronic, there was no information on the chronicity of samples in 16% of the experiments. "Mixed groups" of acute and chronic schizophrenics were used in another 22%. There was great lack of uniformity in the criteria for defining chronicity and acuteness. Length of time in the hospital was the most commonly used criterion for chronicity (51%). Length of hospitalization was supplied in 79%. Seven percent used both "number of hospitalizations" and "length of time in hospital" as criteria. "Number of hospitalizations" was never used as the sole criterion, but 19% included information on this item. Twelve percent simply described their samples as either "chronic" or "acute" without listing specific criteria.

The "acute–chronic" breakdown appears to have many elements in common with two other empirically derived "dichotomies": reactive–process and good–poor premorbid history. It is conceivable that these three dimensions may some day be reduced to a single way of characterizing schizophrenic patients in terms of their background history and the course of their illnesses. The most commonly used prognostic scale was published by Phillips (1953) and is frequently employed when one of the "dichotomous" types is used as the independent variable. Studies are abundant which demonstrate that marked functional differences appear when subjects are so classified.

Yet in the group of studies analyzed, where these "dichotomous subtypes" were not directly under investigation, these data were largely, if not completely, ignored. Eighty-eight percent gave no information on good or poor premorbid history, and 94% had no information on the process–reactive dichotomy.

It might be of value to note here that—even had some of the studies made use of these empirically derived ways of classifying schizophrenic patients—they may well have fallen into a semantic trap (leading to a conceptual trap, culminating in a false conclusion) relative to the "dichotomous" nature of these variables. Acute–chronic, good premorbid–poor premorbid, and reactive–process breakdowns do not refer to homogenous, bipolar batches of patients. All three of these breakdowns are based on a series of continuous variables. In practice, the dimension is customarily broken down in three parts—reactive group, middle group, process group, for example. The two extreme groups are studied, and the middle one is ignored. Many conclusions derived from these kinds of data (for example, that process schizophrenia is inherited while reactive schizophrenia is not) are based on the false belief that reactive–process is a dichotomous, rather than a continuous, variable.

Nevertheless, using this dimensional approach to the study of schizophrenia has yielded some useful information—in the areas of conditionability and rate of responding and learning, as well as treatability and prognosis (see Buss, 1966). Not accounting for these dimensional effects in experiments designed to assess reinforcement practices appears to be a glaring oversight.

The last of these empirically derived, dimensional variables is the paranoid–nonparanoid. Like the other dimensions described, it has a long history, dating back, in fact, to the time of Kraepelin (1909) who insisted that "paranoia" was clearly a separate type of psychosis, distinguishable in three major forms: paranoid schizophrenia, paranoid reaction (paraphrenia, paranoid state), and paranoia. On the other hand, Bleuler (1911) deemphasized the importance of the paranoid element itself, seeing schizophrenia as the overriding condition in which paranoia sometimes plays a small part.

Orgel (1957) found that it was possible to distinguish reliably between paranoid and other types of schizophrenia (interjudge reliability coefficient: .95) when using a detailed set of criteria. Buss (1966), in reviewing the literature on the paranoid–nonparanoid dimension, found that patients at the extreme ends of the continuum differed in a number of significant ways. "Rausch (1952) showed that paranoids manifested overconstancy compared to nonparanoids and normals on a task assessing size constancy. Similar findings were obtained by Hartman (1962) for size changes in afterimages. This kind of perceptual distortion—a failure to adjust to changes in stimuli and a rigid persistence in inappropriate perceptual responses—is precisely what we should expect from paranoids.

"Payne and Hewlett (1960) found that paranoids were less impaired than nonparanoid schizophrenics on several perceptual and conceptual tests. Johannsen, Friedman, Leitshuh, and Ammons (1963) reviewed experiments demonstrating the superiority of paranoids over nonparanoids on such diverse tasks as tapping speed, hand steadiness, Rorschach genetic level, *double alternation learning,* and *conditioning* [Buss, 1966, p. 230]." (Italics ours.) Buss's review suggests that paranoid patients are much more intellectually intact on a wide range of tasks, and it is hinted that prognosis for paranoids is better than for nonparanoids.

Additionally, the Johannsen *et al.* (1963) study showed that the paranoid–nonparanoid dimension was unrelated to the reactive–process and acute–chronic dimensions, but was just as meaningful a variable with relation to intellectual functioning. Yet, in spite of the demonstrated usefulness of the paranoid–nonparanoid dimension, and in spite of the fact that much of the work in empirically deriving it was done prior to the decade of the sixties, only 7% of the experiments in our sample used paranoid–nonparanoid patients in separate groups.

A final item of interest, somewhat related to the dimensions discussed above: The current stage of the patient's illness may be a crucial factor in any investigation of schizophrenic learning. However, 87% of the experiments provided no information on this item, 2% used patients in a moderate-to-good state of remission, 8% had samples of regressed patients, and separate groups of regressed and remitted patients were used in only 3% of the experiments.

C. Major Findings

Using the described procedures for identifying study outcomes and throwing all the "Characteristics of the schizophrenic sample group" items (see Black Code in Coding Manual, Appendix) against study outcomes as though the items were independent variables, there were no major findings ($p < .05$). This is to be expected, considering the highly variegated ways investigators have drawn and identified samples. One could anticipate that, had the subgroup breakdowns been made which were discussed in the previous sections, there might be corroborative evidence for some of the dimensional characteristics of schizophrenia as well as other features. There were some minor trends ($p < .20$) which will be discussed in the following section.

D. Minor Trends

Four "sample-related" items showed minor trends ($p < .20$) when positive reinforcement was used. Where an independent control group was used in the study, there was a tendency in the direction of more *zero* outcomes or "no findings" ($p < .10$). Since it is likely that the better designed studies employed independent control groups, it is ominous to note that performance was not enhanced by positive reinforcement under these circumstances. The failure to observe a trend toward *zero* outcomes under conditions of punishment using a control group might also indicate that learning in "schizophrenics in general" (SIG) is less enhanced by reward than by punishment. This is not particularly borne out by the other data, however (see Sections II and IX).

On the other hand, where a "regressed schizophrenic sample" was used, there tended to be positive results with the use of positive reinforcement ($p < .20$). Two other items, at least one of which may be the result of some capricious statistical fluke—Mixed schizophrenic samples *with* information about subdiagnoses—tended to be related to "no findings" ($p < .20$), while mixed schizophrenic samples *without* information about subdiagnoses tended to be related to positive findings ($p < .20$). These, too, were under treatment with positive reinforcement.

When punishment was used as the treatment, two "sample-related" items appeared marginally significant, duplicating what occurred under conditions of positive reinforcement. Where mixed schizophrenic samples *with* information about subdiagnoses were employed, there was a trend in the direction of "no findings" ($p < .10$), while the trend was in the direction of positive findings ($p < .20$) where mixed samples were used *without* information about subdiagnoses.

It must be borne in mind that the data relating items to outcomes is correlational and does not necessarily have causal implications. Furthermore, the multiple statistical tests with relaxed criteria for rejection of the null hypotheses make it likely that a number of these findings may be simply due to chance. One test of their validity—lacking cross validation —is their "hanging together" in some meaningful fashion, which they appear to do in this case.

Collating the data so far presented, one important trend appears obvious. When a study is better designed, when more care is taken in the construction of the study and the *description* of the sample (e.g., use of an independent control group, providing information about subdiagnoses even though mixed groups of schizophrenics are used), there is a strong likelihood that there will be no significant positive findings. The converse of this is implied: The sloppier the study, the more likely it will get positive findings. This occurs under both positive reinforcement and punishment (see Section XII,A for further discussion).

Finally, investigators identified 39 sample characteristics as independent variables (IVs) among the 90 experiments; our analysts identified four additional IVs which were going unaccounted for and unmeasured.

E. DISCUSSION

In the light of evidence so far presented and that to be presented in the following pages, it is no longer defensible to conduct a study on a group of subjects described simply as "schizophrenic." Aside from the fact that the reliability in diagnosing schizophrenia is perilously low (Schmidt & Fonda, 1956, found 51% interjudge agreement), there is simply too much evidence that schizophrenia involves a wide variety of dimensions, conditions, and phases. Other writers (e.g., Buss, 1966; Garmezy, 1964; Maher, 1966) have pointed this out before, so this is not a new insight. But it is one that bears repeating and repeating.

Schizophrenia does not exist as a unitary disorder. Schizophrenia exists as a wide variety of disorders which as a rule share something which is vaguely described as a "thinking disorder." Future research on "schizophrenia"—whether in the area of reinforcement practices or others, such as drugs, genetics, psychotherapy, etc.—*must* take into account that schizophrenia has some very important dimensional aspects. In addition, it varies over time. Essentially schizophrenia is a remitting-regressing disorder such that one patient may look quite different on two different occasions, especially in the "acute" phase when compared to the "chronic" phase.

Schizophrenia is further capable of being described factor-analytically (Lorr, Klett, & McNair, 1963), wherein several factors appear to take many different forms of interacting roles in disorders all of which have been called schizophrenia.

In the 90 experiments, the following groups of people were over-represented in the samples of schizophrenic subjects: men, veterans, hospitalized patients, schizophrenics on drugs (of unknown types), cooperative patients, chronic patients, long-term hospitalized patients. The findings from any study cannot exceed the limits of the sample.

Because of this lack of specificity in sample drawing (and the limitations described above), it has been necessary to coin a new term to refer to the subjects in our sample of studies. This unique group of people within the American population will be henceforth referred to as "schizophrenics in general" or SIG. It is conceivable that SIG does not refer to anything in the real world and may be the fanciful invention of researchers in schizophrenic research. The reader may judge for himself.

IV. Characteristics of the Experimenter(s)

A. INTRODUCTION

The experimenter, as the principal engineer of the research project, has a number of responsibilities. Usually he is the conceiver of the idea, the formulator of the hypotheses, and the constructor of the design. In practice, he is often also the drawer of the sample and the technician who carries out the experimental tasks. In addition, he may also be the statistician who works up the results and the discussant who describes them.

Rosenthal (1963) has published a series of articles on what may be termed "experimental bias." Even where elaborate controls are devised, often the experimenter's "bias" or "wish" creeps through to inadvertently contaminate the findings. This is especially true where the experimenter is his own technician—where he runs his own study.

Rosenthal has also shown that "knowledge of the hypothesis" on the part of the technician may play a part in "biasing" the findings—even when every human effort is made to retain objectivity.

The purpose of this section of the analysis was to isolate as many experimenter characteristics as possible that might be related to the outcomes of the studies. Two have been mentioned; there may be others.

In the analyses that follow, one assumption must be pointed out. Many of the studies employed were unpublished doctoral theses. Unless otherwise specified, it was assumed that the author was both the experimenter and the technician.

B. FREQUENCY DATA

The majority of investigators were psychologists who both conceived and ran their own studies. Sixty-one percent were male, 12% were female, and 22% went unidentified. In two of the experiments, sex of the experimenter was used as an independent variable, and in two others, both male and female experimenters were used, but the data was not analyzed separately. In the last four experiments, it is not clear whether the investigator himself worked as one of the technicians who administered the experimental task or if he used other people to provide this service.

Among the investigators, 72% were familiar with the hypotheses of the experiment, 2% were not familiar (presumably technicians employed to run the experiment), and no information was available on the remaining 26%.

In spite of the fact that there is some evidence that sex of the experimenter is an effective variable in giving praise and punishment to children (Stevenson, 1961) and even has some differential effects on the performance of normal adults in learning tasks (Stevenson & Allen, 1964), and that some types of people work better therapeutically with SIG than other therapists (Whitehorn & Betz, 1954), 98% of the experiments had no description of the experimenter's personality. In two experiments, the personality description of the experimenter was used as an independent variable.

Overall, investigators identified three independent variables involving experimenter characteristics, one less than identified by our study analysts.

C. MAJOR FINDINGS

There were no major findings in this category. Since the large majority of studies were run by experimenters who were familiar with the experimental hypotheses, it is not possible to replicate Rosenthal's (1963) findings. The difference in sex of investigators did not seem to be related to study outcomes, although male investigators were overrepresented. There is, however, a minor trend related to sex of the experimenter which will be discussed in the next section.

Since there are few instances where the study is run by somebody other than the chief experimenter, it is impossible to determine whether this variable may be important in avoiding experimenter bias. It may be worthwhile noting, however, that if Rosenthal's findings hold for most research, experimenter bias would be expected to play a large part in the experiments analyzed for this project since (1) most studies are run by the experimenters themselves, and (2) they are familiar with their own hypotheses.

D. Minor Trends

All of the minor trends appear in studies using positive reinforcement as the principal treatment modality. The minor trends fall into two classes: sex of the experimenter, and the experimenter's familiarity with the study hypotheses.

If the experimenter is male or if he is a psychologist, which is overwhelmingly the case in most instances, these variables are related to zero outcomes, significant at the .20 percent level of confidence. The item, "no information" on status or identity of the examiner, is related to positive outcome at the same level of confidence.

On the second set of items, the experimenter's knowledge of the study hypotheses is related to "no findings" on outcomes ($p < .10$). On the other hand, "no information about the experimenter's familiarity with hypotheses" is related to positive findings on the study outcomes ($p < .10$).

Combining these fragments of data with those from the preceding section, The theme continues to be borne out: The less precedural information reported, the more positive findings and the greater likelihood it is a published paper than an unpublished doctoral dissertation (see Section XII,A).

E. Discussion

The investigators in this sample of experiments paid little attention to the problems of the experimenter's role in research that have come up in recent years. The studies were so overwhelmingly "one-man shows" that it was impossible to investigate the possible sources of bias due to either knowledge of the hypotheses or to the running of the experiment by the experimenter himself.

More well-controlled experiments these days employ technicians, unfamiliar with the idea or hypotheses of the study but thoroughly versed in the procedures of the study, to carry out the actual collecting of data.

Finally, the personality, sex, and age ratio of the experimenter (relative to the subject) have been the sources of a great deal of speculation and some scattered research outside the area of schizophrenic learning. In a series of studies devoted to understanding the reinforcement effects on schizophrenia, these variables would seem to have some particularly pertinent relevance.

V. Characteristics of the Nonschizophrenic Comparison Group(s)

A. INTRODUCTION

In assessing the performance of schizophrenic patients on a particular learning task, one common research practice is to compare their performance with that of a nonschizophrenic comparison group. The comparison group may be made up of normal subjects, neurotic subjects, brain-damaged subjects, or any other identifiable, nonschizophrenic group.

The comparison group ordinarily undergoes the same experimental treatment regime as the schizophrenic group. This feature distinguishes the comparison group from the "control group" which is an *untreated* group. In the context of this series of studies, a control group would be an untreated group of schizophrenics who were being compared with another group of schizophrenics undergoing the experimental treatment.

The comparison group usually is (or should be) as similar to the schizophrenic group as possible so that the only relevant difference between the two groups would be the presence or absence of schizophrenia. Any other dissimilarity between the two groups would simply act as another independent variable that would have to be assessed in its own right. If the comparison group were younger than the schizophrenic group, or brighter, or came from a higher socioeconomic status, or was largely female while the schizophrenic group was largely male—all or any of these could operate to mitigate against direct comparison of the two groups.

B. FREQUENCY DATA

A comparison group was used in 49 (54%) of the experiments in this analysis. Normal subjects comprised 42 (79%) of the 53 comparison groups. Nineteen (45%) of the researchers screened their normal subjects for a history of any psychiatric disorder, and 2 (5%) screened just for a history of schizophrenia. But alas, no screening was done for schizophrenia or any other psychiatric disorder in *half* of the experiments using normal comparison groups.

Our impressions were that comparison groups were rather loosely drawn with no particular attention paid to careful matching. The failure to get information on psychiatric histories is one indication of the haphazardness of the procedures. Usually groups were matched on sex and, grossly, on age, but rarely on variables like socioeconomic level, intelligence, and educational level. Occasionally, the comparison groups were classes of college sophomores. Consequently, there is virtually nothing to report, either in the case of Major Findings or Minor Trends.

C. Discussion

The inadequacies of both this analysis and the ways in which comparison groups were drawn in the studies point to the conclusion that this is an area to which scant attention is paid. It is common practice to use, as a nonschizophrenic comparison group, volunteers from the ranks of the hospital orderlies or attendants. Orderlies differ from patients in many ways, a major one being that, they are not hospitalized, a condition which appears to make an important difference in rate of conditioning (Chambers, 1965). Also, they are usually not on drugs and lead lives which are probably much more stimulating than the SIG. A less commonly used comparison subject (and appropriately so) is the college sophomore (widely known for their usefulness in university research). They are usually younger and brighter (and better educated) than their schizophrenic counterparts, are not hospitalized, are not on drugs (at least not psychotropic drugs), and are living in a university atmosphere which is attuned to learning and on learning how to learn—which is in sharp contrast to the atmosphere of most large mental institutions.

VI. Situational Variables

A. Introduction

This category attempts to delineate the relevant aspects of the experimental situation in which the subject finds himself. How the idea of participation is broached to the schizophrenic patient, the amount of antecedent contact with the patient before beginning of the experiment proper, the nature of the experimental relationship, the subject's knowledge about the experimenter, the emotional tone of the experimental relationship—all these factors comprise some of the situational elements with which this section is concerned.

There is reason to believe that some of these variables act directly or interact indirectly to influence final results, and, to the extent that they do, contaminate the major findings.

B. Frequency Data

This section includes items particularly relevant to the motivation and subsequent task performance of schizophrenic subjects. However, the data indicate that frequently many of these variables are not analyzed or reported in the research reports. For example, there was inadequate information in 66% of the studies to determine how the investigators described the purpose of the contact to the subject. Was the subject told the contact was for "research," or was a diagnostic test to help the patient, or was a treatment to help the patient, or was it simply left up in the air—ambiguous and undefined? Only 34% of the experiments clearly indicated how the subject of participation was broached to the patients.

Although there were 25 (29%) of the experiments in which the subject was told that he was to participate in a research project, in 3 (11%) of these, there was no report of the subject's being told if the results would personally affect him.

In 87% of the experiments there was no report of a tangible reward offered to the subject for his participation in the experiment. It is apparent that these variables are consistently ignored or, at the very least, not controlled by most investigators.

The "social setting" of the experiment in 91% of the studies consisted of one experimenter—one patient, with social interaction (small talk) occurring during the experiment. However, the emotional tone of the social interaction was not identified in 82% of the studies.

In a closely related area, it would be helpful to know if the subject had any information pertaining to the experimenter's role and/or personality characteristics. Since there is evidence that SIG tend to avoid interpersonal relationships and may be somewhat fearful in an unfamiliar testing situation, these variables may influence his subsequent task performance. However, the subject was not given a description of the experimenter's personality in any of the studies, and in 83% there was no information on the subject's knowledge of the experimenter's role. It should be noticed that in 12% of the sample, there was no social interaction between the subject and the experimenter.

The part of the subject's motivation in the learning task or the experimenter's attempts to motivate the subject are rarely considered by investigators as a whole. In the learning task itself, as described in the next three sections, rewards and reinforcers are built into the experimental procedure, but there is little reported on how the study is described to the patient, how he is encouraged to participate, and what rewards he gets for his participation.

By count, investigators isolated 13 IVs in this category. Our study analysts, on the other hand, isolated a total of 30 IVs—a discrepancy of 17 IVs. Put another way, 57% of the identifiable variation is going unaccounted for in the area of situational variables.

C. MAJOR FINDINGS

There were no major findings in this category. Due to the faulty reporting in this area, it is virtually impossible to ascertain the effects of the coded situational variables on the final outcomes of studies. In this area, probably a good deal more went on than was formally reported (see paragraph above), but this activity was not seen by investigators as relevant to the final reporting of the study.

D. MINOR TRENDS

There was a scattering of minor trends ($.05 < p < .20$), but they were hampered by the small number of experiments involved. Where an asterisk appears, it indicates that the number of experiments involved is less than ten but either equal to or greater than five.

Two items appear worthy of note in considering the outcomes of positive reinforcement. Where antecedent contact was made with the subject (by the experimenter) to secure his participation in the procedure, and where there was no antecedent contact, both related to "no findings." Significance level was .10 for both items. Note that both these items require reporting by the experimenter on items which were rarely reported. This, again, would seem to indicate that the carefully reported studies are those which most frequently come up with zero outcomes.

When considering those outcomes associated with punishment practices, three items qualified as "minor trends," but all suffered from smallness of Ns.

Where the purpose of the contact was described to the subject as diagnostic testing, this item appeared related to "no findings" ($p < .10*$). Under the heading of the social setting of the experiment, the combination of "One Subject and No Experimenter" (the subject working with a machine or materials) appeared related to positive outcomes when punishment was used as the treatment modality ($p < .10*$). When the affective tone of the social interaction was neutral (not friendly and/or not hostile), this item appeared related to positive findings when punishment was used as the treatment modality ($p < .20*$).

The suggested direction of these last two items appears to be toward punishment being more effective in changing behavior when it is delivered in an impersonal or neutral (nonjudgmental) fashion. Section VIII will deal more in detail with the effects of punishment (*versus* reward) on reinforcement learning.

E. DISCUSSION

The findings of this category are, simply, that investigators do not report many items which are potentially significant in interpreting their findings, particularly as these relate to motivating the patient and assessing the setting in which the experiment takes place. The sparse available information suggests that there is ample reason to attend more carefully to situational variables surrounding the actual carrying out of the experiment and to report more fully and completely on the details of these variables. The discovery of 57% more unidentified independent variables alone attests to the "mushiness" of this aspect of research conduct and the great need for more compulsive studies among investigators. Only in one other area (reinforcement practices, Section IX) was an equal amount of uncontrolled variation discovered.

The few findings available in this category are limited by the smallness of the numbers of cases reporting information, and even there some trends appeared.

Certainly, in a task devoted to new learning, it is important to assess how the subject is induced to participate, what he is getting out of it (or thinks he is getting out of it), and the kind of setting in which it takes place. Most investigators found these details too trivial to report.

An important subset of situational variables, the relationship between the subject and the experimenter, will be discussed at greater length in Section XII,B,6 below.

VII. Experimental Task Stimuli

A. INTRODUCTION

This section of the review contains those elements of a study which make up the "structural" variables of the experiment. General classes of items in this section (which can be examined more in detail in the Appendix) are: number of tasks involved, method of presentation of the task or task materials, rate of presentation, specific sense modality stimulated, and nature and characteristics of the task stimuli themselves. This section does *not* include the form and nature of the instructions to the subject (which is the topic of the next section). Also, reinforcing stimuli are not analyzed in this section. These are more properly reviewed in Section IX, on Acquisition and Related Areas.

The "experimental task stimuli" generally differ greatly from one study to the next, which makes comparability of studies testing the same hypotheses difficult to assess. Since all of the items under consideration here have some direct relationship to the dependent variable (if not, they would be analyzed in some other section), these items have critical importance in their bearing on final outcomes of experiments. As will be described in subsequent paragraphs, variation in such elements as "rate of presentation" of the materials and the time limitations put on a task may have as important an impact on rate of learning, as does the specific treatment the subject is undergoing.

B. FREQUENCY DATA

A sheer "percentage count" gives some pictures of the wide diversity of structural elements rampant in this kind of research. At the simplest level, 80% of the experiments used a single experimental task, while two or more tasks were used in the remaining 20%. Both the method of presenting task stimuli and the *rate* of such presentation may be related to the subject's subsequent performance (see Minor Trends); a little more than half of the investigators (59%) used the "personal-instrumental mediation-*E* present" method of presentation. "Personal" in this context means that the experimenter plays a part in the presentation of the task stimuli beyond the initial trial. "Instrumental" refers to mediation of the task stimuli by anything other than the experimenter's person, e.g., cards, blocks, etc. The method of presentation used in 13% of the sample was "Personal-No Instrumental Mediation." The experimenter was not present during the actual tasks presentation in only 7% of the experiments.

The rate of presentation of the task stimuli can be controlled by either the experimenter or the subject (self-pacing). In 50% of the experiments, the experimenter did not limit the time for either a single item or a total task. In an additional 9%, self-pacing of single items was allowed. The experimenter did limit the time in a smaller percentage of the sample (47%). Time for the total task was limited in 19% of the experiments and for 28% time limitations were imposed on single items. The experimenter limited the time for both these variables in only three instances.

In 90% of the experiments the task stimulated the visual sense modality; auditory and tactual accounted for only 21% and 28% respectively. (It should be noted that percentages totaling more than 100% are a reflection of categories in which more than one item can be coded. Such percentages may also be due to the multiple tasks used in some experiments.)

In light of the above data on the visual sense modality, it is not surprising that in 59% of the experiments the experimental task stimuli consisted of graphic or written materials. A mechanic device was used in 43% of the experiments. Only 7% of the sample used no task material, e.g., free-operant conversation.

The remaining categories in this section reflect the various characteristics of the experimental task: Only 14% of the experiments used tasks involving human activity or content; tasks consisting of nonhuman activity or content were used in the majority of the experiments (51%), while a fairly large group (42%) was coded as "indistinguishable" or "mixed" with respect to the "humanness" of the task stimuli.

The sample was fairly evenly divided on the use of verbal *versus* non-

verbal tasks. A verbal task was used in 47% of the experiments, while
nonverbal tasks were used in 53%. Although task structure and content
may be particularly relevant to the problem of contradictory research outcomes, only 2% of the investigators used verbal *versus* nonverbal tasks
as an independent variable. It is noteworthy, also, that scarcely 4% of the
investigators considered human *versus* nonhuman content crucial enough
to be used as an independent variable. Along the same line, the nature of
the "affective tone" of the task stimuli was used as an independent variable
in only 4% of the experiments. Affective tone was reported or identified
in 7% of the studies, making this one of the "least relevant" areas from
the standpoint of the investigators.

In the total sample, 13 independent variables were identified as such
by investigators when considering experimental task variables only. Our
own analysts identified four more independent variables which went unnoticed by the investigators. Since they were unnoticed they, of course,
were not measured, so that it is not possible to directly assess their effects.

In this section, too, the dearth of information provided by the investigators magnifies the problem of comparing task performance of subjects
across studies. It is conceivable that, had more information been reported,
more "unidentified independent variables" could have been isolated.

C. MAJOR FINDINGS

In considering the relationship of items to outcomes, there was only one
"major finding." Under conditions of positive reinforcement, there was
an enhancing effect on learning when the experimenter limited the time
for the performance of the total task ($p < .05$). Considered in contrast
to a finding to be discussed in the next few paragraphs (Minor Trends),
namely that where the experimenter limited the time for a single trial there
tended to be a relationship to nonenhancement of learning ($p < .20$), the
following conclusion might bear subsequent testing in an experimental
situation: SIG appear to function better under conditions of "self-pacing,"
and they become less efficient when they are pressured, item by item or
step by step, to perform at a particular pace. However, they are beneficially
affected when some kind of time limit is placed on the total task. The
practical implications of this are that SIG will work best when left alone,
providing them with an overall time limit and not attempting to keep them
going every inch of the way. If allowed to pace themselves, they appear
to do a more nearly effective job.

D. MINOR TRENDS

Compared to other categories, there is in this category an abundance
of items related to outcomes if one considers marginal statistical significance

worthy of consideration. Many of these should be considered in the light of the finding previously discussed—the positive relationship between time-limiting total tasks and enhancement of learning under conditions of positive reinforcement. Other items which "tended" toward enhancement of learning under positive reinforcement were: (1) where the presentation of the task was personal (presented by the experimenter) without any type of mechanical mediation ($p < .20$); (2) where the sense modality stimulated was auditory ($p < .20$); and (3) where there were no "materials" (blocks, pictures, cards, etc.) used in the task itself ($p < .10*$).

Items related to nonenhancement of learning under positive reinforcement were: (1) where the experimenter limited the time for single trials ($p < .20$); (2) where there was insufficient information provided by the experimenter concerning time limitations (conceivably where no time limits are set); (3) where there was both human and nonhuman content (mixed) in the task materials ($p < .20$); and (4) where graphic or written materials were used in the task ($p < .20$).

When punishment was used as the treatment modality, the use of a single experimental task was positively related to enhancement of learning ($p < .20$), whereas the use of more than one task in the experiment (multiple tasks) was related to nonenhancement of learning ($p < .20$). Using punishment, two other items were related to *non*enhancement of learning: (1) where there was insufficient information about time limitations on trials or tasks (again, conceivably, where there were no time limits) ($p < .20$); and (2) where task stimuli were auditory rather than visual ($p < .20$).

E. Discussion

Where this many variables (items) appear to have some marginal relationship to outcomes, it is quite possible that some of them may be due to chance. In the absence of replication, as discussed previously, it is not possible to ascertain which are more real than apparent. However, where several "trends" hang together and seem to make a kind of thematic sense, they are at least worthwhile hypothesizing about.

From the data of this section, it would appear reasonable to theorize that SIG are most likely to perform effectively in a direct one-to-one personal relationship with the experimenter (at least, under conditions of positive reinforcement). Note that in the previous section, more positive outcomes appeared when the subject worked with a machine or materials under conditions of punishment unhampered by the use of task material (e.g., operant conditioning free conversation) and where the experimenter does not impose strict time limits on single trials, but allows the subject to pace himself—within a time limit for the total task. The task should be a single task rather than multiple tasks.

Under punishment treatments, similar findings obtain, with the additional finding that subjects did more poorly when the auditory sense modality was stimulated in the presentation of the task stimuli.

It has long been believed that SIG have some peculiar needs with relation to information gathering. There is a point here, relative to the minor trends described, that fits in with the "interference theory" of schizophrenia as expounded by David Shakow (1963), Silverman (1964), and others (see Buss, 1966). Interference theory states simply that SIG cannot adequately distinguish relevant from irrelevant cues, that he is so inundated with stimuli—both from within his own body via physiological responses from a chronically aroused autonomic nervous system and from without because he cannot distinguish what is important from what is unimportant—that he is in fact unable to decide what actions are appropriate to take or what decisions to make . . . let alone how to make them. Shakow (1962) has said: "He (the schizophrenic) has difficulty in focusing on the relevant aspects of the defined situation, while being more readily susceptible to the influence of the peripheral. He does not habituate readily . . ." Shakow has demonstrated that where a task is emphasized or pointed up to the schizophrenic—in other words, where his attention is dramatically focused on what is to be done—he performs much better. This perhaps is pointed up by the evidence in this section—where enhancement of learning is observed in single tasks, which are time limited, and which are mediated directly and personally by the examiner (at least in the case of reward learning).

On the other hand, Venables (1964) relates difficulty in focusing attention more to the acute (and possibly reactive and paranoid) schizophrenic, whereas the more chronic (and possibly process) schizophrenics ". . . tend to be characterized by a restriction of the attentional field resulting from elevated states of sympathetic and cortical activation [p. 41]." Once again we are reminded of the folly of contemplating schizophrenia as a single, homogeneous disorder.

VIII. Task Instructions

A. INTRODUCTION

An important element of the experiment—rarely employed as a manipulated or independent variable—are the instructions given the subjects prior to the experimental task. Actually, there are multiple facets to "task instructions," and this section attempts to identify and analyze some of the most salient ones.

Task instructions not only provide the information the subject needs to proceed with the experimental task, they also provide him with the appropriate set, help him focus on the relevant stimuli, and inform him how he is to respond. Identical tasks may be used by numerous investigators, but instructions may differ in regard to motivational set, identification of the correct response, etc., thus raising the question of the validity of referring to such tasks as truly "identical." Sometimes the nature of the task itself may be altered by a change in instructions.

Some of the grosser elements of task instructions are considered in this section. Ignored—largely because they are rarely if ever reported—are such potentially critical issues as: What is the affective tone of the task instructor, are instructions presented personally by the investigator—on tape—or are they read from a card or sheet of paper; does the investigator use identical words from subject to subject; has he memorized the instructions or does he read them from a card; does he demonstrate (behaviorally) any aspect of the task for the subject; what provisions has he made when subjects fail to understand the initial instructions; are instructions given in one lump or are they strewn throughout the experimental task; what provisions are made when the subject makes errors apparently stemming from failure to understand instructions; and others which will occur to the reader.

It is rare that investigators consider task instructions a sufficiently important part of the experimental task to include detailed information in their reports. In analyzing these variables in this section, certain elements of the instructions had to be deduced from the nature of the tasks themselves in many cases. The frequency data in the following paragraphs give a picture of the reporting relative to instructions.

B. Frequency Data

"Set Instructions," items 500 through 509 in the Manual (see Appendix), encompass those kinds of items in which the subject is told what to do, e.g., "work as fast as you can . . . ," "try to get the correct answer," etc. Seventeen percent of the experiments had no information on "set instructions" whatsoever. As might be expected, the most commonly used set instructions were for speed and/or accuracy, with instructions for speed accounting for 35% and instructions for accuracy accounting for 37% of the experiments. Instructions for *both* speed and accuracy were used in 12% of the experiments. The item, "S instructed to surpass his previous performance," shows some degree of overlap with all the variables coded in this category, and this instruction was used in seven of the nine experiments in which set instructions functioned as an independent variable.

Of these nine cases, investigators explicitly identified only three of them; our analysts discovered another six studies in which task instructions were being used as independent variables. Since so few of these instructional effects were measured, we would prefer not to speculate about their influence on learning.

In 72% of the experiments, the subject was told that there was a correct response, and in 48% of this group he was told what the correct response was. The subject was not told the correct response in the remainder of the samples. In another 30%, the subject purposely was not told anything about the correctness of the response as opposed to 2% in which the subject was informed that there were no right or wrong answers.

The next two categories are concerned with the information on reinforcement provided in the task instructions. In the majority of the sample (57%), the reinforcer was not identified to the subject, as compared to 46% in which the reinforcer was identified (e.g., "Green light means you are correct" or "I'll say 'not so good' sometimes"). However, in 11% of the experiments, not enough information was provided to determine whether the reinforcer was identified to the subject or not. Although extinction was employed in only 29% of the experiments, in 10% of this group there was again insufficient information to determine whether or not the subject was told about the cessation of the reinforcer.

The most salient feature of the category, "nature of the task assignment," is that no single item included many experiments. This is not surprising since the category was broken down into 43 items, making this the longest, most detailed category in the coding manual. Despite this, 31% of the tasks were coded as "other." An inspection of the nature of the task assignment in the experiments so coded revealed that 25% used tasks involving reaction times. Although the remainder did not differ radically from those coded on specific items in this category, the variation was great enough to account for their being coded as "other." The group of "other" responders included both verbal and nonverbal tasks.

When specific items were coded in this category, the experiments do not show a predominance of either verbal or nonverbal tasks. For example, in 13% of the experiments, the subject was told to make up a sentence, and in 7% the subject was given a paired-associate task. The subjects were told to perform a simple repetitive task (e.g., marble dropping) in 14%, and a complex repetitive task (e.g., double alternation) was used in another 14%.

The experimental task did involve the discovery of a rule in order to respond correctly in 44 (49%) of the experiments. The subject did not receive any instructions to discover a rule in 32 of these 44 instances, whereas in 12, such instructions were provided. Thus, it appears that tasks involving concept formation may differ significantly in the way the conceptual problem is presented to the subjects.

C. MAJOR FINDINGS

The principal finding which approached statistical significance was Item 522—"S not told of cessation of reinforcer." This item yielded more *plus* outcomes (enhancing learning) under both conditions of positive reinforcement and punishment. (Under positive reinforcement, the item/ outcome relationship was significant at greater than the .05% level of confidence; under punishment, the significance level was .10%, but the N was very small, less than 10.)

The studies included under this item actually represent all experiments using a regular extinction period, and what the finding means, therefore, is that studies using an extinction period are very likely to have first obtained some significant effect of the treatment (i.e., a conditioning effect).

D. MINOR TRENDS

Under conditions of positive reinforcement, plus outcomes were marginally related ($p < .20$) to the following items: The subject was specifically *not* given set instructions, the subject was purposely *not* told anything about the correctness or incorrectness of his responses, and where he was told to perform simple, repetitive tasks.

When the subject was told to do paired-associates, under conditions of positive reinforcement, this contingency resulted in a minor trend ($p < .10$) toward zero outcomes.

Under conditions of punishment, two items showed some relationship to *zero* outcomes. In both cases, tiny Ns (less than 10) were involved, and the significance level was .20 for both. There tended to be nonenhancement of learning (1) when the subject was instructed to surpass his previous performance, and/or (2) when the subject was told to identify or match stimuli.

E. DISCUSSION

What appears most obvious in these findings—and this phenomenon will be further borne out in the succeeding section—is that we are dealing with the interaction of two kinds of reinforcing processes. *Explicit reinforcement* has already been described; it involves the application of a rewarding or punishing stimulus by an external source usually contingent upon some response or series of responses made by the subject. *Implicit reinforcement* refers to those kinds of learning situations where knowledge of results is operative; in other words, the nature of the task is such that the subject learns immediately when he is making a right or wrong response from the task materials themselves.

Frequently, in these experiments, implicit and explicit reinforcement are employed with the same subject on the same task, e.g., paired-associate learning combined with conditioning. Experiments employing this combination of techniques tend to come up with more *zero* outcomes (nonenhancement of learning). This will be demonstrated more dramatically in the next section on Acquisition and Related Areas. The hypothesis arising from this trend suggests that, with the paired-associate learning task, knowledge of results is the most potent factor affecting learning, and that the explicit reinforcement has the effect of disrupting performance. Further evidence for this line of reasoning may be found in a paper by Goldman (1961) who found that explicit reinforcement (both verbal reward and verbal punishment) has an adverse effect on the paired-associate performance of schizophrenic subjects (SIG). In line with the other trends noted in this category, it may be indicative of an emerging general rule: That either explicit or implicit reinforcement can be effective in enhancing learning, but used simultaneously they have the effect of reducing performance. Even "set instructions," when used in an explicit reinforcement study, may have this effect, or motivational instructions (when he is told to surpass his previous performance). These may have the effect of setting up two guidelines to which the schizophrenic subject must attend: (1) the internal, implicit set and/or knowledge accrued through his own mentation; and (2) the information coming at him via the explicit reinforcement practices. Even when consistent, these two sources appear to hamper the subject.

These hypotheses are, again, consistent with the "interference theory" of schizophrenia (at least with relation to acute schizophrenics) which suggests that the patient becomes overwhelmed by too many stimuli and becomes unable to sort out the relevant from the irrelevant details. The minor finding, quoted in the previous paragraphs, that SIG are best able to learn where a simple, repetitive task is used (in contrast to complicated tasks) also bears out this point.

Also relevant to this point is the work done on the high frequency of mixed messages in schizophrenogenic families (Bateson, Jackson, Haley, & Weakland, 1956), where simultaneous messages may be inconsistent and contradictory. One hypothesis might be that SIG "learn" to be gun shy of complicated information input and become confused and frightened in the face of it. Their "inability" to sort out relevant from irrelevant stimuli then becomes a defensive move, since any conclusions to which they may come are punishable (and punished).

Another idea, vaguely suggested by the data, is the inherent suspicion most schizophrenics seem to have of all human information. The more obivously transmitted by another human being a bit of information is, the more suspect it is—from the schizophrenic's point of view. This topic will be discussed further in the next section.

IX. Acquisition and Related Areas

A. INTRODUCTION

In a series of studies on reinforcement practices, this category represents an analysis of the experimentally *manipulated* variables and, as such, should provide more valid information per item than any of the other categories. Some of the general findings, relative to overall outcomes, have been presented in Section II. The following paragraphs will review the analysis of specific items in this category, compared with overall outcomes as described in Section II. Also reviewed in this section will be the results available from the use of two other "treatments"—negative reinforcement and "mixed treatment" (where there is a combination of treatments used simultaneously).

In the previous discussion, a distinction was drawn between implicit and explicit reinforcement, and some problems arising when both are used in the same experimental group were discussed. It is noteworthy that 22% of the experiments analyzed employed implicit reinforcement tasks (such as paired-associates) *in addition to* explicit reinforcement. The hypothesis was formulated that learning fails to be enhanced where both methods are used simultaneously with SIG. Further data in this category should either corroborate or refute this hypothesis.

Finally, several concepts which have not been discussed elsewhere will become more important in this category. Principal among these is the concept of *extinction,* where a conditioned (or learned) response is extinguished through failure to reinforce appropriate responses or series of responses. Other concepts (e.g., counterconditioning and response-contingent reinforcement) will be described as they come up.

B. FREQUENCY DATA

One of the most stunning frequency counts in this series of items (on acquisition and reinforcement practices) refers to the number of times reinforcing stimuli are identified as independent variables (IVs) by investigators contrasted with the number of variables so identified by our research analysts. In the total sample of experiments, investigators identified reinforcement practices as IVs in 24 instances; the research analysts identified a total of 56 such instances, yielding a discrepancy of 32 instances. Thus, in 32 cases (not identical with "experiments" since several unidentified IVs may be operative in a single experiment) reinforcement practices were in fact serving the function of independent variables *without* being so identified, without being measured or controlled.

These unidentified IVs varied from the unavoidable (due to the nature of the variable) to the clearly avoidable contamination. In between these extremes are many borderline cases, the seriousness of which reduces itself to a matter of theoretical or experimental judgment. Examples of these kinds of contaminations will be detailed in the Discussion section.

Among those external reinforcement practices analyzed, by far the most commonly used method of presentation of reinforcement was "personal-direct- with no mechanical mediation." Seventy-one percent of the experiments employed this technique. The second most commonly used method of presentation (28% of the experiments employed it) was "personal-indirect-mechanical mediation" (where the investigator uses some device or machine to present the reward or punishment to the subject).

A smaller percentage of experiments (21%) used the "impersonal-completely mechanical" method of presentation, with the investigator present in 15% and absent in 6% of these experiments. Sixteen percent of the experiments used "method of presentation" as an identified IV.

Although a human (personal) reinforcer was most often used (70%), almost half of the experiments (49%) used a nonhuman (impersonal) reinforcer or punishment.

The nature of the reinforcer (whether it is verbal or nonverbal) is closely related to the item discussed above. It is not surprising, therefore, that the percentages are similar. Verbal reinforcement was used in 67% and nonverbal in 39% of the experiments. Only four experiments used verbal *versus* nonverbal reinforcement as an IV (see discussion of results in Section XI).

As one would expect, the subjects' visual and auditory sense modalities were often stimulated during the reinforcement processes, with auditory stimulation accounting for 79% of the cases and visual for 35%. Of the remaining items in this category, "other" is the only one that accounts for any appreciable number of experiments (21%). Reinforcers such as candy, cigarettes, and money are classified as "other."

Some facets of the time relationship between the emission of the response and the ensuing reinforcement, along with the related question of varying amounts of such reinforcement, are dealt with in the next two categories. A large majority of the experiments (79%) employed a schedule of continuous reinforcement in contrast to 27% that used partial reinforcement schedules. Although the relative effectiveness of different reinforcement schedules may be an important issue in acquisition, only three experiments used such schedules as an IV.

The information on "delay of reinforcement" is consistent with the above data. In 90% of the experiments, reinforcement was not delayed—or delayed only until the end of a logical unit. Reinforcement was delayed until the end of a block of trials and/or the completion of the whole task in a smaller number of experiments (21%).

Although there were no extinction periods employed in the majority of experiments, total cessation of reinforcement (while the subject continued responding) was employed in 29%. A few experiments made use of the techniques of counterconditioning (extinguishing a previously correct response and reinforcing an incompatible response).

The next group of categories provided information on the reinforced response itself (e.g., the type of response reinforced and the response strength). The most striking feature in this batch of data is that, aside from reporting the type of response (behavior) that was reinforced, relatively little information was provided by the writers on other characteristics of the subjects' responses. For example, neither response strength nor affective tone of the reinforced response were specified in 92% of the experiments. Self-referred and other-referred statements were selected as reinforced responses in 13 and 5 cases respectively, were used as an IV by the investigators, but were not applicable in most instances (75 or 83%). Experimenters were almost evenly divided between selecting a spoken or a nonspoken response (50% and 47% respectively).

Reinforcement was contingent upon some aspects of the subjects' responses (e.g., speed of responding, making the correct response, etc.) in 72 (80%) of the experiments. However, a smaller number of experiments 32 (36%) employed noncontingent reinforcement (making the reinforcement independent of any specific response or response class). Although there is a high degree of overlap between these two items and the previously noted items in the category "delay of reinforcement," two different concepts are involved, and they should not be confused.

The last two items in the section on acquisition deal with the issue of the subject's *awareness* of the relationship between his responses and the presentations of the reinforcers. The subjects were tested for awareness of response-reinforcement contingency in 16% of the experiments. This figure tends to be misleading, however, since the question is not relevant in all 90 experiments, because of the nature of some of the experimental tasks. The tasks employed in the small number of studies assessing subject awareness included the Taffel cards (eight studies), paired-associate learning (two studies), Wisconsin card-sorting (two studies), saying words ending with "s" (one study), and group conversation (one study).

The subject's awareness can be tested either indirectly (in which case there is virtually no information on how the investigator assessed awareness) or directly, by asking the subject if he was aware which responses were being reinforced. Only three of fourteen studies asked the subject directly—and all were studies using the Taffel method. The other eleven studies testing awareness give little or no information on how awareness testing was done.

C. Major Findings

In relating specific acquisition items to overall outcomes, there were no significant findings under either positive reinforcement or punishment. But there are some general considerations, relative to reinforcement practices, which bear consideration at this point.

The general effects of treatment manipulations are reviewed in Section II (Overall Outcomes) and are presented in summary form in Tables I–III. Briefly, it will be recalled that the effectiveness of positive reinforcement and punishment with SIG were roughly equal. Table III shows 40 (44%) of the experiments reported enhancement of learning under positive reinforcement and 50 (56%) reported nonenhancement. Under punishment, 31 (48%) showed enhancement, and 33 (52%) nonenhancement.

This split was roughly borne out with "normal" subjects, too, with positive reinforcement appearing a little more effective than punishment in enhancing learning but not significantly so. (Positive reinforcement: 16 (62%) plus, 10 (38%) zero; punishment: 9 (45%) plus, 11 (55%) zero; $\chi^2 = 1.25$, df = 2, $p < .30$.)

Some experiments in this sample were designed with reward versus punishment as an IV. (Some of these were not included in the "across-experiment analysis" because they did not use a control group—either subjects as their own control or a nonreinforced group—and were, therefore, coded as ?.) A number of these experiments also used a normal sample, making it possible to draw comparisons of the relative effectiveness of reward and punishment for normals and schizophrenics.

The procedure used here classified outcomes with respect to the two treatments as follows: (1) Reward and punishment had similar effects on performance or learning; (2) Punishment was more effective than reward; (3) Reward was more effective than punishment (see Table IV).

As can be seen from Table IV, the most frequent outcome for both groups of subjects is "reward equal to punishment." (That is, they were either both effective or both ineffective.) The next most frequent outcome pattern is "punishment more effective than reward." The small number of studies using negative reinforcement precluded the analysis of items in relation to outcomes.

The pattern of outcomes of experiments comparing reward and punishment is the same for SIG and "normals." A chi-square test of the two by

TABLE IV

Classification of Outcomes of Experiments Comparing Reward and
Punishment on the Learning and Performance of SIG and
"Normal" Subjects

	Outcomes		
Subjects	Reward equal to punishment	Punishment greater than reward	Reward greater than punishment
Schizophrenics	24	17	9
"Normals"	11	4	3

three distribution in Table IV yields nonsignificant results ($\chi^2 = .05$, df $= 2$, $p < .30$.)

With "Mixed Type" treatment manipulation, which usually involved rewarding correct and punishing incorrect responses during the same task, the results were less than promising. With SIG, 23% of the studies reported enhancement, 8% reported nonenhancement, and 69% resulted in confused or indeterminate findings (see Table I). With "normal" subjects, 3 (30%) showed enhancement, but in 7 (70%) of the studies the findings were indeterminate (see Table II). There was no attempt to relate items to overall, since the outcome findings were so inconclusive.

D. Minor Trends

Under conditions of positive reinforcement, two items showed a trend toward a *plus* relationship with outcome. When a study employed an extinction period as part of the experiment design, there appeared to be a tendency for the study to have *plus* outcomes ($p < .10$). This, however, may be an artifact. If an extinction period is a part of the design, it would be necessary for subjects to show learning in order for extinction of the learned responses to occur. It is conceivable that subjects who failed to learn were dropped from the study because they did not meet the required performance levels to qualify as subjects for "extinction."

When the experimenter used a *visual* stimulus as a reinforcer, there also appeared to be a tendency toward *plus* outcomes ($p < .20$). This is an interesting finding in the light of some others which will be discussed later.

Finally, in considering the other two treatment manipulations (negative reinforcement and "mixed type"), the picture changes somewhat. It will be recalled that negative reinforcement enhanced learning (in 82% of instances employed) far more effectively than either reward or punishment with SIG. With normal subjects, this effectiveness vanished (14% showed enhancement, 86% nonenhancement), but the nature of the aversive stimulation may have played a significant part in this difference. "White noise" appeared to be enhancing to the general performance level of the schizophrenics, an enhancement not required by the motivationally adequate normal group.

Items related to *zero* outcomes under positive reinforcement were as follows: implicit reinforcement (in conjunction with explicit reinforcement, $p < .10$), the use of nonreinforced control group ($p < .20$), when the nature of the reinforcer was verbal ($p < .20$), and when subjects were tested for awareness of the response-reinforcement-contingency ($p < .20$).

Under conditions of punishment, three items appeared correlated to *plus* outcomes: (1) Learning appeared to be *enhanced* when the method of presentation of the reinforcer was personal but *mechanically mediated* ($p < .20$); (2) when the nature of the reinforcer was *nonverbal* ($p < .20$); and (3) when a response-contingent reinforcer was employed ($p < .20$).

E. DISCUSSION

There are a number of things that need commenting upon relative to the data described in this section. First of all, there appears little evidence to substantiate the hypothesis that SIG learn better under conditions of punishment than do "normals." The differences between these two groups are statistically insignificant, as are the differences between reward-learning and punishment-learning for SIG. For "normals," punishment-learning appears not quite as effective as reward-learning. It is conceivable, of course, that one of the effects of bunching together groups of schizophrenic subjects is the masking of any real differences between different types of schizophrenics in the ways in which they respond to different types of reinforcement practices.

If, on the other hand, there is an underlying core problem in schizophrenia (common to all types of the disorder), and this core is being tapped by our current research methods, then we must content ourselves with the findings we have described on SIG: Reward-learning and punishment-learning show roughly similar effects with punishment having a slight (nonsignificant) edge—even when both treatments are used in the same experiment on the same subjects.

Accepting this latter possibility for the moment, the data in this section suggest some ways in which reinforcers may be made more effective in helping SIG to learn. The "minor trends" described in the preceding paragraphs indicate that learning may be maximized when reinforcing stimuli are visual or in some other way nonverbal, when it is mechanically mediated (rather than socially), and when the reinforcement is response-contingent. The data under conditions of reward-learning and punishment-learning, while not identical, are at least complementary on these points.

These data suggest at least one line of conjecture: SIG are distrustful or fearful of direct social reinforcement, or, put another way, they distrust human information. Perhaps the success of the token economies which have been widely reported (Ayllon & Ayllon, 1959) rests with their use of "tokens" (nonverbal reinforcement, in our terms) rather than their dependence on social reinforcers (such as saying "fine" or "good" or something like that).

The finding concerning the negative effects of combining implicit with explicit reinforcement reappears in the data of this section. Since the effect has been previously discussed, there is no virtue in belaboring the point—beyond one further generalization. It appears that, where information is direct and simply presented (and where the interfering stimuli are reduced), SIG seem to learn more readily. In some cases this is accomplished by providing some kind of "aversive" stimulation (e.g., white noise) during presentation of the task materials, which may have the effect of "drowning out" irrelevant stimuli. In other instances, focusing is done by simplifying the task (recall superiority of single over multiple tasks from Section VII in enhancing learning) and tying reinforcers in closely with the responses to be altered.

Another point is relative to the consideration of reinforcement practices. This group of items relating to the nature of reinforcers in the experimental treatments (along with situational variables) yielded a great number of unidentified IVs. Many reinforcer characteristics were operating as manipulated variables (and going uncontrolled and unmeasured). It was mentioned that some of these instances of unidentified IVs were unavoidable (due to the nature of the experimental design) and others were avoidable.

An example of the "unavoidable" type of confounding may be seen in the considerable overlap found for IV items such as "human *versus* nonhuman," "verbal *versus* nonverbal," and "sense modality stimulated by the reinforcing agent." If, for example, an investigator is studying human (social) *versus* nonhuman reinforcement, he almost necessarily will vary systematically all of the above-listed variables. Some of these it may be possible to manipulate independently, e.g., "verbalness" and "humanness" where the reinforcing stimulus may be presented either interpersonally or mechanically. But whether one does so or not may be a function of the judgment about the importance of the separation of the variables. In this case, for example, one would have to decide whether "humanness" and "verbalness" of the reinforcing stimulus are each significant factors in their own right.

Another kind of contamination, more avoidable than the first, occurs when two behavioral manipulations are compared, e.g., positive reinforcement *versus* combined reward-and-punishment (mixed type), with the two groups receiving task instructions which may differ considerably in content and tone. The same may be true for the manipulation of only "one treatment" *versus* "no treatment," with the treated group receiving motivational instructions which are not given to the untreated group.

Still another avoidable contamination is that occurring between a behavioral manipulation (e.g., reward *versus* punishment) and extinction schedules. The way this may come about is when a study uses one correct response in a first series of trials and then switches to another (different) correct response in a second series of trials. What then occurs is that, during the second series of trials, subjects in the reward condition are having an "incompatible" response reinforced while subjects in the punishment condition are now having a previously correct response punished. Subjects' performances, then, are no longer a test of simple conditioning but of counterconditioning.

In the light of general design problems, which appear significant in this type of research, there is an additional area which seems not to have troubled experimenters to any great degree. All the experiments in this analysis make use of reinforcement practices of some kind as the principal manipulated variables. Much of this work derives from the writing of B. F. Skinner and his associates, employing Skinner's concepts, terminology, and reinforcement paradigm. But they fail to use his research methodology.

Skinner (1959) has spoken against the use of statistics and statistical-type research in the study of animal and human behavior, proclaiming it often irrelevant and obscuring of the critical data. Skinner's research has traditionally used a few subjects (highly defined), tested and treated longitudinally over a series of reinforcement and extinction procedures.

By contrast, all of the experiments in this analysis (and they were not selected by these criteria) use masses of ill-defined subjects, employ brief tasks in a cross-sectional, one-shot design, with "reinforcers" of questionable importance to individual subjects under the experimental conditions. These deviations from Skinner's methodology have not led to replicable results. On the other hand, many of the coding manual items that relate to *plus* outcomes are Skinnerian concepts and methods: rate of response, nonverbal reinforcement (cf. with Skinner's "primary reinforcement"), use of an extinction period, and use of response-contingent reinforcement.

In this analysis, response contingency (under punishment only) was related to *plus* outcomes and nonresponse contingency to *zero* outcomes. Why this trend did not also appear with reward learning is a mystery. Sections XI and XII provide some further clues to the mystery, but it is possible that, as a reinforcer, punishment is slightly more effective throughout the experiments than reward (see Table IV) because punishment functions largely as a primary reinforcer in these experiments, while the rewards had more the properties of secondary (or conditioned) reinforcers. In addition, there is little evidence that what investigators defined as "rewards" were actually rewarding to their subjects. There is a difference between defining rewards *a priori* and empirically establishing them as reinforcing—a distinction rarely observed in this sample of experiments.

X. Dependent Variables

A. INTRODUCTION

The dependent variable represents the heart of the work done by the psychological investigator. It involves the instruments he uses for measuring (quantifying) some behavioral or other psychological variable. This complicates the task of the psychological investigator because measurement in the area of human behavior is, in itself, a highly complicated and, in many ways, primitive scene. The psychological investigator does not have traditional and well-established measuring devices he can fall back on, like foot-inch measurement, degrees of temperature, or weight. In many cases he must devise, for a particular experiment, the measuring instruments with which he hopes to quantify the concepts he is testing. Different measures of a concept are famous for not being as consistent as logic would suggest that they should be. Therefore, deciding what to measure and how to measure it are crucial.

It is helpful to use more than one dependent variable, whenever possible, to avoid a complete wash-out of findings if one of the measures turns out to be noncontributory. Most of the experiments in this analysis did, in fact, use more than one dependent variable, which accounts for the odd and overlapping percentages presented below.

The next part of this section on dependent variables deals largely with the variety of measuring devices used in the experiments we analyzed. The actual validity or sophistication of the devices is beyond the scope of this analysis.

B. FREQUENCY DATA

Of the 19 items in this section, 18 refer to specific dependent variables, and one ("other") is a general item to allow for the coding of less frequently used dependent variables. All but three of the dependent variables listed were used at least once. These three were difference scores-interindividual, reminiscence, and individual learning measured by verbalization of the correct solution.

The two most frequently used dependent variables were difference scores-intraindividual (54%) and frequency of correct responses per block(s) of trials (46%). Latency (reaction times), number of errors, and "other" were used in 18%; generalization in 15%.

C. MAJOR FINDINGS

"Other" included such dependent measures as "number of guesses made," "number correct minus number wrong," "level of aspiration," and scores on questionnaires about the task, etc. It is interesting that this item, "other," is related ($p < .05$) to zero outcomes (nonenhancement) under conditions of punishment. It is not clear why this should be the case. However, of the ten studies involved here, seven used verbal tasks, so that the nature of the task might be a factor. The finding could also be a chance matter, as pointed out earlier in this paper.

D. MINOR TRENDS

Three dependent variable items show some trend under positive reinforcement. "Rate of response" is related to *plus* outcomes ($p < .20$) and, of course, includes studies employing the traditional operant conditioning paradigm. "Resistance to extinction" also shows a trend related to *plus* outcomes ($p < .20$), as discussed in previous sections. To further illustrate, the same studies would be coded under Item 522 (*S* not told of cessation of reinforcer) and under Item 646 (total cessation of reinforcer-extinction), both of which showed similar trends (understandably) because the same studies are being coded.

Another item, "number of trials to criterion," shows a trend toward *zero* outcomes (nonenhancement) ($p < .10$) and strongly overlaps with the paired-associate item from the last section (Item 531) which, of course, also showed a trend toward *zero* outcomes.

Two dependent variable items show a trend under punishment. The item, "other," was related to *zero* outcomes ($p < .05$) and was discussed previously. The final item, "latency of responses (reaction times)," is related to more *plus* outcomes ($p < .20$). Psychomotor tasks are strongly represented on this item.

E. DISCUSSION

Many experimental procedures are coded in several places throughout this analysis. Thus many similar trends, appearing to be corroborative, are simply repetitions of the same information—coded differently. This has been pointed out in several places.

In this section on dependent variables, this artifact becomes more visible than previously. Most of the trends can be explained in terms of previously discussed findings, so that very little is added in this section.

The only really "new" type finding (and this, too, may simply be a statistical quirk) is the relatively highly significant ($p < .05$) relationship of "other" dependent variables to *zero* outcomes under conditions of punishment. This item is the one that picks up all the infrequently used measuring devices: output, guessing strategies, sustained improvement, feelings about the task, etc. Many of them represent exotic, often "far-out" attempts to quantify change. It could very well be that their rarity also reflects their instability as measuring devices, rendering them noncontributory.

On the other hand, the most commonly used dependent variables ("intraindividual difference scores in which the subject is used as his own control;" "frequency and/or number of correct responses per block") do not appear to contribute anything for or against enhancement of learning in and of themselves, which may be a reflection of their stability and effectiveness.

XI. Combinations and Interactions

It was noted in Section I that combinations of items could be related to outcomes in a fashion similar to individual items. One of the limitations in this regard, however, is the requirement that the particular combination of items yield a sufficient number of outcomes for the application of a statistical test. This requirement is not likely to be met in this sample of studies when more than *two* items are combined. However, assuming a combination that yields a sufficient number of outcomes, it is possible by this method to test out specific hypotheses or "hunches" regarding the relationship between certain variables and outcomes. An illustration of this procedure is the following.

It was decided to test out a hypothesis about the relationship between response-contingency and "verbalness" of the reinforcement. References to Section IX (on acquisition and related areas) will show trends for the individual items involved, and it was thought that these trends might be shown to be rather more specific (and perhaps more clear-cut) when outcomes were tested against the combined items. The items involved are 677, 678, 616, and 617 (see Appendix). Verbal (616) and nonverbal (617) reinforcement are the categories in the coding manual which bear the closest similarity to the important concepts of primary *versus* conditioned reinforcement. In general, primary (or similarly here, nonverbal) reinforcement would be expected to enhance learning more than con-

TABLE V

ITEM COMBINATIONS AS RELATED TO OUTCOMES: SUMMARY OF DATA ON
"VERBALNESS" OF REINFORCER AND "RESPONSE-CONTINGENCY" UNDER
CONDITIONS OF POSITIVE REINFORCEMENT AND PUNISHMENT

Item combination	Percent of plus outcomes	p
677/616 R-contingent, verbal reward	(32%)	.05
677/616 R-contingent, verbal punishment	(54%)	n.s.
677/617 R-contingent, nonverbal reward	(47%)	n.s.
677/617 R-contingent, nonverbal punishment	(65%)	.20
678/616 Non-R-contingent, verbal reward	(42%)	n.s.
678/616 Non-R-contingent, verbal punishment	(31%)	.20
678/617 Non-R-contingent, nonverbal reward	(50%)	n.s.
678/617 Non-R-contingent, nonverbal punishment	(33%)	n.s.

ditioned verbal reinforcers. Table V summaries the results. Note that the numbers in parentheses in the column under "directions" are the percentages of *plus* outcomes with the particular combination.

The outstanding finding in this analysis is that there are significantly more *zero* outcomes for response-contingent verbal rewards. Item 677 did not even show up in Section IX (e.g., the outcome split with it is not significant at the 20% level), Item 616 does show some *zero* trend by itself, but—in combination—the two items yield a clear-cut *zero* trend. The above also indicates that the *plus* trend for response-contingent punishment (see Section IX) is borne out mainly for nonverbal punishment, and the *zero* trend for nonresponse contingent reinforcement is borne out mainly for verbal punishment. It may be noted, however, that the trends in each case are the same for verbal and nonverbal punishment, although not reaching significance at the .20 level.

It might be helpful in interpreting the above findings to point out again the difference between R- and Non-R-contingent reinforcement. The former conforms to the typical paradigm for operant conditioning; e.g., the reinforcer is contingent upon a particular response, and the change in rate or frequency of that response is the dependent variable; while the latter (Non-R-contingent) conforms to a model where the reinforcement functions chiefly as a motivator of behavior or performance.

It may be said then that the deficit behavior of schizophrenics suggested in the finding of more *zero* outcomes with verbal rewards holds only in the situation where the reinforcement functions in the relatively strict Skinnerian sense of a "response consequence" and does *not* hold for the situation where the reinforcement has chiefly a motivational function; e.g., praise for preceding performance and exhortation to do better.

Another kind of combination analysis involves dividing experiments into two groups: Type A, in which the subject has no knowledge about the correctness of his responses beyond what information he can obtain through the pattern of reinforcements; and Type B, in which the subject knows which the correct responses are, either by the experimenter telling him directly or by the nature of the task itself, e.g., a knowledge-of-the-results type task.

Type A studies with punishment as the treatment were underrepresented, probably because the Type A tasks tend to be the "pure" operant conditioning studies, and these are less likely to use punishment as a reinforcer. Type B tasks have definite correct and incorrect responses, so that punishment as a reinforcer is just as likely as reward.

Comparing Types A and B on positive reinforcement, Type A tasks tended to have more *plus* outcomes and B more *zero* outcomes ($p < .10$). Type B tasks tested alone against a 50-50 split assumption is significant at less than the 20% level of confidence.

For tasks employing punishment, there were no significant differences. In addition, all negative outcomes occurred with the Type B tasks, under conditions of both reward and punishment. Negative outcomes suggest that learning is actually impaired by the use of Type B tasks with SIG.

When Types A and B tasks are compared with certain selected items, the following findings obtain:

As will be recalled from the previous section, implicit reinforcement studies (Type B, by definition) tended to show a *zero* trend. A test of Type B studies which include the implicit reinforcement item shows a *zero* trend at better than the .10 level, which is somewhat higher than when all Type B experiments are included in the test. A test of Type B with all implicit reinforcement studies excluded no longer yields significant findings, even at a marginal level. Therefore, it seems logical to conclude that knowledge of the results, in and of themselves, is not hampering the performances of SIG, but that implicit reinforcement tasks (e.g., paired-associates) hamper performance only when used in combination with explicit reinforcement.

Two items from the Task Instruction section of the manual appeared to be related to Type A type experiments. The first is: "*S* told there is a correct response, but not told what it is" (510); and the second is: "*S* purposely not told anything about correctness of R" (513). When these items were tested against each other, using only Type A tasks, they turned out to be significantly different ($p < .05$), with the first (510) associated with more *zero* and the second (513) associated with more *plus* outcomes. When all experiments were included, the trend remained the same, but the significance level dropped ($p < .20$).

Another pair of items related to the Types A-B classification is response-contingency. Type A experiments are always response-contingent, while Type B may be either response-contingent or nonresponse-contingent. It may be recalled that this variable showed little direction under positive reinforcement, but under punishment showed minor trends toward *plus* outcomes with response-contingency and toward *zero* outcomes with non-response-contingency. Earlier in this section, in combining contingency items with verbal-nonverbal items, it was found that the combination of response contingency and verbal reward yielded more *zero* outcomes at a significant level ($p < .05$). Response-contingent nonverbal punishment tended ($p < .20$) toward *plus* outcomes, and nonresponse-contingent verbal punishment tended ($p < .20$) toward *zero* outcomes.

Using only Type B tasks in order to help clarify the issues, it was found that positive reinforcement combined with response contingency still tended to show a *zero* trend ($p < .10$). (Nonresponse-contingency under reward learning continued to show nothing.) Response-contingent punishment, by itself, does not show a significant trend; however, when response contingency under both reward and punishment was tested out, it was found that they differed significantly ($p < .05$), with reward having more *zero* outcomes and punishment having more *plus* outcomes. This difference is also supported by a chi-square test at the same level of significance. Nonresponse-contingent punishment still tended to show a trend toward *zero* outcomes at less than the 20% level.

This Rube Goldbergian approach to clarifying some of the variables in reinforcement practices did manage to amplify some of the findings relative to response-contingency and implicit reinforcement practices, but the effort involved is far more than the output justifies.

Several other such combinations were tested out, following "hunches" or hypotheses of the investigators, but in all other cases the *N*s were too tiny to apply statistical tests. With a larger sample of experiments, it might have been possible to sift out the contributions of other combinations of items.

Section IX (on Acquisition and Related Areas) reports an instance where item combinations ended up in an unavoidable confounding of item effects, rendering the outcomes questionable. The example used was the confounding of "humanness" and "verbalness" in the reinforcing stimulus, such that the effects of neither characteristic is clearly demonstrated. The "unavoidability" of such confounding may, in the last analysis, be a function of the kind of research design used for this type of experimentation, a topic which will be discussed in the following section.

Although interesting, it is problematical whether or not pursuing item combinations and interactions is a useful occupation so long as sampling, task instructions, and situational variables contribute so much to the un-controlled variance in experiments such as have been sampled. It is con-ceivable that simplification of designs may put interactions and combin-ations more in their proper perspectives.

XII. Implications for Future Research

A. LIMITATIONS OF LITERATURE REVIEWS[3]

It is one of the traditions of our profession that, in fields where there is abundance of experimental literature, review articles become a conven-ient way of drawing together the findings of diverse studies and encapsulat-ing them in a covey of summarizing statements. This is a tradition, unfortunately, more honored in the observance than in the breach, and there are journals among us who even cater primarily to "reviewists."

The field of learning in schizophrenia is one which has been very adequately served by review articles, and it is certainly apt at this point to ponder the service they have provided.

The source materials for most reviews are published papers. Most journals have space limitations and usually require authors to write ab-breviated or shortened versions of their experimental reports. In the sample of studies incorporated in the current analysis (which includes both published papers and unpublished doctoral dissertations), it was ob-served that more *plus* outcomes were obtained for studies providing "no information" in some important item categories. (Specifically this involved Items 040 *versus* 041, 100 *versus* 104, 105 *versus* 111, and 112 *versus* 114—items involving subject and experimenter characteristics.) In general, more information could be obtained for coding purposes from dissertations than from articles, and this was particularly true for the items in question.

It was, therefore, hypothesized that the relationship between informa-tion/no information and outcomes might be due to a possible association between theses/articles and outcomes. This was not only confirmed, but it also turned out that there was a significant relationship between theses/articles and outcomes such that unpublished theses obtained significantly more *zero* outcomes and published articles significantly more *plus* out-comes. The relationship was significant between the .05 and .10 levels for both positive reinforcement and punishment tested separately—and at the .01 level when tested for all four treatments combined.

---

[3] For those who would like to read a brief literature review, based on the current analysis of those variables *other* than reinforcement practices considered by the studies in this sample, see Appendix. Do not say, however, that you were not forewarned about the utter folly of such reviews.

One conclusion deriving from this long chain of events is that dissertation papers tend not to get published (even when highly abbreviated) unless they have positive results (*plus* outcomes) to report. Consequently, it may be concluded that (1) studies reporting positive findings are more likely to be published than those reporting negative findings; (2) review articles are most frequently based on published (rather than unpublished) studies; (3) *ergo,* review articles tend to give a biased account of the findings extant in the field of learning in schizophrenia, inasmuch as they tend not to include studies reporting negative findings.

The reviewer may get into trouble on another count also. He must make at least one additional major assumption in confronting his task: the assumption of comparability among studies. This assumption may or may not be justified, depending upon the area of research and the studies involved. In the field of schizophrenic learning, as has been suggested in the preceding sections, assumed comparability is an invalid base from which to start. Studies certainly vary in quality and cannot be assumed comparable on these grounds. It has been suggested in previous sections that the better designed studies appear more likely to obtain negative results and (reprising a previous point) are more likely to go unpublished and unreviewed.

Other data speak against the validity of assumed comparability. It is highly unlikely that we can make very many statements about "schizophrenics in general." The schizophrenic population appears to be a far more complex entity than previously supposed (at least by researchers) and probably involves a wide variety of disorders, hung together by only a slender thread of similarity. Until researchers are more conscientious about drawing their population samples and are more descriptive about what they have drawn, it is difficult (even for a reviewer) to assess what kind of a sample is being researched.

Further, researchers are many times naive about the source of their main effects. Note that, in the total of 90 experiments, authors had identified a total of 95 independent variables, while our study analysts identified 149 independent variables—a discrepancy of 54 IVs, presumably going unrecognized by researchers. This being the case, it is unlikely that even the most scrupulous of reviewers can account for the great amount of variability from this source alone.

In addition, "findings" may be related to many more elements than simply the designated (or undesignated) IVs and may in fact be related to anything from the wording of the task instructions to the nature of the reinforcer to whether or not the subject is on drugs at the time of the study. The thrust of this entire analysis has been that a wide number of design and procedure variables can effect (in greater or lesser amounts) the outcomes of studies, making an assumption of comparability highly questionable.

The failure of experimenters to report critical data (particularly with respect to the sample) leaves the reviewer with only the sketchiest data on which to compare and combine studies. It is appalling to recall that even some of the most basic data (current mental status, whether or not patients are on psychotropic drugs, whether or not they are hospitalized at the time of the study, whether or not they are male) go unreported in many studies.

In view of these serious shortcomings, it is difficult to understand what actually is being reviewed in review articles. The fact that there have been many superior review articles written (even in the field of schizophrenic learning) attests more to the ingenuity of reviewers than to the completeness or veracity of the studies themselves.

One counter argument that could be presented against some of the previous points is that any behavioral phenomenon (*qua* phenomenon) should be able to manifest itself under a number of conditions and should not be so precious (if it is of any account) that it can be demonstrated only under special procedures in a sterile environment. But it is conceivable that in the field of human behavior there are no phenomena of such a magnitude; that behavioral influences have a subtle effect and act differently on different people in different circumstances. That being the case, it would be a matter of some importance for the investigator to be unusually precise and conscientious in dealing with his subject matter.

This brings up a final point—one which *has* been discussed by several reviewers. The art of replication is virtually a lost one in psychological research. It is difficult to find even a few instances in which an experiment has been repeated with another sample. Even when similar designs are employed, individual investigators add their own innovations, rendering the two studies noncomparable. To find a single task (or procedure) which has been used on a wide variety of samples (even within the relatively restricted schizophrenic population) is a virtual impossibility. And yet it is this kind of data for which there is the most desperate need at this time.

The building upon previous research—so widely and successfully used in the physical sciences—is not really a viable technique in this field, so long as much of the work is undefined and ill-constructed. Powerful research guidelines are needed to remind the neophyte investigator of his research responsibilities and the criteria he must maintain in order to make a reasonable contribution to the data of his field.

The following and concluding section of this monograph is a primitive attempt—based on this analysis and on other sources—to establish a manual of procedure for doing research on schizophrenic learning. Readers may disagree on some of the elements of the outline, but they certainly cannot disagree on the necessity for its existence.

B. GUIDELINES FOR THE RESEARCHER

1. Introduction

Two types of errors are common in research. Type One errors attribute an observed effect to what was done (treatment) when, in fact, it is merely due to chance. In Type Two errors, one may attribute the observed effect to chance when, indeed, it is the result of the treatment (Schoolman *et al.*, 1968).

Research design is intended to minimize controllable error. Its purpose is to hold all experimental elements constant (or at least quantitatable so that they may be subtracted from the main effects), allowing only the critical variables (treatments) to vary.

Many experimenters founder on the very first step: How to ask a researchable question. *"Which is more effective, positive reinforcement or punishment, in enhancing the learning or performance of a schizophrenic patient?"* is not, as it stands, a researchable question. Starting from the end of the question and proceeding backward to the beginning, the question of the nature of the "schizophrenic patient" comes immediately to the fore.

2. The Subject Pool and the Research Model

No textbook on psychiatry or clinical psychology purports to have an operational definition of schizophrenia. It is usually considered a generalized condition which manifests itself in many states, not only from person to person but from time to time in the same individual.

Investigators, in facing the problem of researching schizophrenia, are confronted with the problem of *which* "schizophrenic state" to deal with. Before any further research steps can be taken, the investigator must answer some fundamental questions about his own concept of schizophrenia.

Some empirical data on the nature of schizophrenic states were presented in Section I. Dimensional differences in schizophrenic states were discussed (acute *versus* chronic, paranoid *versus* nonparanoid, good premorbid *versus* poor premorbid, and so forth) which appeared to have some heuristic value in describing at least some types of schizophrenic states. The schizophrenic states which characterize the life history of a single patient are quite another problem. It is a common clinical observation that schizophrenic patients alter states from time to time, depending on a wide number of variables, not least of which is the nature of the disorder itself which remains unknown and undefined at the present time.

Another problem relating to schizophrenic states concerns the environment in which the patient finds himself. Like everyone else, schizophrenic patients are affected by their surrounding and the stimuli impinging upon them. Since most of the studies on schizophrenia and schizophrenic learning have been done with hospitalized patients, it is important to recognize that a schizophrenic "state" is being dealt with which may not obtain in an unhospitalized schizophrenic. Ullmann and Krasner (1968) in their book review the data on schizophrenics' responses to hospitalizations and the differences that have been observed—traceable largely to the *fact* of hospitalization. This "state" problem becomes of particular importance where a comparison group of "nonhospitalized subjects" (normal or whatever) is employed. Differences between group performances (usually attributed to the presence and absence of mental disorder) may be seriously influenced by the fact that one group is hospitalized, the other not.

Collecting homogenous groups of subjects who share similar schizophrenic states but who have their own individual schedules of variant states is a problem of great magnitude for the experimenter. In fact, most experimenters ignore it and simply draw a sample of "schizophrenics in general." The experimenter has a choice of drawing a sample of schizophrenic patients who have many "state" characteristics in common, yet vary in a good many other state characteristics, *or* doing intensive investigation on a single schizophrenic patient whose state characteristics are well known and charted over the course of the experiment. The first choice maximizes the likelihood of making Type One errors in assessing findings; the second choice obviously cuts down on the generalizability of his findings.

Whichever approach he chooses, it would appear imperative that researchers should, first, not only carefully select and draw their samples, but that they be boldly and frankly detailed in their descriptions of their samples. At least, then, readers would have some idea concerning limits that should be placed on the interpretation of the findings. Editors of journals who insist that investigators shorten their research reports to meet space limitations should also be aware of the importance of detailed sample descriptions.

Second, it would appear important for the researcher initiating a new project to be very much aware of previous literature, building upon information obtained by other workers to define more clearly his own samples. The rather marked differences, for example, between "acute" and "chronic" schizophrenic patients that have been repeatedly demonstrated should suggest to the researcher that perhaps he should be wary of randomly mixing these two types together.

A strikingly similar "state" problem arises when "learning" is the variable to be assessed. Bush and Mosteller (1955) state:

> Data on animal and human learning present peculiar problems to the statistician; since irreversible changes take place while the data are being collected, repeated sampling is seldom possible. Organisms that can be considered "identical" at the start of an experiment do not remain completely "identical" because each has a different history during the course of the experiment. Observations such as these often throw doubts on the routine application of standard statistical procedures. More important, they suggest that, if methods specifically designed for handling these data were available, considerable gains in efficiency and meaningfulness would obtain. . . .

Skinner's original work (Ferster & Skinner, 1957) with animals in evaluating reinforcement and extinction procedures employed a stochastic model in which repeated procedures and measurements were taken over a period of time with the same organism (or organisms). He had the luxury of using organisms (rats and pigeons) whose states varied little from subject to subject and so felt freer to generalize to a far broader population than he was able to sample. The compounding of the problem in human learning (and especially in schizophrenic learning) where subject states (both intra- and interindividual) and learning states vary simultaneously presents an awesome research problem. Add to this, the phenomenon of some subjects learning more rapidly than others, some subjects attaining a concept and others failing to attain, and the problems extant in using an extensive (small group) model become astronomical.

Consequently, every researcher aspiring to do research in the area of schizophrenic learning should give more than passing attention to the use of intensive stochastic models (Chassan, 1959, 1960) in constructing his designs. His lack of freedom in generalizing from his restricted sample may be compensated for by the fact that what he does find has some greater validity than if he had used an extensive model.

Researchers are usually interested in a particular subject pool (like schizophrenia) and in a particular phenomenon or phenomena related to the subject pool before they arrive at the stage of asking specific research questions concerning both elements. It is important that the researcher be aware of the limitations that each imposes on the questions he is able to ask. In dealing with schizophrenic subjects the nature of the subject pool itself is so undefined and virtually nondescript that he seems almost safest dealing with a few individuals who unmistakably fall into that subject pool. The previous practice—used by the vast majority of studies in this analysis—of lumping together an undescribed batch of patients who have, through some device or series of devices, been labeled "schizophrenic" is untenable as a research technique. In understanding the contribution "sample drawing" makes on research results, it would be elucidating to construct one simple reinforcement study, and to replicate it *ad nauseum* on a number of different schizophrenic samples (or individuals), cut up in as many ways as possible: Dimensionally, factorially, sexually, socially, in-and-out of hospital, on-and-off drugs (specified), in remission and in regression, old and young patients. As Buss (1966) has stated: "It no longer suffices to compare a schizophrenic sample with a normal sample. There must be specification of the premorbid history, the presence or absence of delusions, and the chronicity of psychosis [p. 306]." Among many other things!

3. The Research Question

Once the subject pool and behavioral phenomena to be studied have been ascertained, the researcher faces the task of asking a relevant and testable question. The question posed in the previous paragraphs is un-researchable because, for one thing, it is too vague. Once the subject pool and the particular design problems posed by the assessment of "learning" have been dealt with, the researcher must answer the questions: What *kind* of positive reinforcement? What *kind* of punishment? What *kind* of task to be learned? And *what* measures of effectiveness? At least part of these must be modified to conform to the available techniques. The remainder may be clarified by answering some questions about the research question.

"What is the primary objective of the study? Is its purpose to explain or to provide practical applications?"[4]

Often, because the researcher wants to do too much with a single study and to answer too many questions (or answer questions which are too broad), he ends up with gross treatments, gross measurements, and consequent fuzzy findings. It is conceivable that a study may be well worth doing if all it contributes is something practical or managerial and contributes little to the esoterica of current theory. Most of the studies in our sample attempted to extend the findings toward both theoretical and practical implications. Advisers often require this of graduate students when they are writing the Discussion section of their dissertations. This may be fine as an exercise in mentation as long as the study itself is not serving the Discussion section when it should be the other way around.

[4] Segments of a research outline (Best, 1970) will be used extensively throughout the following discussion. The outline is an unpublished manuscript constructed by the Midwest Research Support Center, Veterans Administration, and is used with permission of the author.

A study does *not* have to serve both theoretical and practical needs; very few studies can serve both equally well.

"What specific questions are implied by this (overall) objective? Which of these specific questions is the key question?"

The author states: "You should plan to answer one or a small number of questions definitively rather than trying to answer everything, and, as is so often the case, answering neither with certainty."

"Will a definitive answer to the key question satisfy the objective? What specific action will be taken as a result of this trial [Best, 1970, p. 1]?"

It is possible that no action *need* be taken; that the research contribution is simply an explanatory one.

"Can the key question be answered with available resources?"

Too often, work is done with pathological groups using tools and measurements not completely tried and tested. This use of "made up" or contrived tasks contributes to the uncontrolled variance in the experiment and renders interpretation of the findings impossible. Many studies in the current sample were not only manipulating treatments but were standardizing tasks and measurements as well. It is not possible to do all this simultaneously. Each is a separate task and requires separate experimentation.

"If the key question cannot be answered with available resources, how may the question be modified to permit a definitive answer."

"Will this modified question satisfy the overall objective [Best, 1970, p. 1]?"

It was observed repeatedly throughout the analysis of the studies in this sample that a great many uncontrolled variables affected outcomes to a greater or lesser degree. Often these uncontrolled variables were "trivial" aspects of the experimental design or procedure; for example, the wording of task instructions. Apparently these "trivial" aspects are bypassed by experimenters as "too trivial" to research out. And yet, it is conceivable that a well-controlled study on the effects of various kinds of task instructions may have far-reaching value—not only for subsequent research studies but for learning about communication with schizophrenic subjects.

Consider, for a moment, the range of research questions that could be raised about the wording of task instructions: (1) by tape or in person; written or oral; if oral, male or female; if male or female, young, old, or middle-aged; (2) simple wording or complicated wording; using examples or not using examples; using one example or several; (3) trial runs included in instructions; one trial or repeated trials until the subject gets them right; (4) affective tone of the instructions: hostile, agreeable, neutral; (5) expectation level of the instructions; high or low; patronizing or grandiose; (6) are task instructions used for motivational reasons as well as information giving; if so, how is the subject being motivated and to what extent is the motivational element successful (as over against no motivational element); (7) what purposes for doing the task are implied in the instructions; if none, are the purposes explained elsewhere to the subject; if not how is this justified; (8) are task instructions given in one lump or are they distributed over a task or trial task; if this choice is possible, what are the relative merits of each approach.

There are probably many others that can be spun out of this one single "trivial" element. Add to this the combinations of possibilities when the subject pool is considered (schizophrenic states, etc.) and it is possible that a researcher could carve a lifetime career out of answering some relatively important questions about research procedure.

The conclusion is that the researcher must see that his design and procedure are well anchored down at each step along the way. Difficult as this is in research on human behavior, it must be conceded that any amount of uncontrolled variation will affect the outcome to some extent. The first anchoring point is in posing a sharp, focused, researchable question, keeping the subject pool, the nature of the behavioral phenomenon (such as learning), and the available resources clearly in mind.

It is *not* noncontributory to ask a simple, straightforward, even naive research question.

It is *not* a terrible thing to construct a simple, straightforward design using well-known tasks and common measurements.

In fact, it is *not* heretical to collect a great deal of controlled data, over time, on a single, well-diagnosed schizophrenic patient. Not only might a great deal be discovered about the patient, something might even be found out about "schizophrenia."

4. Independent and Dependent Variables

An experimental study invariably focuses on some treatment or treatments which the subjects will undergo, the effects of which will be measured by some device or devices arrived at by *a priori* decision. Results of this analysis suggest that IVs were often not clearly thought through; that, on the one hand, the task or treatment itself was of questionable potency to bring about change under the best of conditions and that, on the other hand, so many diverse and frequently unidentified IVs were operating simultaneously that any forthcoming main effects were badly contaminated.

Good experimental design usually involves some yardstick against which learning or performance can be measured. This might involve an untreated control group or a comparison group of some kind. There are a number of possibilities. The first is serial comparison of a patient with himself. This is the kind employed in stochastic models of the type Skinner employed.

> This design assumes that after a trial with one treatment, a patient will return to essentially his prior state, and that he will respond to a second treatment in a fashion unrelated to whether or not he had received the first. Changing environmental factors tend to be balanced out through randomization of order for the first two regimens and through simultaneous testing of different orders. The similarity of the patient to himself from one time to another under these assumptions is generally greater than the similarity of one subject to another, leading to greater power in analysis with this design [Best, 1970, p. 4].

A second method is simultaneous comparison of matched patients.

> If pairing is done on irrelevant factors known to affect the response and pair members are randomly assigned to contrasting regimens, one might reasonably expect to gain greater power than through the use of unmatched samples. However, the intra-pair variability under similar treatments must be expected to be considerably less than the inter-pair variability to adequately compensate for the appreciable decrease in degrees of freedom with this design [Best, 1970, pp. 4–5].

A third is simultaneous comparison of one group of subjects with another. When one or more of the assumptions obtaining under the first method are not met, this is generally useful. Changing environmental and ancillary treatment factors which might affect the response are balanced out, thus reducing this potential source of bias.

A fourth is simply a variation of the above, in which a schizophrenic group is compared with a nonschizophrenic group. The problem arises when it becomes necessary to see that the two groups do not differ in any relevant way except for the presence or absence of schizophrenia. This is frequently next to impossible to achieve.

The comparison group problem is a difficult one. Even when well matched on demographic-type variables with the patient group, there are situational differences in performance on learning tasks. There is a real methodological question concerning the applicability of comparison group research to hospitalized schizophrenic patients. Where there is no appropriate kind of group, which differs from the patients only on the dimension of schizophrenia, perhaps the whole concept of comparison group research should be abandoned in favor of a control group or several control groups in those instances where single subject (intensive) models seem less appropriate.

Even when there has been an attempt at comparability in comparison group design, there is often little attention paid to the potency of the treatment itself. Preliminary pilot work may help screen out impotent treatment methods. A study which uses either on impotent treatment or gives insufficient trials for a potent treatment to become effective may lead investigators to forfeit knowledge, not only of the treatment, but also of the boundary conditions within which it and similar treatments operate.

The second part of the potency problem is selecting measures which will adequately reflect the effects brought about by the treatment manipulation. Often in the current analysis, dependent variables were trivial if not irrelevant. It has become popular recently to use multiple measures in the hope that what one will fail to pick up another will be successful at reflecting.

> An *a priori* decision as to what will constitute the key response criteria is far preferable to measuring everything in sight and deciding after the fact which will be emphasized. This latter is a 'boot-strap' operation in which calculated 'probability' values may be far from true probabilities. An arbitrary index defined before the study on the basis of judgment or from a pilot study is an unbiased method of quantifying response. However, one should always consider how acceptable such an index will be to his professional peers [Best, 1970, p. 3].

Generally, normally distributed, continuous measures permit the greatest power in statistical analysis; other continuously distributed or ranked measures are next; ranked categories with ties are somewhat less; and categorization by attributes, such as dead *versus* alive, are least (see Best, 1970).

A virtue of a good measure (in addition to its being accurate) is its reproducibility. Often where ranking or categorizations were used in the experiments of this analysis, the criteria by which subject-performances were judged were not sufficiently described so that another experimenter could reproduce the measure. This mitigates against rerunning the experiment on another sample or another group of subjects and thereby limits the usefulness of the original study, no matter how valid its methods may have been.

In studying learning phenomena with schizophrenic patients, the criterion measures tend to be somewhat simpler than those usually employed in other kinds of behavior studies. Number of errors is a common measure which is built into the task and which is a continuous measurement. It lends itself well to statistical treatment, and there is a great deal of data on learning curves from other sources. In these kinds of studies, there is less reason for sloppy independent variable and measurement work than there could be in other types of psychological studies.

When more esoteric measures were used—usually concocted at the time of the study with little pilot or standardization work—this type of dependent variable tended to be related to *zero* outcomes in our analysis; this suggests that there is some virtue in remaining with the better developed and more commonly used performance or error measurements.

5. *The Structure and Procedure of the Experiment*

In relation to the structure and procedure of the experiment, probably more care should be given to the design of the study and the step-by-step conducting of the experiment when dealing with psychopathological groups than with other types of subjects. This is particularly true in dealing with schizophrenic subjects where reams have been written about the distractibility of such patients, their difficulties in focusing, their inabilities to respond to relevant cues, and their difficulties in responding appropriately under even the best of circumstances. Since it appears to be the case with SIG that they have these peculiar attention problems, it would appear useful to construct designs and procedures which would lessen the impact of these characteristics so that they do not contaminate the main effects. This means keeping the preexperimental, experimental, and post-experimental contacts as simple and clear-cut as possible. Loosely constructed procedures in which subjects are asked to free-associate or respond-at-random appear particularly prone to stimulating schizophrenics' discursive responses. The use of single rather than multiple tasks, the use of focusing devices of various kinds, the avoidance of prolonged and complicated tasks may aid in the designing of more useful studies. Unless the investigator is particularly interested in studying schizophrenic distractibility, allowing this tendency to manifest itself unnecessarily in the experimental situation will do little to clarify his findings.

To judge from our analysis, the briefer and simpler the instructions the better. And, for the sake of replication, the wordage should be kept as constant as possible from subject to subject (even with normal comparison groups) and should be reported in toto.

There seems, in our analysis, almost an inverse relationship between simplicity of design and procedure and clarity of findings. There appears, however, to be a fine line between keeping the experiment simple and dropping out variables (for the sake of simplicity) which might better be tested out experimentally. It is clear, for example, that SIG perform better to multiple or single reinforcers in the same task. There is also a question whether SIG cannot generalize from something they have learned, or whether they have not learned it sufficiently well to generalize.

It would appear highly desirable that the investigator justify every step of his design or procedure with reference to previous research wherever possible. There is more justification for this approach than for his spending many preliminary paragraphs and much work in going over the broad areas of schizophrenic functioning so frequently summarized in "Introductory" paragraphs.

The tendency for investigators to make schizophrenic learning studies far too complicated is reflected, not only in the vast number of indeterminate results extant in our sample, but in the number of unidentified IVs ferreted out by our analysts. Complicated tasks and ornate procedures often concealed far too many uncontrolled variables and contaminated the main effects.

One of the virtues of using single subject or stochastic models is the rigidity with which one can regard the conducting of a single task. Where a single task is conducted with a number of subjects, it can usually be assumed that there is sufficient unmeasured variation from subject to subject involved in the actual conducting of the task to render the findings questionable. Add to this the massive amount of variation extant in the SIG samples and it is amazing that any kind of consistent finding is ever possible.

No doubt many procedural aids have been overlooked by previous incomplete experimentation. Referring again to the negative reinforcement studies employing "white noise," it is conceivable that "white noise" might become a common procedural measure to help distractible subjects attend to tasks; but, as has been previously pointed out, the actual function of "white noise" with SIG has never really been resolved. Does it function as negative reinforcement or does it mask distracting stimulation, or both?

The point remains that much of the research in the area of schizophrenic learning has focused on the effects of reward and punishment on performance when, in actuality, there are many more basic variables related to the circumstances and the nature of the learning task which appear to have as profound an impact on performance. When most investigators assay to experiment in this area, they make many unwarranted assumptions about the nature of the experimental procedure and their relationship with their subjects which unquestionably influence the experimental results. It might very well be that the influence of reward and punishment on learning and performance may be a direct function of the setting, the task, and the relationship between the subject and the experimenter.

6. The Relationship between the Subject and the Experimenter

There has been some interest, particularly in recent years, on the relationship of the experimenter (or technician) to his SIG subjects, but these have usually been incorporated as a part of a larger study in which effects of reward and/or punishment have been studied. Very little work has been done directly and exclusively on the many components of the subject-experimenter relationship.

In most studies the exact nature of the subject-experimenter relationship goes unreported. Usually task instructions will be reported, and several studies have dealt with antecedent contact with the subject; but the exact nature of the continuing contact before, during, and after the experiment proper has not been sufficiently studied.

It is possible that, as is the case with children, learning may be affected by the interpersonal relationship between teacher and child, or between experimenter and subject. And it is possible that this influence may be as important (or nearly as important) as the employing of reward and/or punishment as tools in the learning task.

Our previous sections dealing with the subject-experimenter relationship contain enough hints, minor trends, and suggestions to arouse suspicion of a great deal of uncontrolled variation assignable to this source.

There is reason to suspect from this analysis (Berkowitz, 1964; Ells, 1967) that antecedent contact between experimenter and subject, if its purpose is to insure the subject's cooperation, tends to obviate positive findings. In fact, motivational instructions on the part of the experimenter tend, in general, to have generally nonenhancing effects on learning by SIG (see Section XI). In fact, the less the experimenter does with the subject directly and interpersonally (including reinforcing him verbally), the better SIG appear to perform. This is somewhat of an overgeneralization based on a zealousness from finding four or five trends fitting together, but nonetheless is a piece of quasi-data which should not go totally ignored.

SIG tend to do better where the presentation of materials for a task is mediated mechanically, even though the experimenter is in the room and is obviously the prime mover.

All of the above goes to suggest that there is more than meets the eye in the subject-experimenter relationship, and it cannot be discounted by surrounding the relationship with ornate experimental variables and esoteric treatments. It would appear that the less the human experimenter has to do directly with SIG, the better they learn and perform. This is an hypothesis, but an eminently testable one, provided that it can be set up in the form of a researchable hypothesis!

Future investigators in the area of schizophrenic learning might well pay special attention to this set of variables. It is possible that many interesting things might be discovered if, for example, reward were held constant and some of the interpersonal elements varied. But if the investigator persists in studying reinforcement practices as such, he must still account for his role in the experimental procedure. It should, by all means, remain a *constant* if he is dealing with a number of subjects and is going to, in the end, depend on small group statistics for his outcome information. Since he does *not* know the total effect of his impact on the subject's performance, he should subtract himself out of the experimental situation as much as possible, knowing that he may very well be reducing the effectiveness of verbal rewards plus contributing to the uncontrolled variance. The contacts he by necessity has with the subjects should be constant, brief, and completely reported so that subsequent investigators can build on his experience.

In the present analysis, there are unlimited possibilities suggested for the interaction of the subject-experimenter relationship with other variables. Smallness of N has prohibited most of them from being considered in Section XI, where interactions and combinations were briefly dealt with. It has been noted, for example, that there tends to be a zero trend ($p < .20$) when the sex of the experimenter is male under conditions of positive reinforcement. Considering that the vast majority of subjects were male SIG, the hypothesis is suggested that male SIG do not respond well to male reinforcing agents where rewards are used. This may, additionally, have implications for the poor performance of motivating instructions and for the better performance of mechanically mediated reinforcers. Perhaps the use of female reinforcing agents with male SIG might alter the picture sufficiently, in one direction or another, to promote new outcomes.

The internal structures (design and procedure) of most experiments in this analysis were such that it becomes more fruitful to ponder the vast number of uncontrolled variables probably affecting outcomes than to reflect too deeply on the outcomes. It is one of the facts of psychological research life that every brick of every experiment must be shaped and understood with great clarity before any faith can be put in possible "main effects."

7. Interpreting the Findings or "The Trouble with Outcomes . . ."

Schoolman, Becktel, Best, and Johnson (1968), conclude their paper on the use of statistics in medical research with the following two paragraphs:

> If it is a good answer we seek to find and publish, we must be first concerned with whether we are asking a good question. Second, will our plan answer the question with predetermined risks of mistakes? Third, have we executed the experiment in such a fashion that there is reasonable justification for quantitating those results? If the answer is important, the question is important. Conceivably, an answer may be more useful when $p < 0.05$ than when $p > 0.05$, but surely it is not more important. *The importance of the answer is a function of the question and not whether the answer is yes or no.* (Italics ours.) Thus we would urge that criteria for publication be revised

so that they are based upon whether or not it is a well-conceived, meaningful question which the experiment may be expected to answer, rather than upon what the answer is.

Finally, we would gently offer some general suggestions to editors which result perhaps more from our consultative experience with investigators than from review of the Journal. Do not insist upon statistics for statistics' sake. The interpretation of adequately planned experiments is usually obvious. The calculations of p values or inclusion of elaborate analysis does not necessarily add anything meaningful to the presentation. Analysis is not an information-generating operation. The information lies in the data and the purpose of analysis is an aid to data presentation and interpretation. If, as is frequently the case, the analysis (even though appropriate) does not add anything to the data presentation, don't use it. In the vast majority of cases where investigators have sought our help because editors have insisted upon the inclusion of statistical analysis in their papers, none was appropriate, none was necessary. The real value of statistical methods lies not in analysis but in planning [Schoolman *et al.*, 1968, pp. 366–367].

It has also been pointed out by other authors (e.g., Chassen) that one of the great disadvantages of the extensive research model (used exclusively in the group of studies which were sampled in this analysis) is that it is biased in the direction of the null hypothesis.

When an investigator is conscientious enough to try to pull together a sample of schizophrenics who are similar (homogeneous) with respect to some set of disease variables, he is usually confronted with a tiny sample, making it necessary for a treatment to be extraordinarily effective in order to be statistically significant. Where he is less particular in drawing his schizophrenic sample and goes for large numbers rather than homogeneity, he is more likely to get positive (significant) results but is less likely to procure a clear-cut outcome, due to the heterogeneity of the sample.

In the first case, there is an unnecessary bias in the direction of accepting the null hypothesis. Frequently it is forgotten that failure to obtain a statistically significant result is not a finding for or against any kind of an hypothesis; it is an indeterminate finding. It leaves the question still unanswered. And, in the second case, even though a question has been answered, the answer is unclear because of the vagueness of the question (in this case, not clearly specifying the population from which the sample is drawn).

Clearly, the trouble with the outcomes in the experiments from this analysis is that they are uninformative. Often lacking clear-cut statistical significance (even when the sample is large), authors clutch and grab at passing minor trends (near significance) as has been done in this analysis. The findings section (or more usually, the Discussion section) of most papers then becomes an hypothesis-generating exercise which reveals more than anything how inadequately the original question was asked in the first place.

Trends and fads have also played a large part in the kinds of research questions investigators (particularly dissertation writers) have asked and hoped to answer. Like all fads, the reason for their existence is often more emotional than rational, but they clog up the journals for a time, more out of persistence than quality (for example, the "fad" among researchers regarding "unconscious perception" back in the 1950s and the popularizing of "verbal conditioning" studies in the 1960s).

There are hopeful signs (mainly astrological) that the fad is fading in reinforcement studies with schizophrenia; their contributions to our knowledge about schizophrenia as a disorder and about how schizophrenic patients learn have been less than overpowering. In most cases, the experiments have not even been worthwhile exercises in conducting research, which is, after all, what doctoral dissertations are intended to be.

Perhaps we are entering an era in which researchers will take a long, hard look at the experimental work with *all* psychopathological groups and realistically assess what our current research models and practices have bought us in terms of new knowledge. Perhaps now we can go back to a more rational approach to psychopathological research and begin again at ground zero.

Appendix

Review of the Literature: A Consideration of the Effects of Experimentally Manipulated, Nonreinforcement Variables on the Learning and/or Performances of Schizophrenics in General

In addition to the effects of treatments (e.g., rewards and punishments) on SIG, many experiments in this analysis investigated the effects of other variables on learning and/or performance. Although there was a fairly large number of such nontreatment IVs, the number of experiments investigating any particular variable was quite small. For example, the largest group assessing any single variable was nine. Consequently, there were few such areas that lent themselves to "review."

As is customary in review articles, no statistical tests have been used in collating these findings. Following tradition, simply a subjective summary of the findings in each of the areas will be presented.

In general, the effects of the nontreatment IVs do not seem to form any sort of pattern. In contrasting items (such as human *versus* nonhuman), effects seem to be equal, overall, rather than unequal. The clearest finding seems to involve the use of antecedent contact between subject and experimenter under conditions of positive reinforcement, and this finding must be viewed with caution because of the small N (four experiments). The trend suggests that *no* antecedent contact is better than antecedent contact in enhancing learning. But, where antecedent contact is employed, negatively toned antecedent contact is more effective than positively toned contact.

In experiments using human *versus* nonhuman (social *versus* nonsocial) reinforcers, the two types appeared to be generally equal to each other in effects; neither had an advantage over the other (nine experiments).

With respect to the affective tone of the reinforced response, negative tone appeared to be better than either neutral or positive tone. However, only two studies were involved—both employing positive reinforcement.

In a number of experiments, nontreatment IVs involved the nature of the schizophrenic sample itself. On the severity of illness items (eight experiments), the performances of high-severe and low-severe groups were the same in the majority of cases. When they differed, the low-severe groups appeared to have the advantage.

Paranoid and nonparanoid patients (four studies) were generally equal to each other in performance. Similarly, in considering good premorbid history *versus* poor premorbid history (seven experiments), these two groups were also more often equal in performance than not equal. When they differed, the advantage appeared to be with the good premorbids.

One final variable: The scant information available from our data on complex *versus* simple tasks indicates that in *no* circumstances do SIG perform better on complex than on simple tasks. This is based on six experiments using simple *versus* complex tasks as an IV.

As has been previously mentioned, there were many additional IVs (particularly in the areas of Situational Variables, Task Instructions, and Acquisition) that were not so identified by the investigators but which become apparent when experiments were coded by our analysts. In fairness to the investigators, it should be pointed out there is a great deal of confounding (or overlap) among the variables in these three sections— partly because of the nature of the variables themselves and partly from the way the data was cut up for purposes of this analysis. However, the largest amount of uncontrolled variance in this regard results from sloppy experimental design.

CODING MANUAL FOR RESEARCH ON SCHIZOPHRENIC LEARNING

General Instructions to Raters

This is a manual for classifying and codifying information gleaned from research papers on schizophrenic functioning. Raters are assumed to have a certain amount of basic knowledge of research terminology and procedures. Most of the information needed for this manual may be obtained from sections of papers called "Sample" and "Procedure." Raters may generally ignore sections called "Introduction," "Results," or "Findings," "Discussion," and "Summary." The following cautions are important:

1. DO NOT INFER. If the report of the experiment does not specifically mention an item of information that should be rated, circle the code number for "Insufficient information." There are two exceptions to this rule:
   a. If a psychological test is used, but insufficiently described in the report, consult outside sources for a description of the test before making your rating unless you are quite familiar with the test.
   b. Under "Sex of Experimenter," you may infer that the author is the experimenter (E) if study is based upon a Ph.D. dissertation (unless otherwise explicitly stated).
2. "Unassigned" items are not to be used for rating purposes and may be ignored. "Unassigned does not mean the same as "Insufficient information."
3. READ CAREFULLY! Always keep track of the title of the broad section in which you are coding. (The title is at the top of the page.)
4. Make your rating by CIRCLING THE CODE NUMBER of the item you are choosing on the answer sheet ONLY.
5. The category instructions ("Select *one*" or "Select as many as necessary") are intended only as guidelines. Individual studies may force you, occasionally, to ignore them in the interest of coding adequate information. The general rule to follow in all categories is to select the minimum number of items per category.

BLACK CODE: CHARACTERISTICS OF THE SCHIZOPHRENIC SAMPLE GROUP

Sex (Select *one*)

000	No information regarding sex of sample
001	Male
002	Female
003	Male and female in separate groups
004	Mixed male and female in same group

Kind of Information Reported in Describing Sample (Select as many as necessary)

005	Age
006	IQ
007	Visual acuity

008	Education
009	Socioeconomic status
010	Shock, absence of
011	Race
012	Neurological disorder, absence of
013	Extreme response sets
014	Number of hospitalizations
015	Length of hospitalization
016	Preexperimental habit strength test (operant level, base rate, common usage)
017	Preexperimental personality test variables
018	Literacy or reading ability test
019	Cooperative (as reported before study)
020	Awareness of reinforcer or punishment response contingency
021	Awareness of the purpose of the experiment
022	Other restricting and/or descriptive characteristics
023	Treatment regimen—past and/or present
024	Severity of illness

Restrictive Items Used as Independent Variables
(Select as many as necessary)

025	Not applicable
026	Age
027	IQ range
028	Education
029	Socioeconomic status
030	Electroconvulsive shock
031	Extreme response sets
032	Preexperimental habit strength test
033	Preexperimental personality test variables
034	Other

Hospitalization Status (Select *one*)

035	No information on status
036	Inpatient
037	Outpatient
038	In- and outpatients in separate groups
039	Mixed in- and outpatients in the same group

Subdiagnosis (Standard nomenclature) (Select *one*)

| 040 | Mixed schizophrenics in one group, *with* information about diagnostic subtypes |

041	Mixed schizophrenics in one group, *without* information about diagnostic subtypes
042	Paranoid schizophrenics only
043	Nonparanoid schizophrenics only
044	Paranoid and nonparanoid in separate groups
045	Other subtypes used in separate groups

Symptoms (Schizophrenic sample divided into comparison groups on basis of symptoms) (Circle if YES; leave blank if NO) (If YES, select as many items below as are necessary)

046	Circle if YES; leave blank if NO
047	Delusional *vs.* nondelusional
048	Withdrawn *vs.* not withdrawn
049	Unassigned
050	Unassigned
051	Unassigned
052	Unassigned
053	Unassigned
054	Unassigned

Premorbidity (select *one*)

055	Good premorbidity (Phillips or comparable scale)
056	Poor premorbidity (Phillips or comparable scale)
057	Good and poor premorbidity in separate groups (Phillips or comparable scale)
058	No information

Process-Reactive (Select *one*)

059	Process schizophrenics only
060	Reactive schizophrenics only
061	Process and reactive schizophrenics in separate groups
062	No information

Chronicity-Acuteness (Select as many as necessary)

063	Sample defined as chronic by time in hospital (greater than 12 months)
064	Sample defined as acute by time in hospital (less than or equal to 12 months current hospitalization)
065	Sample defined as chronic by number of hospitalizations (two or more)

066	Sample defined as acute by number of hospitalizations (first hospitalization)
067	Sample defined chronic by investigator without explicit criteria
068	Sample defined acute by investigator without explicit criteria
069	Sample rated chronic by staff of judges
070	Sample rated acute by staff of judges
071	Sample defined chronic by clinical folder
072	Sample defined acute by clinical folder
073	Chronicity used as an independent variable
074	Sample mixed on chronicity (e.g., both acute, chronic; may be inferred if length of hospitalization and/or number of hospitalizations is given)
075	Insufficient information

Stages of Remission (Select *one*)

076	Moderate-to-good state of remission
077	Regressed or severely decompensated
078	Separate groups of remissed and regressed
079	Mixed groups of remissed and regressed patients
080	No information regarding current stage of remission

Source of Diagnosis (Select *one*)

081	Diagnosis of schizophrenia based on clinical folder (hospital staff and/or psychiatrist in charge of case)
082	Diagnosis of schizophrenia based on psychometrics *only*
083	Diagnosis of schizophrenia based on judges' opinion
084	No information regarding source of diagnosis of schizophrenia
085	Unassigned
086	Unassigned

Drug or Medication Status (Select *one*)

087	All on psychotropic drugs
088	None on psychotropic drugs
089	Separate groups of on-drug and off-drug patients
090	Mixed groups—some patients on drugs and some off drugs
091	Drugs used as independent variable
092	No information regarding drug or medication status of patients

	Division of Sample into Control and Experimental Groups
093	Circle if YES; leave blank if NO

	Members of Schizophrenic Sample Used as Own Control
094	Circle if YES; leave blank if NO

BROWN CODE: CHARACTERISTICS OF THE EXPERIMENTER(S)

Sex (Select *one*)

100	Male
101	Female
102	Mixed male and female, data separately analyzed
103	Mixed male and female, data not separately analyzed
104	No information regarding sex of *E*

Status (Select as many as necessary)

105	*E* is a psychologist
106	*E* nonpsychologist, but professional (psychiatrist, social worker, nurse, therapist, etc.)
107	*E* nonprofessional (aides, secretaries, clerks, etc.)
108	Peer acts as *E* (fellow patient)
109	Research technician acts as *E*
110	Status used as an independent variable
111	No information

Experimenter's Familiarity with Hypotheses (Select *one*)

112	*E* FAMILIAR with hypotheses
113	*E* UNFAMILIAR with hypotheses
114	No information
115	Unassigned

Personality (Select *one*)

116	No description of *E*'s personality
117	*E* described as extrovert and/or aggressive
118	*E* described as introvert and/or timid
119	Personality of *E* described in ways other than above
120	Personality description of *E* used as independent variable

RED CODE: CHARACTERISTICS OF THE NONSCHIZO-
PHRENIC COMPARISON GROUP(S)

	(NOTE: "Comparison group" refers to any group to which the schizophrenic sample is compared, such as normals, neurotics, organics, etc. Comparison group is not synonymous with Control group, which refers to a group receiving no treatment—See item 236)
200	Nonschizophrenic comparison group used (Circle if YES; leave blank if NO) If NO, skip this section: Characteristics of the Nonschizophrenic Comparison Groups

Diagnosis (Check more than one if necessary)

201	Normal—not screened, or no report of screening, for history of schizophrenia
202	Normal—screened for history of schizophrenia
203	Normal—screened for history of ANY psychiatric disorder
204	Neurotic
205	Character disorder
206	Mixed psychiatric, nonpsychotic
207	Mixed psychiatric, not specified
208	Other psychotic
209	Brain injured
210	Other

Chronicity (Select as many as necessary)

211	Not applicable
212	Sample defined as chronic by time in hospital
213	Sample defined as acute by time in hospital
214	Sample defined as chronic by number of hospitalizations
215	Sample defined as acute by number of hospitalizations
216	Sample defined chronic by investigator without explicit criteria
217	Sample defined acute by investigator without explicit criteria
218	Sample rated chronic by staff of judges
219	Sample rated acute by staff of judges
220	Sample defined chronic by clinical folder
221	Sample defined acute by clinical folder
222	Chronicity used as an independent variable

223	Sample mixed on chronicity (may be inferred if length of hospitalization and/or number of hospitalizations is given)
224	Insufficient information

Hospitalization Status (May circle more than one if more than one comparison group)

225	Not applicable
226	Inpatient
227	Outpatient
228	In- and outpatients in separate group
229	Mixed in- and outpatients in the same group
230	No information

Sex (May circle more than one if more than one comparison group)

231	Male
232	Female
233	Male and female in separate groups
234	Mixed sexes in the same group
235	No information

Division of Comparison Sample into Control and Experimental Groups

236	Circle if YES; leave blank if NO

Members of Comparison Sample(s) used as Own Control

237	Circle if YES; leave blank if NO

ORANGE CODE: SITUATIONAL VARIABLES

Reward for Participation (Select *one*)

300	Tangible reward offered for participation in experiment
301	No report of tangible reward offered for participation in experiment
302	Reward for participation in experiment used as independent variable
303	Unassigned

Defining Purpose of Contact (Select as many as necessary)

304	Purpose of contact with *S* described as "research," but

S told *prior to experiment* that results WOULD NOT personally affect him

305   Purpose of contact with *S* described as "research," but *S* told *prior to experiment* that results WILL personally affect him

306   Purpose of contact with *S* described as "research," but no report as to whether or not *S* told prior to experiment how results will personally affect him

307   Purpose of contact with *S* described as *diagnostic* test, or just a test, to help *S*

308   Purpose of contact with *S* described as treatment to help *S*

309   Purpose of contact with *S* ambiguous—*S* given no reason for appointment

310   Purpose of contact with *S* used as independent variable

311   Insufficient information to define purpose of contact with *S*

312   Research to help understand mental illness or personality, etc.

Antecedent Contact with S (Tasks where the results are *not* used as dependent variables and which come prior to the dependent variable task are rated as antecedent contact)

313   Report of antecedent contact between *S* and *E* not relating to experiment (Circle if YES; leave blank if NO)

314   Report of antecedent contact between *S* and *E* relating to experiment (other than task instructions) (Circle if YES; leave blank if NO) (Yes also includes operant level determination)

315   Report of antecedent contact between *S* and *non-E* relating to experiment (Other than task instructions) (Circle if YES; leave blank if NO)

Nature of Antecedent Contact with S Relating to Experiment (Select as many as needed. Answer this category only if you have answered YES to 314 and/or 315)

316   Antecedent contact with *S* to secure his participation in experiment

317   Antecedent contact with *S* characterized by attempt to gain rapport

318   Antecedent contact with S characterized by attempt to antagonize, irritate, intimidate, or frighten S

319   Antecedent contact with S characterized by practice or warm-up task, or establishing of operant level or base rate, or testing to classify Ss.

320   Nature of antecedent contact with S used as an independent variable

321   Insufficient information

Continuity of Antecedent Contact (Select *one*)

322   Not applicable (Use 322 if neither 314 nor 315 were checked)

323   Antecedent contact continuous with treatment trials

324   Antecedent contact not continuous with treatment trials

325   Continuity used as an independent variable

326   Insufficient information

Subject's Knowledge of Experimenter's Role (Select *one*)

327   No information regarding S's knowledge of E's role and/ or status

328   S given prior information regarding E's role and/or status

329   S given NO prior information regarding E's role and/or status

330   S's information about role and/or status of E used as independent variable

Personality Description of Experimenter to Subject
(Select *one*)

331   No information on this point

332   S given POSITIVE personality description of E before meeting

333   S given NEGATIVE personality description of E before meeting

334   Personality description of E to S used as independent variable

The next two categories should relate to the period after the Experimental Task instructions.

Social Setting of Experiment (Select as many as necessary)

335   One S, no E

336   One S, one E

337   One S, multiple E's
338   Multiple S's, one E
339   Other
340   Social setting used as an independent variable

           Social Interaction (Select as many as necessary)

341   No social interaction
342   S-S interaction
343   S-E interaction
344   E-E interaction
345   Social interaction used as independent variable
346   Insufficient information

           Affective Tone of Social Interaction Beginning with Task Instructions (Select *one*)

347   Positive (supportive, reassuring, approving)
348   Negative (antagonizing, intimidating, censuring, disapproving)
349   Neutral
350   Affective tone used as independent variable
351   Insufficient information

           Antecedent Contract Between Subject and Subject (Applicable only if S-S interaction is present)

352   Not applicable (Use 352 if 342 not checked)
353   Report of antecedent contact between S and S not relating to experiment (Circle if YES; leave blank if NO)
354   Report of antecedent contact between S and S *relating to experiment* (Other than task instructions) (Circle if YES; leave blank if NO)
355   Insufficient information

YELLOW CODE: EXPERIMENTAL TASK STIMULI (In a classical conditioning study, the conditioned stimulus should be rated in this section. Do not rate reinforcing stimuli in this section)

           Number of Tasks (Select *one*)

400   Single task
401   Multiple tasks

           Method of Presentation (Select as many as necessary)

Definitions:

Personal—*E* plays a part in the presentation of the task stimuli and materials beyond the initial trial

Impersonal—*E* does not present materials or stimuli beyond the initial trial

Instrumental—Presentation of stimuli that is mediated by anything beyond *E*'s person

No instrumental—Presentation of stimuli by *E*'s voice, gestures, touch, etc.

402	Personal—no instrumental mediation
403	Personal—instrumental mediation—*E* present
404	Impersonal—instrumental mediation—*E* not present
405	Impersonal—instrumental mediation—*E* present
406	Method of presentation used as an independent variable
407	Insufficient information

Control of Rate of Presentation (Select as many as necessary)

408	*E* limits time *S* is to respond to total task or subtask
409	*E* limits time *S* is to respond to single item
410	*E* does not limit time *S* is to respond to total task or subtask (self-pacing)
411	*E* does not limit time *S* is to respond to single item (self-pacing)
412	Control of rate of presentation used as independent variable
413	Insufficient information

Sense Modality Stimulated (Do not include reinforcing stimuli here) (Select as many as necessary)

414	Visual
415	Auditory
416	Tactual
417	Vestibular (balance)
418	Nociceptive (pain and pressure)
419	Kinesthetic
420	Other sense modalities
421	Sense modality of experimental task stimuli used as independent variable
422	Insufficient information

Nature of Materials (Select as many as necessary)

423   Graphic or written materials
424   Auditory materials
425   Blocks, puzzles, pieces, marbles, cards
426   Mechanical device
427   No material—e.g., free operant conversation

Characteristics of Task Stimuli: Humanness (Select one unless there are two or more tasks)

428   Human activity or content; human references
429   Humanoid: Objects or animals in humanlike activity, and symbolic references to human activity (e.g., proverbs)
430   Nonhuman activity or content; nonhuman references
431   Stimuli indistinguishable or mixed on above three items (e.g., personal pronouns—unless otherwise stated—are involved here)
432   Humanness of task stimuli used as independent variable
433   Insufficient information

Characteristics of Task Stimuli: Verbalness (Select as many as necessary)

434   Verbal task
435   Nonverbal task
436   Mixed verbal and nonverbal task
437   Verbal and nonverbal materials used as independent variable
438   Insufficient information

Characteristics of Task Stimuli: Meaningfulness (Select one)

439   Meaningful content, relatively nonambiguous
440   Content-free, relatively ambiguous; e.g., projective test materials
441   Both meaningful and content-free materials used in tasks (mixed)
442   Meaningful and content-free stimuli used as independent variable

| 443 | Insufficient information |
| 444 | Unassigned |

Nature of Affective Tone (Specific items in this category are to be checked only if 445 is answered YES)

445	Affective tone of task stimuli used as independent variable (Circle if YES; leave blank if NO)
446	Physically threatening
447	Ego-threatening
448	Prejudicial
449	Sexual
450	Hostile (verbally)
451	Pleasurable
452	Neutral
453	Other
454	Mixed affective tone

Characteristics of Task Stimuli: Association Value

| 455 | High *vs.* low association value used as independent variable (Circle if YES; leave blank if NO) |

Characteristics of Task Stimuli: Complexity

| 456 | Complex *vs.* simple task stimuli used as independent variable |

Characteristics of Task Stimuli: Similarity

| 457 | Similar *vs.* dissimilar task stimuli used as independent variable (Circle if YES; leave blank if NO) |

GREEN CODE: TASK INSTRUCTIONS

Set Instructions (Select as many as necessary)

500	S instructed for speed ("Work as fast as you can" or "Give first response which comes to mind")
501	S instructed for accuracy ("Do as well or the best you can")
502	Set instructions used as independent variable
503	Unassigned
504	S instructed to surpass his previous performance
505	S instructed to cooperate with one or more Ss
506	S instructed to compete with one or more other Ss

507	S instructed for competition between teams
508	S specifically not given set instructions
509	No information about set instructions

Instructions Concerning Correct Response (Select as many as necessary)

510	S told there is a correct response, but he is *not* told what it is
511	S told there is a correct response, but he *is* told what it is
512	S told there are no right or wrong answers
513	S purposely not told anything about the correctness of response in task instructions
514	Insufficient information

Reinforcer Identification (Select *one*)

515	Not applicable
516	Reinforcer identified to S (e.g., "Green light means you are correct," or "I'll say 'not so good' sometimes")
517	Reinforcer not identified to S
518	Insufficient information
519	Unassigned

Cessation of Reinforcer (Extinction) (Select *one*)

520	Not applicable
521	S told of cessation of reinforcer
522	S not told of cessation of reinforcer
523	Insufficient information on this variable

Nature of Task Assignment (Select any number) *Read Each Item!*

524	S told to make up story
525	S told to make up a sentence
526	S told to complete sentences
527	S told to associate to stimulus word (free)—single response
528	S told to associate to stimulus word (free)—two or more responses
529	S told to associate to stimulus word (controlled)—specified content single response

530	*S* told to associate to stimulus word (controlled)—specified content two or more responses
531	*S* told to do paired associations (numbers, words)
532	*S* told to say words (no stimulus-word, free)
533	*S* told to say words (types of words specified)
534	*S* told to respond to standard interview questions (personal matters and problems)
535	*S* told to respond to standard interview questions (impersonal problems, attitudes, opinions)
536	*S* told to respond to nonstandard interview questions (personal matters and problems)
537	*S* told to respond to nonstandard interview questions (impersonal matters and problems)
538	*S* told to respond to standardized tests
539	*S* told to state general rules used to discriminate or sort stimuli or objects
540	*S* told to identify or match stimuli
541	*S* told to interpret proverbs
542	*S* told to learn lists of words (serial learning)
543	*S* told to guess or predict
544	*S* told to indicate ones that are similar
545	*S* told to indicate ones that don't belong
546	*S* told to free-sort (e.g., sort these into piles)
547	*S* told to control-sort (e.g., sort these into two or more piles)
548	*S* told to fit in pieces (e.g., puzzles or form boards)
549	*S* told to perform repetitive simple task (e.g., marble-dropping, lever-pushing)
550	*S* told to perform repetitive complex task (e.g., double alternation or one or more complex prearranged patterns)
551	*S* told to free-draw (figure drawing, HTP)
552	*S* told to mirror-draw
553	*S* told to follow target
554	Threshold instructions—"Tell me when you see/hear/feel it"
555	Threshold instructions—"Tell me when you can identify it"
556	*S* told to discriminate relevant from irrelevant cues (figures from ground, scanning, embedded figures)
557	*S* told to report what he sees

558   *S* told to judge magnitudes (size, brightness, loudness, weight)
559   *S* told to discriminate differences (in color, shape, pitch, etc.)
560   *S* told to judge spatial relations (rod and frame test, tilted room or chair, depth perception)
561   *S* told to judge body orientation (vestibular studies)
562   *S* told to report body image perceptions (from figure drawings or descriptions)
563   *S* told to report social perceptions (describing aspect of social environment, e.g., recognizing new *vs.* old patients or personnel, awareness of psychological or social characteristics of the other patients or personnel; adjective check list data)
564   *S* told to report fantasy perceptions (dreams, hallucinations, daydreams)
565   *S* told to report kinetic perception (autokinetic movement phi-phenomenon, necker cubes, etc.)
566   Other
567   Unassigned
568   Unassigned
569   Unassigned

           Rule Instructions (Circle 570 or 571 if the task involves the discovery of one or more rules which, if known to *S,* would automatically enable him to give the correct response) (Circle 572 for all other tasks)

570   *S* given set and/or instructions to discover rules
571   *S* not given set and/or instructions to discover rules
572   Not applicable

           Mode of Response (Select as many as necessary)

573   *S* instructed to speak response
574   *S* instructed to write response
575   *S* instructed to make a motor response
576   Autonomic responses (e.g., heart beat, respirations, etc.)
577   Insufficient information on this variable
578   Unassigned

BLUE CODE: ACQUISITION AND RELATED AREAS

600	Study employing Classical (Respondent) conditioning (Circle if YES; leave blank if NO)
601	Study employing Instrumental (Operant) conditioning— Explicit reinforcement (i.e., reinforcement manipulated by E) (Circle if YES; leave blank if NO)
602	Study employing Instrumental (Operant) conditioning— Implicit reinforcement (i.e., reinforcement built into tasks, e.g., knowledge of results) (Circle if YES; leave blank if NO)
603	Use of Nonconditioned control group (Circle if YES; leave blank if NO)

If answers to all four of above are "NO," skip over to the next section (*Purple Code*); otherwise proceed.

Instructions for Remainder of This Section

If you are rating a classical conditioning study, the US (unconditioned stimulus) should be considered equivalent to reinforcement or punishment, as the case may be; and CS (conditioned stimulus) should have been rated above under the Experimental Task Stimuli Section. With those studies employing both classical and instrumental conditioning choose as many items as necessary in all of the following categories under this section, Acquisition and Related Areas.

Method of Presentation of Reinforcement or Punishment (Select *one*)

604	Personal-direct-face-to-face no mechanical mediation
605	Personal-indirect-mechanical mediation-E present
606	Impersonal-completely mechanical-E not present
607	Impersonal-completely mechanical-E present
608	Method of presentation used as independent variable
609	Implicit reinforcement (see 602) (e.g., paired association or serial learning will fall here)
610	Insufficient information on this variable

Nature of Reinforcer or Punishment—Personal/Impersonal (Select *one*)

611	Human (personal)
612	Nonhuman (impersonal)
613	Personal/impersonal used as independent variable

| 614 | Personal and impersonal mixed in one session |
| 615 | Insufficient information on this variable |

Nature of Reinforcement or Punishment—Verbal/Nonverbal (Select *one*)

616	Verbal
617	Nonverbal
618	Both verbal and nonverbal in one session (mixed)
619	Verbal/nonverbal reinforcement used as independent variable
620	Insufficient information on this variable

Type of Behavioral Manipulation (Select as many as necessary)
(Definitions: *Positive* reinforcement or reward refer to stimuli which increase the strength of preceding responses; *Negative* reinforcement refers to stimuli which when removed increase the strength of preceding responses) (*Punishment* refers to the presentation of aversive stimuli or the removal of positive reinforcers)

621	Positive reinforcement or reward
622	Negative reinforcement
623	Punishment
624	Combination (at least two) of Positive reinforcement, Negative reinforcement, and Punishment used in same group in one session (mixed) (include here studies where "knowledge of correct response" is method of reinforcement)
625	Single reinforcer or punishment used in one session
626	Varieties of reinforcers or punishments in one session
627	Type of behavioral manipulation used as independent variable (when only one of the items in this category is checked, check 627 if 094 or 093 or 603, e.g., use of control group, is checked). If only 094 is checked, check 627 only if there is a no treatment—treatment comparison

Sense Modalities Stimulated in Reinforcing or Punishing (Select as many as necessary)

| 628 | Visual |
| 629 | Auditory |

630	Tactual
631	Vestibular (balance)
632	Nociceptive
633	Kinesthetic
634	Sense modalities used as independent variable
635	Other
636	Insufficient information

Reinforcement or Punishment Schedules
(Select as many as necessary)

637	Continuous reinforcement
638	Partial reinforcement (e.g., VI, FI, VR, FR, etc.)
639	Probabilistic reinforcement schedule (where both correct and incorrect responses are reinforced, but at differential rates)
640	Reinforcement schedules used as independent variable
641	Insufficient information on this variable

Delay of Reinforcement and/or Punishment

642	No delay
643	Delayed reinforcement following end of logical unit
644	Delayed reinforcement following block of trials and/or completion of whole task

Extinction Schedules (Select one)

645	No extinction period
646	Total cessation of reinforcement (extinction)
647	Counterconditioning
648	Punishing previously correct response(s)
649	Extinction schedule used as independent variable
650	Insufficient information

Type of Response Chosen by Experimenter to Be Reinforced or Punished (Select one)

651	Insufficient information
652	Spoken
653	Nonspoken
654	Both spoken and nonspoken (mixed)
655	Spoken—nonspoken used as independent variable

Response Strength (Select as many as necessary)

656   Not specified
657   Response strength used as independent variable
658   High
659   Medium
660   Low

Affective Tone of Reinforced or Punished Response
(Select as many as necessary)

661   Not specified or identified
662   Physically threatening
663   Ego-threatening
664   Prejudicial
665   Sexual
666   Hostile (verbally)
667   Pleasurable
668   Neutral
669   Affective tone of reinforced response used as independent variable
670   Mixed affective

Reference Direction of Reinforced or Punished Response

671   Not applicable
672   Self-referred statements
673   Other-referred statements
674   Both self-referred and other-referred statements in the same experimental group (mixed)
675   Self- and other-referred statements used as independent variable

Reinforcement of Nondelusional Speech

676   Circle if YES; leave blank if NO
677   *Response-Contingent Reinforcement:* reinforcement is contingent upon some particular aspect of *S*'s response, e.g., speed of responding, making correct response, etc.
678   *Nonresponse-Contingent Reinforcement:* reinforcement is not contingent on any particular aspect of *S*'s response
679   Unassigned
680   Unassigned

Subjects Tested for Awareness of Response-Reinforcement or Response-Punishment Contingency

681   Circle if YES; leave blank if NO

Subjects Asked When Reinforcers Occurred

682   Circle if YES; leave blank if NO
683   Unassigned
684   Unassigned
685   Unassigned
686   Unassigned
687   Unassigned

PURPLE CODE: DEPENDENT VARIABLES (Select as many as necessary)

700   Latency of responses (reaction time)
701   Rate—frequency of response per unit of time
702   Frequency and/or number of correct responses per block(s)
703   Difference scores—intraindividual (increment or decrement in performance)
704   Difference scores—interindividual (between pairs of individuals)
705   Number of trials to criterion
706   Time per trial/or total time
707   Amplitude or magnitude (e.g., autonomic response)
708   Number of errors
709   Retention
710   Resistance to extinction
711   Reminiscence (increment in recall following rest)
712   Individual learning measured by number of consecutive correct responses or solution
713   Individual learning measured by verbalization of correct solution
714   Individual learning measured by comparison with control group performance
715   Individual learning measured S's awareness of response-reinforcement/punishment contingency
716   Mean ratings
717   Generalization

718	Other
719	Unassigned
720	Unassigned

TABLE A

SUMMARY OF ITEMS *Versus* OUTCOMES FROM EXPERIMENTS ON POSITIVE
REINFORCEMENT WITH SCHIZOPHRENICS IN GENERAL

Item No.	Coding manual description	Direction of trend	p
040	Mixed schizophrenic sample *with* information about sub-diagnosis	0	.20
041	Mixed schizophrenic sample *without* information about subdiagnosis	+	.20
077	Regressed schizophrenic sample	+	.20
093	Independent control group used	0	.10
100	Sex of E: male	0	.20
105	Status of E: psychologist	0	.20
111	Status of E: no information	+	.20
112	E familiar with hypotheses of study	0	.10
114	No information about E's familiarity with hypotheses	+	.10
316	Antecedent contact with S to secure participation in experiment	0	.10
322	Continuity of antecedent contact not applicable (i.e. no a/c)	0	.10[a]
402	Method of presentation of task: personal, without instrumental mediation	+	.20
408	E limits time for total task	+	.05
409	E limits time for single trial	0	.20
413	Insufficient information about time limitation	0	.20
415	Sense modality stimulated: auditory	+	.20
423	Graphic or written materials used	0	.20
427	No materials used	+	.10[a]
431	Mixed human nonhuman content in task materials	0	.20
508	S specifically not given set instructions	+	.20
513	S purposely not told anything about correctness or incorrectness of responses	+	.20
522	S not told of cessation of S^r (i.e. extinction period used)	+	.05
531	S told to do paired-associates	0	.10
549	S told to perform repetitive simple task	+	.20
602	Implicit reinforcement used	0	.10
603	Nonreinforced control group used	0	.20
616	Nature of S^r: verbal	0	.20
628	Sense modality stimulated by S^r: visual	+	.20
646	Extinction period used	+	.10
681	S's tested for awareness of the R-S^r contingency	0	.20
701	Rate of responding	+	.20
705	Number of trials to criterion	0	.10
710	Resistance to extinction	+	.20

[a] $10 > N \geq 5$.

TABLE B

SUMMARY OF ITEMS *Versus* OUTCOMES FROM EXPERIMENTS ON PUNISHMENT
WITH SCHIZOPHRENICS IN GENERAL

Item No.	Coding manual description	Direction of trend	p
040	Mixed schizophrenic sample *with* information about sub-diagnosis	0	.10
041	Mixed schizophrenic sample *without* information about subdiagnosis	+	.20
307	Purpose of contact with S described as diagnostic testing	0	.10[a]
335	Social setting of experiment: One S, no E	+	.10[a]
349	Affective tone of social interaction: neutral	+	.20[a]
400	Single task used	+	.20
401	Multiple tasks used (i.e., more than one)	0	.20
413	Insufficient information about time limitation	0	.20
424	Auditory task materials used	0	.20
504	S instructed to surpass previous performance	0	.20[a]
522	S not told of cessation of reinforcer	+	.10[a]
540	S told to identify or match stimuli	0	.20[a]
605	Method of presentation of S^r personal but mechanically mediated	+	.20
617	Nature of S^r: nonverbal	+	.20
644	Delayed S^r after block of trials	0	.10
677	Response-contingent S^r used	+	.20
678	Non-R-contingent S^r used	0	.20
700	Latency	+	.20
718	Other	0	.05

[a] $10 > N \geq 5$.

References

American Psychiatric Association. *Diagnostic and statistical manual of mental disorders.* (2nd Rev. ed.) DSM-II. Washington, D. C.: APA, 1968.

Ayllon, T., & Ayllon, M. The psychiatric nurse as a behavioral engineer. *Journal of the Experimental Analysis of Behavior*, 1959, **2**, 323–334.

Bateson, G., Jackson, D. D., Haley, J., & Weakland, J. H. Toward a theory of schizophrenia. *Behavioral Science,* 1956, **1**, 251–264.

Berkowitz, H. Effects of prior experimenter-subject relationships on reinforced reaction time of schizophrenics and normals. *Journal of Abnormal and Social Psychology*, 1964, **69**, 522–530.

Best, W. R. Development of an experimental design for a clinical trial. Class notes from course, Clinical Trials in Cooperative Studies, May 11–15, 1970. Sponsored by the Midwest Research Support Center, Veterans Administration, Hines, Illinois.

Bleuler, E. *Dementia praecox or the group of schizophrenias.* New York: International Universities Press, 1950 (1911).

Bush, R. R., & Mosteller, F. *Stochastic models for learning.* New York: Wiley, 1955.

Buss, A. H. *Psychopathology.* New York: Wiley, 1966.

Chambers, D. A. Conditioning in psychotics. *Acta Psychiatrica Scandinavica*, 1965, **41**, 1–41.

Chassan, J. B. On the development of clinical statistical systems for psychiatry. *Biometrics*, 1959, **15**, 396–404.

Chassan, J. B. Stochastic models of the single case as the basis of clinical research design. *Behavioral Science*, 1960, **6**, 42–50.

Ells, E. M. Effects of operant level, interview with experimenter, and awareness upon verbal conditioning of chronic schizophrenics. *Journal of Abnormal Psychology*, 1967, **72**, 208–212.

Ferster, C. B., & Skinner, B. F. *Schedules of reinforcement.* New York: Appleton, 1957.

Garmezy, N. Some determiners and characteristics of learning research in schizophrenia. *American Journal of Orthopsychiatry*, 1964, **34**, 643–651.

Goldman, A. R. *The effects of dependency and dependency-anxiety on schizophrenics' rate of learning under conditions of reward and punishment.* (Doctoral dissertation, Stanford University) Ann Arbor, Mich.: University Microfilms, 1961. No. 61-4132.

Hartman, A. M. The apparent size of afterimages in delusional and non-delusional schizophrenics. *American Journal of Psychology*, 1962, **75**, 587–595.

Johannsen, W. J., Friedman, S. H., Leitshuh, T. H., & Ammons, H. A study of certain schizophrenic dimensions and their relationship to double alternation learning. *Journal of Consulting Psychology*, 1963, **27**, 375–382.

Kraepelin, E. *Psychiatry.* Leipzig: Barth, 1909.

Lorr, M., & Klett, C. J. Cross-cultural comparison of psychotic syndromes. *Journal of Abnormal Psychology*, 1969, **74**, 531–543.

Lorr, M., Klett, C. J., & McNair, D. M. *Syndromes of psychosis.* Oxford: Pergamon, 1963.

Maher, B. A. *Principles of psychopathology.* New York: McGraw-Hill, 1966.

Orgel, S. A. Differential classification of hebephrenic and paranoid schizophrenics from case material. *Journal of Clinical Psychology*, 1957, **13**, 159–161.

Payne, R. W., & Hewlett, J. H. Thought disorder in psychotic patients. In H. J. Eysenck (Ed.), *Experiments in personality.* Vol. 2. London: Routledge & Kegan Paul, 1960. Pp. 3–104.

Phillips, L. Case history data and prognosis in schizophrenia. *Journal of Nervous and Mental Diseases*, 1953, **117**, 515–525.

Rausch, H. L. Perceptual constancy in schizophrenia. *Journal of Personality*, 1952, **21**, 176–187.

Rosenthal, R. On the social psychology of the psychological experiment: The experimenter's hypothesis as unintended determinant of experimental results. *American Scientist*, 1963, **51**, 268–283.

Schmidt, H. O., & Fonda, C. P. The reliability of psychiatric diagnosis: A new look. *Journal of Abnormal and Social Psychology*, 1956, **52**, 262–267.

Schoolman, H. M., Becktel, J. M., Best, W. R., & Johnson, A. F. Statistics in medical research: Principles versus practices. *Journal of Laboratory and Clinical Medicine*, 1968, **71**, 357–367.

Schor, S. S. *Fundamentals of biostatistics.* New York: Putnam, 1968.

Shakow, D. Segmental set: A theory of the formal psychological deficit in schizophrenia. *Archives of General Psychiatry*, 1962, **6**, 17–33.

Shakow, D. Psychological deficit in schizophrenia. *Behavioral Science,* 1963, **8,** 275–305.

Silverman, J. The problem of attention in research and theory on schizophrenia. *Psychological Review,* 1964, **71,** 352–379.

Skinner, B. F. *Cumulative record.* New York: Appleton, 1959.

Stevenson, H. W. Social reinforcement with children as a function of CA, sex of E, and sex of S. *Journal of Abnormal and Social Psychology,* 1961, **63,** 147–154.

Stevenson, H. W., & Allen, S. Adult performance as a function of sex of experimenter and sex of subject. *Journal of Abnormal and Social Psychology,* 1964, **68,** 214–216.

Ullmann, L. P., & Krasner, L. *A psychological approach to abnormal behavior.* New Jersey: Prentice-Hall, 1969.

Venables, P. Input dysfunction in schizophrenia. In B. A. Maher (Ed.), *Progress in experimental personality research.* Vol. 1. New York: Academic Press, 1964.

Vestre, N. D. Relative effects of phenothiazines and phenobarbital in verbal conditioning of schizophrenia. *Psychological Reports,* 1965, **17,** 289–290.

Veterans Administration. *Cooperative studies in psychiatry: An anotated bibliography summarizing fifteen years of cooperative research in psychiatry, 1956–1970.* Washington, D. C.: Department of Medicine and Surgery, Veterans Administration, 1970.

Whitehorn, J. C., & Betz, B. J. A study of psychotherapeutic relationships between physicians and schizophrenic patients. *American Journal of Psychiatry,* 1954, **111,** 321–333.

Analyzed Studies

Aisenberg, R. B. *The cumulative differential effects of reward and punishment on the performance of schizophrenic and normal subjects.* (Doctoral dissertation, Boston University) Ann Arbor, Mich.: University Microfilms, 1957. No. 21–587.

Atkinson, R. L. *Paired-associate learning by schizophrenic and normal subjects under conditions of verbal reward and verbal punishment.* (Doctoral dissertation, Indiana University) Ann Arbor, Mich.: University Microfilms, 1957. No. 24–545.

Benton, A. L., Jentsch, R. C., & Wahler, H. J. Effects of motivating instructions on reaction time in schizophrenia. *Journal of Nervous and Mental Diseases,* 1960, **130,** 26–29.

Berkowitz, H. *The effects of prior experimenter-subject relationships on reinforced reaction time of schizophrenics and normals.* (Doctoral dissertation, University of Connecticut) Ann Arbor, Mich.: University Microfilms, 1964. No. 65–2695.

Bernd, S. M. *Changes in the verbal productions of schizophrenics as a function of changes in ascribed examiner characteristics.* (Doctoral dissertation, New York University) Ann Arbor, Mich.: University Microfilms, 1961. No. 61–2642.

Brennan, J. *The effect of type of stimulus and reinforcement on verbal generalization in normals and schizophrenics.* (Doctoral dissertation, New York University) Ann Arbor, Mich.: University Microfilms, 1964. No. 65–6622.

Brooker, H. *The effects of differential verbal reinforcement on schizophrenic and non-schizophrenic hospital patients.* (Doctoral dissertation, Indiana University) Ann Arbor, Mich.: University Microfilms, 1962. No. 62–5015.

Brown, R. L. *The effects of aversive stimulation on certain conceptual error re-*

sponses of schizophrenics. (Doctoral dissertation, Southern Illinois University) Ann Arbor, Mich.: University Microfilms, 1960. No. 61-2076.

Campbell, J. M. *Verbal conditioning as a function of the personality characteristics of experimenters and subjects*. (Doctoral dissertation, University of Washington) Ann Arbor, Mich.: University Microfilms, 1960. No. 60-1862.

Cavanaugh, D. K. *An investigation of motivation and content as factors influencing the performance of schizophrenics on concept formation tasks*. (Doctoral dissertation, University of Buffalo) Ann Arbor, Mich.: University Microfilms, 1957. No. 23–474.

Cavanaugh, D. K., Cohen, W., & Lang, P. J. The effect of "social censure" and "social approval" on the psychomotor performance of schizophrenics. *Journal of Abnormal and Social Psychology*, 1960, 60, 213–218.

Cohen, B. D. Motivation and performance in schizophrenia. *Journal of Abnormal and Social Psychology*, 1956, 52, 186–190.

Cohen, E., & Cohen, B. D. Verbal reinforcement in schizophrenia. *Journal of Abnormal and Social Psychology*, 1960, 60, 443–446.

D'Allessio, G. R., & Spence, J. T. Schizophrenic deficit and its relation to social motivation. *Journal of Abnormal and Social Psychology*, 1963, 66, 390–393.

DeLuca, J. N. *Cognitive task performance in schizophrenia as a function of premorbid history, evaluation and set to improve*. (Doctoral dissertation, Catholic University of America) Ann Arbor, Mich.: University Microfilms, 1963. No. 63-8060.

Dimauro, J. T. *The effects of verbal censure on the conceptual ability of process and reactive schizophrenics*. (Doctoral dissertation, Temple University) Ann Arbor, Mich.: University Microfilms, 1964. No. 65–1404.

Dinoff, M., Horner, R. F., Kurpiewski, B. S., Rickard, H. C., & Timmons, E. O. Conditioning verbal behavior of a psychiatric population in a group therapy-like situation. *Journal of Clinical Psychology*, 1960, 16, 371–372.

Dinoff, M., Horner, R. F., Kurpiewski, B. S., & Timmons, E. O. Conditioning verbal behavior of schizophrenics in a group therapy-like situation. *Journal of Clinical Psychology*, 1960, 16, 367–370.

DiVittis, A. L. *The effect of hospitalization on the verbal conditioning of schizophrenic subjects*. (Doctoral dissertation, University of Pittsburgh) Ann Arbor, Mich.: University Microfilms, 1965. No. 66-8118.

Ebner, E. *Verbal conditioning in schizophrenia as a function of the degree of social interaction*. (Doctoral dissertation, Purdue University) Ann Arbor, Mich.: University Microfilms, 1961. No. 61–2468.

Ells, E. M. *Verbal conditioning of chronic schizophrenics as a function of operant level and experience with the experimenter*. (Doctoral dissertation, University of Minnesota) Ann Arbor, Mich.: University Microfilms, 1963. No. 64-4092.

Fischer, E. H. Task performance of chronic schizophrenics as a function of verbal evaluation and social proximity. *Journal of Clinical Psychology*, 1963, 19, 176–178.

Foley, M. A. *Effect of response-contingent termination of noxious stimuli on the performance of schizophrenics and normals on tasks involving relevant and irrelevant stimuli*. (Doctoral dissertation, Catholic University of America) Ann Arbor, Mich.: University Microfilms, 1965. No. 65-5553.

Friedman, H. A comparison of action patterns of schizophrenic and normal adults. *Journal of Clinical Psychology*, 1958, 14, 142–146.

Fulk, R. H. *Premorbid variables and learning parameters in schizophrenia*. (Doctoral dissertation, Ohio State University) Ann Arbor, Mich.: University Microfilms, 1964. No. 65-3856.

Garmezy, N. Stimulus differentiation by schizophrenic and normal subjects under conditions of reward and punishment. *Journal of Personality,* 1952, **20,** 253–276.

Gelburd, A. S. *Increments and decrements in schizophrenic performance as a function of presence of the experimenter.* (Doctoral dissertation, University of Tennessee) Ann Arbor, Mich.: University Microfilms, 1965. No. 65-10113.

Goldman, A. R. *The effects of dependency and dependency-anxiety on schizophrenics' rate of learning under conditions of reward and punishment.* (Doctoral dissertation, Stanford University) Ann Arbor, Mich.: University Microfilms, 1961. No. 61-4132.

Goodstein, L. D., Guertin, W. H., & Blackburn, H. L. Effects of social motivational variables on choice reaction time of schizophrenics. *Journal of Abnormal and Social Psychology,* 1961, **62,** 24–27.

Guevara, C. I. *The effects of success and failure experiences and schizophrenics' rate of learning under conditions of high and low expectancy of success.* (Doctoral dissertation, Stanford University) Ann Arbor, Mich.: University Microfilms, 1965. No. 65-12783.

Hagen, J. M. *The conditioning of verbal affect responses in two hospitalized schizophrenic diagnostic groups during the clinical interview.* (Doctoral dissertation, Washington State College) Ann Arbor, Mich.: University Microfilms, 1959. No. 59-5450.

Hartman, C. H. *Verbal behavior of schizophrenic and normal subjects as a function of types of social reinforcement.* (Doctoral dissertation, State University of Iowa) Ann Arbor, Mich.: University Microfilms, 1955. No. 12-897.

Holz, W. C., Azrin, N. H., & Ayllon, T. Elimination of behavior of mental patients by response-produced extinction. *Journal of the Experimental Analysis of Behavior,* 1963, **6,** 407–412.

Huston, P. E., & Shakow, D. Learning capacity in schizophrenia. *American Journal of Psychiatry,* 1949, **105,** 881–888.

Irwin, M. L. *The effects of praise and censure on the performance of schizophrenics.* (Doctoral dissertation, University of Pennsylvania) Ann Arbor, Mich.: University Microfilms, 1965. No. 66-272.

Johannsen, W. J. *Responsiveness of chronic schizophrenics and normals to social and nonsocial feedback.* (Doctoral dissertation, University of Wisconsin) Ann Arbor, Mich.: University Microfilms, 1959. No. 59-1393.

Johannsen, W. J., & Campbell, S. Y. Verbal conditioning in chronic schizophrenia: Effects of reinforcement class and social responsiveness. *Psychological Reports,* 1964, **14,** 567–572.

Karras, A. The effects of reinforcement and arousal on the psychomotor performance of chronic schizophrenics. *Journal of Abnormal and Social Psychology,* 1962, **65,** 104–111.

Kelly, J. A. *The effects of self-reinforcement on paired-associate learning by schizophrenic and normal subjects.* (Doctoral dissertation, Indiana University) Ann Arbor, Mich.: University Microfilms, 1965. No. 65-10853.

Kilberg, J. *The differential effects of nonverbal and verbal rewards in the modification of verbal behavior of schizophrenic and normal subjects.* (Doctoral dissertation, Columbia University) Ann Arbor, Mich.: University Microfilms, 1962. No. 62-3697.

Knopf, I. J., & Brown, R. A. The effects of social and nonsocial censure on stimulus generalization in neurotics and schizophrenics. *Journal of Consulting Psychology,* 1966, **30**, 315–319.

Koppenhaver, N. D. *The effects of verbal and nonverbal reinforcement on the performance of schizophrenic subjects.* (Doctoral dissertation, Purdue University) Ann Arbor, Mich.: University Microfilms, 1961. No. 61–2488.

Kugelmass, N. *Operant conditioning of words having "good" and "bad" connotative meaning in schizophrenics and non-psychotics.* (Doctoral dissertation, University of Connecticut) Ann Arbor, Mich.: University Microfilms, 1965. No. 66-865.

Ladd, C. E. *The digit symbol performance of schizophrenic and non-psychiatric patients as a function of motivational instructions and task difficulty.* (Doctoral dissertation, State University of Iowa) Ann Arbor, Mich.: University Microfilms, 1960. No. 60-1560.

Lair, C. V. *The effect of praise and reproof on learning and retention of nonpsychotics and schizophrenics.* (Doctoral dissertation, Vanderbilt University) Ann Arbor, Mich.: University Microfilms, 1954. No. 9207.

Latz, A. *The modification of schizophrenic performance by drugs and positive reinforcement.* (Doctoral dissertation, Boston University) Ann Arbor, Mich.: University Microfilms, 1963. No. 63-6575.

Letchworth, G. E. *Studies in efficiency: Verbal conditioning in schizophrenia.* (Doctoral dissertation, University of Pennsylvania) Ann Arbor, Mich.: University Microfilms, 1963. No. 64-7385.

Leventhal, A. M. *The effects of differential verbal reinforcement on psychiatric and nonpsychiatric hospitalized patients.* (Doctoral dissertation, State University of Iowa) Ann Arbor, Mich.: University Microfilms, 1958. No. 58-2973.

Long, R. C. Praise and censure as motivating variables in the motor behavior and learning of schizophrenics. *Journal of Abnormal and Social Psychology,* 1961, **63**, 283–288.

Losen, S. M. The differential effects of censure on the problem-solving behavior of schizophrenic and normal subjects. *Journal of Personality,* 1961, **29**, 258–272.

Lydecker, W. A. Effects of different reinforcement conditions on the learning of schizophrenics and normals. *Proceedings of the Annual Convention of the American Psychological Association,* 1966, **74**.

Maginley, H. J. *The effects of the "threats" of failure and disapproval upon the conceptual learning performance of hospitalized mental patients.* (Doctoral dissertation, University of Pittsburgh) Ann Arbor, Mich.: University Microfilms, 1956. No. 16-518.

Marchionne, A. M. *Cognitive and drive properties of censure in schizophrenic learning.* (Doctoral dissertation, Washington State University) Ann Arbor, Mich.: University Microfilms, 1961. No. 61-3241.

McCarthy, J. E. *The differential effects of praise and censure upon the verbal response of schizophrenics.* (Doctoral dissertation, Catholic University of America) Ann Arbor, Mich.: University Microfilms, 1963. No. 64-355.

Norman, R. P. *Level of aspiration in chronic schizophrenics as a function of social desirability and threat of failure.* (Doctoral dissertation, University of North Carolina) Ann Arbor, Mich.: University Microfilms, 1961. No. 62-3144.

O'Brien, B. A. *The effects of various amounts of information supplied by reward and censure upon the performance of schizophrenics.* (Doctoral dissertation, Catholic University of America) Ann Arbor, Mich.: University Microfilms, 1964. No. 64-8250.

Olson, G. W. *The effects of success and failure instructions on the subsequent per-*

formance of schizophrenics and normals. (Doctoral dissertation, State University of Iowa) Ann Arbor, Mich.: University Microfilms, 1957. No. 20-928.

O'Neill, D. F. *Probability estimation, awareness of sequential dependency, and desire for certainty in schizophrenic disorders.* (Doctoral dissertation, Fordham University) Ann Arbor, Mich.: University Microfilms, 1964. No. 64-13228.

Page, R. A. *The effects of different conditions of reinforcement on the problem solving and ward behavior of schizophrenic patients.* (Doctoral dissertation, Boston University) Ann Arbor, Mich.: University Microfilms, 1958. No. 58–438.

Pascal, G. R., & Swenson, C. Learning in mentally ill patients under conditions of unusual motivation. *Journal of Personality,* 1952, 21, 240–249.

Potash, H. M. *Schizophrenic interaction and the concept of the double bind.* (Doctoral dissertation, Michigan State University) Ann Arbor, Mich.: University Microfilms, 1964. No. 65-2052.

Pugh, L. A. *The effects of praise, censure, and noise on electrodermal and reaction time measures in chronic schizophrenic and normal women.* (Doctoral dissertation, University of Oklahoma) Ann Arbor, Mich.: University Microfilms, 1965. No. 65-1250.

Ralph, D. E. Social reinforcement and stimulus generalization in schizophrenic and normal subjects. *Proceedings of the Annual Convention of the American Psychological Association,* 1966, 74.

Reisman, J. M. *Response differences between process and reactive schizophrenics as induced by magazine photographs.* (Doctoral dissertation, Michigan State University) Ann Arbor, Mich.: University Microfilms, 1958. No. 58-2330.

Reynolds, R. D. *Operant response as a function of the premorbid adjustment of schizophrenic subjects.* (Doctoral dissertation, Purdue University) Ann Arbor, Mich.: University Microfilms, 1964. No. 65-5040.

Robinson, N. L. *Paired-associate learning by schizophrenic subjects under personal and impersonal reward and punishment.* (Doctoral dissertation, Stanford University) Ann Arbor, Mich.: University Microfilms, 1958. No. 58-1304.

Rosenfeld, J. G. *The effects of social reinforcing variables on the ward recognition responses of schizophrenic and non-psychiatric patients.* (Doctoral dissertation, Temple University) Ann Arbor, Mich.: University Microfilms, 1961. No. 61-1509.

Ryan, L. R. *An exploratory study of some aspects of listening of schizophrenics.* (Doctoral dissertation, University of Colorado) Ann Arbor, Mich.: University Microfilms, 1960. No. 61–841.

Salzberg, H. C., & Williams, J. T. Effect of three types of feedback on concept formation in chronic schizophrenics. *Psychological Reports,* 1966, 18, 831–837.

Salzinger, K., & Portnoy, S. Verbal conditioning in interviews: Application to chronic schizophrenics and relationship to prognosis for acute schizophrenics. *Journal of Psychiatric Research,* 1964, 2, 1–9.

Sermat, V., & Greenglass, E. Effect of punishment on probability learning in schizophrenics. *British Journal of Social and Clinical Psychology,* 1965, 4, 52–62.

Sherman, M. *The responsiveness of chronic schizophrenics to social reinforcement as a function of subject variables, situation and performance criterion.* (Doctoral dissertation, Stanford University) Ann Arbor, Mich.: University Microfilms, 1964. No. 64-7683.

Sommer, R., Witney, G., & Osmond, H. Teaching common associations to schizophrenics. *Journal of Abnormal and Social Psychology,* 1962, **65,** 58–61.

Spence, J. T., Goodstein, L. D., & Lair, C. V. Rote learning in schizophrenic and normal subjects under positive and negative reinforcement. *Journal of Abnormal Psychology,* 1965, **70,** 251–261.

Strain, G. S. *Some short-term effects of subject and reinforcement variables on concept formation by schizophrenic subjects.* (Doctoral dissertation, Purdue University) Ann Arbor, Mich.: University Microfilms, 1965. No. 66-2324.

Tilton, J. R. *The use of instrumental motor and verbal learning techniques in the treatment of chronic schizophrenics.* (Doctoral dissertation, Michigan State University) Ann Arbor, Mich.: University Microfilms, 1956. No. 16-755.

Toal, R. A. *Social reinforcement and stimulus generalization in schizophrenic groups.* (Doctoral dissertation, University of Tennessee) Ann Arbor, Mich.: University Microfilms, 1962. No. 63-2186.

Topping, G. G., & O'Connor, N. The response of chronic schizophrenics to incentives. *British Journal of Medical Psychology,* 1960, **33,** 211–214.

True, J. E. *The verbal conditioning of abstract responses in process and reactive schizophrenic patients.* (Doctoral dissertation, Purdue University) Ann Arbor, Mich.: University Microfilms, 1962. No. 62-3492.

Waters, T. J. *Censure reinforcement, cue conditions and the acute-chronic schizophrenic distinction.* (Doctoral dissertation, University of Missouri) Ann Arbor, Mich.: University Microfilms, 1962. No. 62-6428.

Wilson, F. S., & Walters, R. H. Modification of speech output of near-mute schizophrenics through social-learning procedures. *Behaviour Research and Therapy,* 1966, **4,** 59–67.

Wing, J. K., & Freudenberg, R. K. The response of severely ill chronic schizophrenic patients to social stimulation. *American Journal of Psychiatry,* 1961, **118,** 311–322.

Woodbury, J. M. *The reinforcing value of verbalization as a function of anxiety.* (Doctoral dissertation, Washington State University) Ann Arbor, Mich.: University Microfilms, 1960. No. 60-1522.

Young, H. D. *The effects of oral censure on the conceptual performance of chronic schizophrenics as a function of premorbid adjustment and current mental health.* (Doctoral dissertation, Columbia University) Ann Arbor, Mich.: University Microfilms, 1962. No. 62-3708.

AUTHOR INDEX

Numbers in italics refer to the pages on which the complete references are listed.

SUBJECT INDEX

A

Achievement behavior, locus of control and, 17–19

Acquisition, in schizophrenics, reinforcement procedures and, 181–189

Age
behavior change and, 76
imitation and, 100

Anxiety, *see also under* Computer-assisted learning
effects in programmed instruction, 116–117

Anxiety reduction
modeling and, 46–49
roleplaying and, 53–54

Appropriateness
modeling and, 49–50
roleplaying and, 57–59

Arousal
modeling and, 46–49
roleplaying and, 53–54

B

Behavior, *see specific behaviors*

Behavior change, 41–81
age of subject and, 76
elicitation of criterion behavior and, 67–69
generalization of, 71–72
group *vs.* individual treatment and, 72–73
interpersonal-noninterpersonal and verbal-nonverbal behaviors and, 65–67
modeling and
cognitive variables and, 49–50
information and, 42–45
motivational variables and, 46–49
rehearsal and, 45–46
modeling, modeling plus roleplaying, and roleplaying and, 59–61
number, duration, frequency and spacing of sessions and, 72–73

participation and modeling plus participation and, 61–64
persistence of, 69–71
repetition, sequencing and pacing of behaviors and, 72–73
roleplaying and, 50–51
cognitive variables and, 57–59
information and, 51–52
motivational variables and, 53–57
rehearsal and, 52–53
sex of subject, experimenter, model and assistants and, 73–76

C

Cognitive activity, locus of control and, 8–15

Computer-assisted learning, 109–148
effects of anxiety on, 117–118
Florida State University CAI system and, 120
future directions in research on, 140–144
studies of, 120–140
systems and procedures in, 118–120
Spence-Taylor drive theory and, 113–116
trait-state anxiety theory and, 110–112
inventory for, 112–113

Control, 1–39
achievement behavior and, 17–19
changes in locus of, 27–31
deferred gratification and, 15–17
cognitive activity and, 8–15
resistance to influence and, 2–8
response to success and failure and, 19–22
sources of
familial, 22–25
social, 25–27

D

Deferred gratification, locus of control and, 15–17

Drive, Spence-Taylor theory of, 113–116